Testimonials

We were close to divorce, and in a last ditch effort to save our marriage. Our communication was almost non-existent (except when we were fighting). Graeme and Annette didn't give us solutions: they gave us something better. They helped us understand ourselves, and showed us how to be vulnerable again with open hearts. In doing so, they reminded us what love truly was.

Grant, QLD

After researching possibilities around the world, we discovered Annette and Graeme. We came to their retreat seeking to enhance the foundation of our loving and devoted relationship. We found an even deeper love; and on the last day, we shared a dream of ours in the most beautiful commitment ceremony we could ever imagine, which manifested in only a few short hours.

Derek and Susan, United States

I was attracted by a piece Annette wrote about sexual shame that resonated totally with my experience. It was a crack in the deep, foreboding dark I'd always felt in this area. Some light got in, and I can still feel the relief in discovering that I wasn't alone and that there was a way to change. I discovered a pride in the truth of my innate sexuality and sensuality.

Lizzie, QLD

I was holding myself back from a deeper, loving sexual connection with my husband. I discovered a wonderful freedom: learning to switch off from the outside world, connect in the moment and have Tantric-type experiences. I appreciate Annette and Graeme's honesty, compassion, understanding, professionalism, knowledge and experience. I also appreciated the wonderful practices they teach, and their commitment to this sacred work.

Marie, WA

I felt ashamed and embarrassed to ask for help on such a personal issue. The fear that I might be stuck forever in this space and lose my wife became so overwhelming that I chose to act. It's been a process untangling the web, but I now feel more alive and I have a greater sense of myself. With our three children now grown up, we've sold our home and are traveling around the world for 18 months. I believe we're able to do this because meaningful intimacy is now back at the centre of our relationship.

Greg, NSW

We'd been together for 40 years since we were 14. At 17, the pain, loss and anger of the enforced adoption of our first daughter caused us both a bitterness that we couldn't seem to shake off. It was scary putting our real selves and hurt out there, but we learned to reconnect as the young lovers we had once been; and our open communication has enhanced our relationships with our three beautiful children.

S & T, QLD

After 20 years and three children together, I felt I no longer loved my husband. We'd tried mainstream counselling, which didn't help, and I was desperate. Annette and Graeme were very 'real' people, which made it easy for each of us to work with them. Now, ten years later, my relationship with my husband is stronger than ever, as is my relationship with myself. We've learned the benefits of being vulnerable with each other, which opens our hearts and leads to blissful lovemaking.

Bernadette, NSW

My partner had just moved to Jakarta for work, and we were trying to find a way to keep connected whilst apart. My concern, believing everything significant must be subject to scientific analysis, was that this seemed far too New Age-y for my tastes. However, we took your New Age teachings; and with them have consistently achieved intimacy despite the distance. Therefore, as applied to us, the woo-woo works!

KG and DW, Indonesia

After 14 years of marriage, all of our issues had risen, putting us into crisis. We took a leap of faith by investing in ourselves, and we're very glad that we did. Writing down our priorities in the relationship is something we still revisit regularly, over two years later. We have so many fond memories of our time with Annette and Graeme, but deeper than that is the memory that we actually did it – we prioritised our relationship enough to take that step.

M & L, Australia

Our 20-year relationship was strained to near breaking point due to differences in libido and attitudes to sex. It took an enormous amount of courage for my husband and I to enrol in work we thought would be extremely alternative. The benefits we've gained have been beyond our greatest expectations, resulting in a deepening and strengthening of our relationship from the sexual right through to the spiritual.

Robyn, NSW

We both felt a bit stuck and didn't know how to get out of our rut. I have now truly come to appreciate how much my wife means to me, and how much more I could have been doing to help our relationship. I have had quite a few lightbulb moments, not only in my relationship but also as a man who wants to look after his family, contribute to society, and so much more. Annette and Graeme have played a huge role in that.

Lee, SA

We had fallen apart on every level; and sadly, it had been years since we had actually been 'making love'. After attempting to do everything I could to 'fix' the marriage myself, I was asking for a divorce. At this point, my husband finally agreed to get some outside help. Annette and Graeme's wholistic approach felt like the best fit for us. They are incredibly authentic humans who showed me that the real relationship lies with 'me' and 'me'.

Carmen, NSW

For all those who feel the longing...

Acknowledgements

Our clients have helped to make this book a reality

We're extremely grateful to our clients, who've opened themselves to exploring intimate relationship in unique and vulnerable ways that have left us awed and humble. Without them, this book wouldn't be possible.

Getting real with each other is about the scariest thing we can do as human beings, yet time after time our clients have gone to their depths and come through into greater love and understanding.

We're grateful to ourselves as well

In this book, Graeme and I have thrown our relationship under the microscope and explored all areas of ourselves in order to learn the art of relationship and make it relevant to everyday reality. We want to recognise ourselves for having the courage, naivety and willingness to choose and stay on our path.

For, just like our clients, we have moments when we want to pull our heads under the covers and take all the possible theories about relationship and stuff them where the sun don't shine. Yet after retreating, we always seem to find a way to come back into ourselves and into each other.

And many thanks to our support team

Big hugs and gratitude go to Alex Fullerton at authorsupportservices.com for helping us believe in our book and to her team: Tanja Gardner who helped us sort the 'we's' and the 'we all's': Sylvie Blair for the fabulous design and to our friend Nenad Stojadinovic for believing in the book enough to proof read it for us. Many thanks also to Ally@moshers.com.au plus the terrific team at InHousePublishing for their final touches, and to all who helped steer us through the unknown of our first book.

Coming Together

Solving the Mystery of Intimate Sex and Relationships

Annette Baulch & Graeme Sudholz

Coming Together: Solving the mystery of intimate sex and relationship
Author – Annette Baulch and Graeme Sudholz

Copyright © Oztantra 2018

www.oztantra.com
info@oztantra.com

This book is sold with the understanding that the authors are not offering specific personal advice to the reader. For professional advice, seek the services of a suitable, qualified practitioner. The author disclaims any responsibility for liability, loss or risk, personal or otherwise, that happens as a consequence of the use and application of any of the contents of this book.

The client stories we mention are composite stories of real-life people in order to maintain their confidentiality and our integrity. Our own stories are definitely ours!

All rights reserved. This book may not be reproduced in whole or part, stored, posted on the internet, or transmitted in any form or by any means, electronic, mechanical, photocopying, recording, or other, without permission from the authors of this book.

Editing and design by AuthorSupportServices.com

National Library of Australia Cataloguing-in-Publication
Authors: Annette Baulch & Graeme Sudholz
Title: Coming Together
Edition: First
ISBN: 978-0-6481146-0-4

Foreword

Relationships have the capacity to take us to the heights of ecstasy or the depths of despair, they can break us down and they can open us up, they can lead us to pain or be a catalyst for growth. For such an important aspect of life it is amazing that we don't receive any formal training.

I am blessed to have had the opportunity to discover, explore and teach the wonders of heart-centred relationships in my 26 years conducting Emotional Intelligence Trainings, coaching couples around Australia, and the world, and in my 20 years journeying with my beautiful wife Susan which is as passionate, connected and loving as ever, today.

It is inspiring to see two of my students go on to demonstrate such commitment to heart centred relationships as Annette and Graeme. I have had the privilege of watching them translate their own healing journey into a passionate way of living and service to others. And I have witnessed their great courage and commitment to be willing to show up and engage with each other in a climate of honesty, curiosity and kindness to themselves and each other. They have demonstrated not just a strong devotion to their truth, and each other, but also to love.

Annette and Graeme are the real deal. Having grown up in the country, they are down to earth and straightforward. They demonstrate great integrity by living what they teach. They teach a down to earth, practical and inspiring approach to creating and maintaining passionate, loving relationships. They are a bright beacon in a world where much sexual exploration gets lost in self-indulgence and fantasy that ultimately strands us in a quicksand of delusion, disappointment and separation.

Humans are social animals. We have evolved in relationships personal and social. We all long for the experience of comfort, connection, companionship and fulfilment that deep, abiding love promises. And yet so many people struggle to realise this possibility.

There probably has never been a tougher time in history than now to create and sustain a passionate, loving relationship.

Stress and anxiety levels are at an all time high and nothing kills love like stress. We live in a world of increasing demands and expectations where everything is speeding up and we are under mounting pressure to perform and achieve.

All these demands on us draw us out of relationship, not just with our partner, but also with our self. It is too easy to go on autopilot and begin to live as a machine, just going through the motions, not really connecting to others and not really feeling what is happening within us.

As well as this, we live in a world of increasing independence. People now question: "How do I relate to my partner now, as an independent being?", "How do we get on the same page and form a team without compromising my independence or losing my self in the relationship?"

Plus our culture has an increasingly 'disposable' attitude. This short-term view of things has resulted in the tendency to dump a relationship if it starts to struggle, rather than working on restoring it.

More and more there is a gap opening up, not just in our relationships but also within us. In our haste to get things done we are losing touch with the tender, vulnerable, sensitive part of our self. Many people are feeling a kind of emptiness, a soullessness that is being expressed as a loss of meaning and passion in life. Couples with young families are struggling to keep their relationship with each other alive, professional couples are drawn out of intimacy by corporate demands. Too often empty nesters look at each other as strangers and wonder where the love went.

Foreword

We all long for and fear that state of intimacy in which we dissolve into one. So we open up and then close down, we come in close and then run away. Each time we do we weaken the foundation on which loving relationships are built: our commitment to each other. As the commitment weakens we withdraw more quickly when painful and difficult situations arise. This leaves us creating more and more unresolved hurt and more and more caution and armouring.

What we lack are the skills and understanding and self-awareness to be our self fully, to connect deeply, to heal hurt, to unite sex and intimacy and to celebrate love.

Thank goodness Annette and Graeme have written this lovely book. In it you will find a clear and straightforward path for traversing the landscape of relationships and coming home to love as Annette and Graeme lay out the ground rules for engaging deeply in relationships.

Having built a foundation of intimate loving connection Annette and Graeme focus on celebrating loving relationships through our sexuality. They guide us with gentleness, humour and sensitivity through what has been for many a painful landmine of shame and broken dreams. They articulate the differences that men and women experience in their approach to, and experience of sexuality. This helps us to deepen our understanding of our self and have greater patience and tolerance to support and nurture our partner. They give clear and simple instructions on exercises for sexual healing.

This book is a guide for us to return our sexuality to its natural innocence, beauty and proper expression of love in intimacy. Many of the potholes on the path to spiritual lovemaking are identified and solutions presented in ways that are gentle, non-shaming and encouraging.

Unlike many books on Love and Sexuality Annette and Graeme share in detail their own struggles and triumphs and this helps us to feel more OK about our own personal challenges in our relationships. The wisdom shared here has come from Annette and Graeme's own personal experiences of sexual union in a committed relationship. Committed relationships offer us the container to go to depth because they provide the safety to take the risk of showing up in honesty, passion and vulnerability. To be able to work through difficult, awkward and even hurtful feelings until a place of harmony and reconnection is established.

I honour their desire to make the world a more open hearted and loving place. This book will help you to open your heart and live your life fully. Enjoy.

Kind Regards,
Nicholas de Castella
Director, Institute of Heart Intelligence
W: www.eq.net.au

Contents

Foreword xiii

Preface xix
    How to get the most out of this book xxii

Introduction 1
    Coming Together is a roadmap 2

Chapter 1: Setting the Stage for Intimacy

1.1	Finding the value in an intimate relationship	5
1.2	Understanding the Relationship Landscape	9
1.3	What Actually IS Intimacy?	22
1.4	Learning to Feel (and Yes, There's a Reason for It)	26
1.5	Vulnerability: The Blessing and Curse of Intimacy	32

Chapter 2: Surrender and Freedom

2.1	The ABC of Coming Together	39
2.2	Developing Feeling Intelligence	46
2.3	The Nature of Mind and the Games that it Plays	58
2.4	The Longest, Most Worthwhile Journey from the Head to the Heart	68

Chapter 3: Connection, Separation and Control

3.1	Me, You and Us: The Dance Of Intimacy	77
3.2	Using your ABC as a relationship tool	86

3.3	Dealing with Emotional Triggers	91
3.4	Ending The Power Play	100

Chapter 4: Self, Self and Self

4.1	Know Thyself First: Acceptance is the Key	105
4.2	Your Relationship Begins with You	108
4.3	Trust Your Essence	109
4.4	Yes, You are Fascinating: Your Beliefs, Values, Needs and Desires	111
4.5	Surviving Letting Another Person in Close: The Importance of Boundaries	127
4.5	The Importance of Inter-Generational Boundaries	135

Chapter 5: The Fine Art of Communication

5.1	Known as the Finer Art of the Shit Fight	141
5.2	Finding the Passion	157
5.3	Men and Woman are Different	165
5.4	So, Let's Talk About Sex, Baby!	172

Chapter 6: Stuckness and State Change

6.1	Activities to Shift Your State When You Get Stuck	181
6.2	Dealing With the Great Debilitator – Shame	185
6.3	The Ultimate Art of State Change: Dissolving Your Ego	191

Chapter 7: Sexeptance

7.1	Acknowledging What Lies at Our Core	205
7.2	Sex - What's in it For Me as a Woman? (by Annette)	209
7.3	Actually, Men DON'T Want Just Sex (by Graeme)	235

Chapter 8: Sexploration

8.1	When Two Become One	259
8.2	Mmmm... Turn Your Volkswagen Into A Ferrari!	288

| 8.3 | Identifying Your Unique Blocks to Pleasure | 295 |

Chapter 9: The Shadow and the Spy

| 9.1 | Embracing The Shadow | 319 |
| 9.2 | Doing Jigsaws: How To See The Unseen | 333 |

Chapter 10: Managing The Other

10.1	Porn vs Romance	341
10.2	How to Turn Jealousy Into a Gift	345
10.3	When Your Partner's Had an Affair	350
10.4	Monogamy, Screwing Around, Open Relationships and Polyamory	354

Chapter 11: What About Love?

11.1	The Universal and Personal Heart	361
11.2	The Differences between Men and Women in Love	366
11.3	The Hidden Person Inside of Us Worthy of Our Love	371
11.4	Letting Love In	373

Chapter 12: Shine and Sustain

12.1	Creating a Solid Relationship Framework	383
12.2	Trust the Process	391
12.3	When is it Time For a Relationship to End?	402
12.4	Signs You're Creating a Sacred, Intimate Relationship	405

Annette, Graeme and Oztantra 413

Suggested Reading 415

Preface

In a world where less and less is held sacred, Annette Baulch & Graeme Sudholz have a passion for awakening the world to the full potential of committed intimate relationships.

They've developed a framework for exploring relationship, intimacy and sexuality at a multi-dimensional level in a way that's profound, yet straightforward. Their work is clear, non-judgmental, real and inspiring – kind of like themselves. Because of the depth of their own journey, Annette and Graeme aren't afraid to be upfront about subjects that have most of us cringing in our seats. And their matter-of-factness then allows us to become more comfortable in our own skins.

Their own relationship began in 2001 at an emotional intelligence workshop where both of them were trying to learn why their former marriages had ended. Annette (then a nurse) says that meeting Graeme (then a farmer) was like, "stepping into a hurricane," because he "lives his life at a level of intensity that both challenges and excites me". Meanwhile, Graeme says that Annette has "taught me – and continues to teach me – who a woman is and what she's really capable of".

Many personal development workshops later, the couple somehow discovered Tantra: an ancient eastern philosophy about living life (including sex) as an art that they've explored and adapted to their own learnings. Making the shift from a traditional rural life of farming and nursing to being world-class relationship counsellors and workshop facilitators has been a huge one, as you can imagine (or maybe you can't). It has also taught them the skills they bring to you here.

Some words from Annette

This book has ultimately come about through a little 'feeling magic' of my own. One day, I found myself feeling overwhelmingly depressed at how badly my relationship of 20 years was going. How could it be this hard, when both of us were giving it everything we knew? Maybe we didn't really love each other? I knew this wasn't true, but love just didn't seem to be enough, even *with* a couple of counsellors helping to fix our problems.

That relationship eventually ended, and seeking to learn from my mistakes, I was lucky enough to find some great teachers. Gradually, learning stopped being about 'fixing' myself, and instead became a process of self-love and healthy exploration of life, relationship and feeling. I learnt about the place in me where love, trust, courage, empathy, compassion, gratitude and many other qualities necessary for real relationship (and life) arise. After so many years of suffering, it felt like magic.

During this time I tentatively moved into a new relationship with my current partner Graeme, and was *that* ever a whole new world! But amazingly, many of the exact same struggles started arising as in my previous relationship. I slowly learnt the truth of what was happening – that a relationship (of any kind) is ultimately about how I'm being in my relationship with myself. In other words, I needed to 'do relationship' from inside me.

Along the way I discovered a fascination with sex (because this also lives inside me), and its mysterious power. It took me many years to learn just how powerful sexual feelings are, and how they can either be the biggest gift, or the biggest hurt in any intimate relationship.

This is the basis of my story. Magic, sex and discovering my sense of self have led me into my life's work. Alongside Graeme, I now support couples and individuals in finding their own unique relationship roadmap for a relationship first with *themselves* and then with their significant other.

Preface

Some words from Graeme

I remember standing in front of the workshop of my successful farm in late 1996, looking around at all I'd achieved, yet feeling empty and bitterly disappointed. I'd lost my direction. I was a father and husband, but totally clueless in understanding myself, let alone knowing how to be in relationship.

Because of this, my marriage ended, which was the catalyst that exploded me out of my complacency. The months following my separation were a very dark and scary time. I was lucky to have caring friends who supported and 'pushed' me into the personal development workshop where I first met Annette.

Here the lid came off everything I'd bottled up my whole life, and I realised I had some serious work to do on myself. My greatest fear was "Take the farm out of the boy, and who am I?" I measured my self-worth in material achievements, attaching very little – if any – value to self-awareness. It wasn't until eventual bankruptcy and total financial annihilation hit me that the penny finally dropped.

In my relationship with Annette, we both chose to go full-on into this work. We did every workshop we could find, sharing our lives and our passion together. I soon realised the importance of healthy sexuality, and how I'd limited mine as a result of early childhood experiences. I also really began to understand and appreciate the gift of being in a committed relationship where personal growth is encouraged and supported, especially in developing happy, healthy intimate longevity.

Along the way, I've met many people who've all had one thing in common: emotional stuff. And I discovered that what makes the difference in successful relationships is choosing to do something about that emotional stuff. It's a choice that we all have.

This book is Annette's 'baby', and during her process of writing it, I've stopped and taken stock of exactly what I've achieved for myself. Getting to know myself better since that time of desolation feels like a worthwhile achievement, and one I share with others who are challenged by life – even if there's no tractor or paddock in sight any more. (Although I do still indulge my fetish for driving 'big yellow Tonka toys'.)

How to get the most out of this book

This book contains lots of information about a very personal and intense subject. (The 4 years it's taken to write it has felt like doing our own personal Phd). Our suggestion is to take in as much as you need at any one time, then keep coming back to it when you're ready for more. There are some parts that may take more than one reading, for what they're appealing to lies beyond your ordinary thinking mind. Use it as a resource for when you want some affirmation, inspiration or answers to a challenge. You can delve as lightly or as deeply as you desire, for there is enough on offer here to last you a lifetime!

This book is about doing

Knowledge and understanding are very helpful tools, but they're NOT the lived experience. As Mahatma Gandhi said, "Knowledge gained through experience is far superior and many times more useful than bookish knowledge." Because of this, we offer a minimal amount of scientific data in this book (though we do refer to people who do offer it). Instead, we focus on your experience (and reflecting on these experiences). So become your own experimenters and find your own solutions to your unique relationship challenges. We support you by offering a range of different activities so you can find your own combination.

To bring in something new and break old habits, you need to take action. Give yourself permission to get it wrong: even if you make mistakes, you'll always learn something – and this is much, much better than doing nothing. Simply reading this book won't help your relationship like doing something about it will! So, read the book and then practice, practice, practice, learning something new each time.

A couple of final words about this book

This book is a unique document covering some of what Graeme and I have learned about relationship (the bits that are suitable for printing!) As we've said, much of it is based on our own personal experience, our clients' experiences, reading hundreds of books and learning from other professionals.

Because we started out as two very mainstream folk the people who've been attracted to our work have mostly been of a similar ilk (although we've met many and varied other people along the way). This means that we most often talk from a male/female relationship dynamic – it's where our experience is based. It *doesn't* mean that we don't accept or value people and relationships of all types, be they cis-gender, transgender, gay, lesbian, queer, asexual or questioning. Nor does it mean that this book won't be able to help people outside of male/female relationships: much of what we cover is just about being human.

And because this book includes sexuality we need to talk about genitals, which brings us a dilemma. People are very different in how they relate to this part of their bodies, including the names they give them. As we can get into trouble whichever way we choose to describe genitals – whether in functional, poetic or common slang terms, we've chosen to use the words which are most familiar to us. We invite you to substitute your own.

Additionally, it's important to mention that Graeme and I wrote this book together. But then, when we got it to the editing stage, we realised that if we only ever used the word 'we' to talk about ourselves, it quickly got confusing for you as a reader. It became ambiguous as to whether any given 'we' meant us specifically, or human beings in general.

Because of this, you'll often see us use the words 'Graeme and I'. That's just for clarity, and doesn't mean Graeme was any less involved in writing the book than Annette was.

Introduction

Welcome.
Come in, sit down and make yourself comfortable.

It's great to have you here. Welcome to the world of intimate relationships.

From here on, when Graeme and I refer to 'relationship' we're referring to an intimate relationship. An intimate and sexual relationship that exists between two adults who share a commitment to being together, married or not, living together or not.

We know it's your deeply instinctual longing for a satisfying, intimate, sexual and loving connection that's brought you here. You want to love and be loved. To desire and be desired. It's what *all* of us want more of. According to researcher Helen Fisher, the need for romantic love and sex is as much a part of our survival system as thirst or hunger.

It's a longing that attracts and terrifies us in almost equal measure.

The good news is that there's a reason for this apparent conundrum. We'll show you how it's all part of being simple-yet-incredibly-complex human beings. We'll also show you how to navigate your way through the minefields of intimate relating. Whether you're looking to fix a troubled relationship or build an extraordinary one, the tools are the same.

For once you've made this commitment to your significant other, how do you continue to feel satisfyingly close to them? How do you feel seen, valued, loved and desired after the initial magic has gone? Is there really magic to love, or is this just an old-fashioned fantasy?

We believe magic IS possible when you address your relationship in a holistic way. Relationships, like life, are an experience lived on many levels: mental, physical, emotional, sexual, heart and soul. This book is a roadmap for relationships at all of these levels (even if you don't believe in souls).

Coming Together is a roadmap

This book is a roadmap that turns your struggles into *pathways* to what you seek, rather than the immovable obstacles they often seem. Not pathways to a Hollywood happy-ever-after, but instead to something real, tangible and lasting.

Most couples try (as we did) things that either don't work or make things worse:

- They think 'if my partner would just... everything would be ok'
- They focus on their children, or on things outside the home like family, friends, work, sport, sex or hobbies to reduce their suffering, at the expense of each other
- They shut down emotionally to avoid hurt
- They mask their fears and frustration by performing in the bedroom rather than co-creating pleasure and connection
- They do the same things and hope for different results.

But Graeme and I have identified that you benefit from connecting *with yourself first*, rather than overly focussing on your partner or the relationship.

This is because you can only be in a relationship with another person to the extent you're in a relationship with yourself.

If this sounds selfish, it's actually the opposite – as you'll find out.

We've developed a simple self-connection process that takes you beyond selfishness, which we call **The ABC of Coming Together**. The ABC stands for Attention, Breath and Connection – a mindful connection with yourself – and this one core teaching underpins each of the learnings we've identified in **12 Key Areas of Intimate Relationship**. We've found that the desire for a healthy connection and relationship with another person springs automatically from this deeper connection with the self.

You'll start to turn the light on

If you want satisfying intimacy and sex, you need to be prepared to look not only at your relationship but also inside yourself. You won't find what you most want in the outside world; instead, you'll find it begins within you. You can either look inside together or begin alone, hopefully inspiring your partner to get on board along the way.

You'll find that you're 'normal'

We've found that the only normal thing in relationships is the setting on the washing machine! No matter what you might think, you, your relationship and your sex life (no matter how crazy they might seem at times) are unique, rather than abnormal.

People (especially 'experts') don't often share what really goes on inside their intimate relationships. But we can tell you from experience that what happens on the inside can look very different to what you might see on the surface of relationships at the restaurant, school or office. It seems that all really is fair in love and war.

We've learnt, though, that successful relationships aren't about trying to be perfect because perfection doesn't actually exist. It's about having the courage to be real – to be yourself and trust in the love that brought you together, without letting it wilt away under the pressures of domesticity (or at least not to stay there). If you can get comfortable with your relationship being messy, uncomfortable and uncertain at times, you'll find the most amazing gifts within it.

So as you journey through the pages of this book with us, Graeme and I invite you to give yourself permission to get a bit messy. Trust us: the results will be worth it.

Setting the Stage for Intimacy

1.1 Finding the value in an intimate relationship

If you're like most of us, you've entered into your intimate relationship in a state of openness and desire. You have a heady feeling that despite the odds, you've somehow found something uniquely special that will last, and see a lifetime of blissful togetherness stretching ahead of you.

Unfortunately, relationships too often descend over time into a source of hurt, fear and frustration that feels like a betrayal of the happy-ever-after you were somehow 'promised'. Even if your relationship is relatively happy, you can still be left with the feeling that there's 'more' you're missing out on.

It can seem easier to say "this is not for me" and walk away, often into the next relationship hoping to find new answers, or to suffer on in silence.

Intimacy is about so much more than ending our aloneness. If 'not being alone' was *all* we needed, there would be no suffering in relationships. We'd just get together and be happy. The reality is so often different, yet we continue to seek relationships in some form or other despite their difficulties. The modern challenge is to find new meaning and purpose within our intimate relationships. It's to find the 'more' we all suspect is there.

Graeme and I believe that it *is* possible to have it 'all' in relationship, but that this 'all' looks different to what most people think. It's not about getting everything you want. Instead, it's about a greater uncovering of your authentic selves: your multi-layered 'whole selves' (some would even say soul selves). These are the selves that you can enjoy discovering through each other, over the years it takes them to emerge.

What do we mean by your authentic self? You're being authentic when your external self reflects your internal self: when what you say and how you act matches how you feel and what you believe inside you. We've found that greater authenticity offers greater happiness in intimate relationship because it reveals the love that lives at our core. It's the adventure of a lifetime!

Human beings are built to heal

In my 30-odd years as a registered nurse, I (Annette) learnt how our amazing human bodies are built to heal. Our psyches (who we think we are) are built the same way. Through intimate love and sex, our psyches seek opportunities to rejuvenate the parts of ourselves that have become unavailable due to emotional wounding, or that have simply lacked an opportunity to blossom.

Our intimate relationships are our psyches' unconscious attempts to heal unresolved hurts from our past and realise our potential. Relationships are *unconsciously designed* to trigger us into our deepest places in order to heal, awaken or reveal the love that lives within us. Think of them as being like lancing a wound to remove the pus, or providing a warm spot in the sun for a flower to open. If we handle it correctly, bumping up against our partners in the challenge of intimacy removes both the rough edges of our hurts and our unseen limitations. This then reveals more of our diamond selves shining within. It's how we need each other in the deepest of ways that lie beyond the obvious.

We get a taste of this healing and awakening when we first fall in love, as two of the most powerful natural forces in the world – love and sex – unite. We somehow feel bigger, brighter, smarter, more capable and even omnipotent because we love this person, and they love us.

This is the inherent (and awesome) magic that lives within each relationship, and within each of us as individuals. It's magic that, at some level, we all still want to believe in. Our task then is to see the true nature of this magic, to cultivate its 'bigness' and minimise the moments that dim its glow.

Relationships make sense when we see them this way: as an intimate system for awakening and healing ourselves, for sharing the gifts of who we are. And for supporting our partner to do the same.

We're shown what love can be

Even more than this, when we look up from earning our next dollar, accumulating our next possession or getting our next need met, our intimate relationships remind us of the existence of love in the world.

Relationships are like life: not just a concept of our minds but an experience to be lived. Whilst we live our lives alone in the stories of our minds, baffled by our own bullshit, it's easy to consider ourselves completely self-sufficient, independent and fair-minded beings. Having someone move into our cave, see us right up close and tell us where to clean up our act puts our beliefs about who we think we are to the ultimate test.

When we experience the gritty, everyday face of intimacy as an opportunity for growth, we really *get* life at a profound level. We understand the vastness of real love. Love that shows us moments in our humanity so precious that we're blown away by their divinity. Without being able to explain it, we see that 'falling in love' is just the first step, and there's so much more to it.

We're also shown the true potential of sex

Part of relationship magic is taking ownership of our sexuality and the gifts it offers beyond mere procreation and itch scratching. In its fullest potential, sex is about allowing ourselves to be fully vulnerable, seen, loved and loving. In it we open ourselves up to heart-connected, healing and life-sustaining pleasure. We get glimpses of total freedom, expanded love and ecstasy.

In this way sexual pleasure and connection are much more than a self-indulgent act. They're a pathway for healing – a place to safely open in places where we've been contracted, sometimes for a lifetime. It offers us unlimited experiences of our inner mysteries and life-force energy. It's where the magic and longevity of intimacy for the long run lives. That's worth being alive for.

It's the work of a lifetime

It takes time to get all these layers – a lifetime, in fact. That's why Graeme and I believe in the value of committed, long-term intimate relationships for offering unlimited potential in achieving love, connection, pleasure and meaning in life to those who seek them. When you take charge of yourself in your relationship and sexuality in this way, you move a long way toward becoming all you can be in life. This is how a long-term relationship becomes a never-ending exploration of what's possible, maintaining its spark long after its point of ignition.

1.2 Understanding the Relationship Landscape

No matter how intimate it might seem, your relationship isn't just about you sitting across from your partner at dinner, sharing a smile, feeling desire and perhaps wondering who's going to pick the kids up from school tomorrow. It's influenced by the many generations that have gone before you, and the current world you live in.

Stephanie Cootz, author of *Marriage, A History: How Love Conquered Marriage*, says that couples originally got together to propagate the survival of the species, and then to build family alliances and strategic property ownership. It's only in the last 250 years that relationships have become about individual romantic love, and only in the last 50 that they've involved any sort of equal partnership.

We're all now freer to create our own relationship styles and we're as influenced by our peers and the world around us as we once were by our parents, our cultural and traditional family values.

Like it or not, relationships have entered the age of 'me', with a belief in our specialness and our right to happiness. We now enter relationships with higher expectations than ever before. We want our spouses to be partners, lovers, soulmates, friends, providers, nurturers, buddies, therapists, mind readers, financial planners and a place to belong. And we need them to be all these things with less support from our traditional support networks, and for longer as our average life expectancy increases.

> *"In the modern industrialised Western world where I come from, the person whom you choose to marry is perhaps the single most vivid representation of your own personality"*
>
> Committed, Elizabeth Gilbert

As we've made great strides in creating physical safety, along with social and financial security for ourselves we're now less likely to seek it from our romantic relationships. Instead, our focus is on our more personal, intangible, but equally important, internal reality. We expect our intimate relationships to provide seemingly paradoxical qualities like:

- Security/Support/Comfort/Belonging
- Familiarity/Identity/Fidelity/Longevity
- Fun/Pleasure/Adventure/Excitement
- Intimacy/Connectedness/Freedom/Autonomy
- Love/Sex/Mystery/Meaning/Happiness.

We no longer seek to disappear into the comfort of coupledom. Instead, we want to remain ourselves *as well as* having all the benefits of being in a relationship. And in the age of unlimited choice, we not only want it all, we want it *now*.

As a result, we're at much more immediate risk of suffering from emotional wounding to our ego than we are from global warming or international terrorism. And the answers to the painful paradoxes in the things we desire can only be found inside us. So how do we go about finding these answers?

Gaining the required knowledge and skills

> *"Most of the time, we fall in love but can't remain there. The world then calls this state we were in delusion or infatuation. But we were not deluded. We were not just infatuated. We merely lacked, or someone else lacked, the emotional skills to hold onto the magic when the morning came"*
>
> Enchanted Love, Marianne Williamson

As relationships become more complex, most of us still receive very little (if any) training for them, even though they're the potentially most important and fulfilling parts of our lives. Let's face it: if we were offered an extremely exciting yet challenging job that required multiple skillsets we didn't have, very few of us would be willing to sign on without negotiating some training and ongoing support. This is particularly true if our income was to be based on the quality of our daily performance, as our relationship happiness often is.

So why do we do *exactly* this with our relationships?

It's largely because almost everyone around us does exactly the same, including our parents, whom we learn the most about relationships from. This lack is what creates the dreaded 'loss of spark' in a relationship, leaving us thinking that we've fallen 'out of love'.

Getting the training you need to address the challenges in your relationship allows you to choose understanding over suffering.

Relationship training like you find here helps you to see your partner as a person just like you: someone who dearly wants connection, and who is probably trying just as hard, and hurting just as much as you, rather than as your enemy. It helps you to give them a warm hug rather than a cold shoulder.

Your first relationship skill is to challenge any myths you've been sold about relationships that may be getting in your way. We start here:

It's our Relationship That's the Problem

Most people believe that their relationship is the cause of their problems. It isn't. Graeme and I see that relationships merely become battlegrounds for what is actually going on within the people themselves. That's why trying to fix a relationship will never fully do the job. Of course it's less challenging because the focus is outside of you and on your relationship, but it won't bring you the results you're looking for. As we've said, people unconsciously choose to be in relationships with those whose personalities challenge whatever is unresolved or unseen within them. This is *real* togetherness! So when things 'go wrong' it's not a relationship problem. It's actually a flag for people to look *inside themselves* to see what's being invited to grow. It's like the airlines say… we all need to fit our own oxygen masks before helping others.

Rather than blame our partner or our relationship,
we need to take the opportunity to learn something
about ourselves: most of our 'stuff' in our relationships
began even before we met each other.

When we become more comfortable in ourselves we get more authentic and available for love, life and our relationship with our significant other. Note: this doesn't mean living in denial of our partner's behaviour. Rather, it means getting clear in our own, so we can deal with theirs more effectively.

Building relationship glue

It's easy to pay lip service to the idea that relationships take work to be successful. Unfortunately, most of us leave doing that work until things go really wrong – perhaps even until our partner is about to walk out (or has walked out) the door. Working on our relationships is much more pleasurable and successful when we start before we're struggling.

It allows us to build a 'glue' that will keep us together when normal relationship challenges arise. Instead of sorting out problems with the dreaded 'We need to talk…' conversations, we choose to communicate in ways that invite each other into our respective worlds and create a safe space for relating. It's vulnerable, but it works.

Research by John M. Gottman, Ph.D has shown that couples who make the effort to connect with and truly know each other have consistently better relationships than those who don't. This effort gives us a sense of being on the same team before we get into opposing corners. And the more connected we are with ourselves, the more we have to share – and the more we see the value in learning about our partner.

Letting go of the fairy tale

Despite how modern we've become (unless we've grown fashionably cynical), most of us still carry the old-fashioned idea of the perfect fairy-tale relationship in the back of our minds. This happy-ever-after looks unique for each of us, but it usually has a common flavour of effortlessness. We come to a relationship believing that if we start with the right person, claim ownership of them, then set up house and have a family, we'll somehow effortlessly grow old together into our twilight years... all the way to a shared burial plot.

Holding onto this fantasy makes us lazy. We take our relationship, our partners and even love itself for granted, making them our last priority instead of our first. It's like we believe that once we're in a relationship, everything will magically be OK because we love each other. We do the same with our sex lives, believing they should just happen spontaneously.

Yearning for this impossible mental picture drains our energy and attraction for what's real, causing us to – either consciously or unconsciously – devalue what we have, or look around for something better. But real-life relationships don't have to be less than perfect. They can actually be better than we've ever imagined – literally beyond our wildest dreams!

Having an ideal fantasy makes the future seem safe and comforting, because we assume it's certain. Yet it's as if we're saying to life, "I know what's coming, I know what to do and I don't need any help." That means we close ourselves off to the vast potential of life that's so much more than our minds could plan. We keep trusting in the fantasy, rather than in ourselves and in love. Yet falling in love with not knowing opens us up to the magic of what lies beyond us.

What do Graeme and I mean by magic? We don't mean anything woo woo, just things that happen mysteriously and are impossible to explain or understand. This magic could be newness, surprise, chance, serendipity or merely coincidence, but it adds interest and even enchantment into our relationships. Believing in magic means we don't need the safety of knowing the end result, we can trust what lies on the other side of fear and certainty. It means we trust that each step is creating the next step, and that each step also creates our future.

 Letting Go of the Fairy Tale

Recognise and be willing to grieve the loss of your idealised fantasy relationship. For your relationship to last, your childlike ideals must die in the face of reality to allow what's genuine, authentic and magical to grow. Take a breath and relax. Nothing is wrong here.

1. Together or separately, write all your dreams of perfection down on a piece of paper. The more you come up, with the better. Depending on how attached you've been to your fantasy, this might bring up some fear and sadness. Know that this is healthy, and let yourself have a good cry if you need to.
2. Light a candle in a safe place and burn your paper.
3. See yourself leaving these limitations safely behind you and visualise a fresh new page for you to create on.

Once you've done this, you'll open up to the unknown possibilities of your real-life relationship and get excited about them. And if your

> relationship isn't all you've dreamed of, you'll be motivated to take some of the actions in this book to help it become so!

Other Relationship myths

These myths can become sacred cows that aren't open to question, but we need to question them if they aren't working for us. For example:

- I'll be in one relationship for my whole life. *This is statistically not as likely as it used to be.*
- My relationship needs to involve someone of my 'opposite' gender plus children. *Look around you, there are gender diverse relationships everywhere.*
- I have a 'twin flame', and all I have to do to live happily ever after is find them. *This can be true, but much time is wasted in wishing for it to happen.*
- My partner will complete me, and I'll never be alone again. *Loneliness still happens in relationships, and another person can never complete you the way you can complete yourself.*
- If someone truly loves me, they'll automatically know what I need and want without me having to ask. *Your partner is not your parent, and you are no longer an infant.*
- It's wrong to hurt my partner's feelings, so I should avoid being honest. *Avoiding honesty hurts more in the long run, because it builds walls and denies your partner the real 'you' to be in relationship with. If we're really honest, we do this more to protect ourselves from being seen than to protect our partners.*
- I must hold onto my relationship no matter what. *Being willing to let a relationship go means you're willing to take a risk on what's real rather than hold on to a fairy tale.*

- A good relationship is about denying myself to make my partner happy. *As you become more strongly based in your ego self, this one-sided approach simply doesn't cut it.*

- If I can't love my partner enough, there's something wrong with me. *Your partner needs to love themselves first, just like you do.*

- Habits and routines are the death of a relationship. *It's normal to create habits, our brains teach us to do this, as it would be terrifying to have to continually start everything from scratch. The important thing is to create habits and routines that work for you.*

- Disagreeing with my partner means something is wrong with the relationship. *It just means something more is being revealed, if you know how to look.*

- Good relationships are about 50/50 compromises. *In fact, continual compromise creates resentment. Try each giving 100/100 and notice your results.*

- Having a break will bring me closer to my partner. *This is true only if you make time to look at the challenges in your relationship whilst you're taking the break. Otherwise, it's statistically the beginning of the end.*

- An affair means my relationship is over. *If you're willing to sort it out, your chances of survival – and even having a better relationship than before – are excellent.*

- Once I'm in relationship I will/should not feel attracted to anyone else. *You're human, so that's not how you're made. It's what you do with the attraction that counts.*

- I should never let the sun go down on my anger. *Sometimes getting a good night's sleep can help you resolve things more easily the next day.*

- Having counselling for my relationship means that it's over. *The right relationship counsellor can mean that the good bit is just about to begin.*

1: Setting the Stage for Intimacy

 Exploring Your Beliefs About Relationship

Bringing your own beliefs to light will help you to decide which ones are serving you.

1. Without censoring them, write a list of as many of your beliefs about relationships as you can, leaving a gap between each belief.
2. Ask yourself where each one came from. Is it a myth, or is it true for you? If so, write down the evidence you base this on.
3. Taking each belief one at a time, imagine how would your life would be if you dropped it. How would you feel? What would be different?
4. Rewrite your list with only the beliefs that you now find relevant. Notice how you feel about yourself and relationships afterwards. Freer? Safer? Clearer? Challenged?

The important thing here is to become aware of the beliefs you're operating from, and that the ones you choose support – rather than limit – you.

Doing' relationship from the *inside* ...

We all long to feel close and connected to our partner. But it feels even better – and it's more powerful – when we can let go of unrealistic ideals and experience this through connection with ourselves instead. In fact, connection with ourselves is vital to good relationship.

*We can only be connected to another person to
the degree we are connected with ourselves.*

Being in connection with ourselves means becoming more actively aware of our thoughts, feelings and physical bodies. It means being at home inside ourselves, living from our authentic centre. From our centre, we waste minimal energy creating suffering or pain, and blaming our partner or ourselves for it. Instead, we create a greater abundance of love, understanding, support, respect, fun, creativity, pleasure and all the things that make a relationship work.

Another aspect of 'doing relationship' from the inside

A young couple comes to see us. They're both disconnected and hurting. She's fed up with his insensitive attempts at sex and wants something more intimate. He's bored with being told he's 'doing it wrong' and is about ready to give up, yet can't because he loves her. She's feeling hurt and frustrated and he's feeling rejected, shamed and lost.

Do Men = Sex, Women = Love?

What these two are acting out is a very common relationship scenario that's driven by the idea that men bring sex into a relationship and women bring love.

Graeme and I see this belief as another myth, and believe that challenging it transforms the potential for intimacy between men and women. It brings the walls of separation tumbling down and forms a part of the foundation we work from.

The stereotypical belief that men want sex and women want love works fine in the early days of relationship when both sex and love are abundant. But as the effortlessness of a new relationship fades, this view becomes at least a limitation and at worst a power-driven nightmare. This is because it puts the power within your relationship *outside* of you, and *into* the other.

As a man, you're left seeking what your woman controls – sex, for she has the ultimate veto rights. And as a woman, you're left seeking what you most desire from your man – his intimacy and his love, which has fallen away. This leaves both of you open to the deepest wounds of relationship:

emotional abandonment and rejection. This dynamic can and does, of course, happen the other way around, but the underlying premise is the same – that what we most want lies outside our control. It's a very painful place to live.

What you might not realise in this equation is that when a man shuts down sexually from too much sexual rejection, he also shuts down emotionally, and you'll understand why shortly. His partner then chastises him for wanting sex whilst not being emotionally available.

The other side of this equation that is a woman who closes her heart from a lack of intimacy (both in sex and outside of it) shuts her sexuality down. Again, you'll understand why soon. Her partner then invalidates her for not being sexually available.

As a result, both partners try to micro-manage the other to get their needs met, playing out the old saying that 'women fake orgasms and men fake relationships'. Each person is left needing what the other has and feeling incomplete without it, like two halves seeking each other to make one whole. Or if you're playing out the opposite dynamic where men have the low interest in sex and women the high you might both be faking relationship and orgasms.

This is because each person is playing from their weaknesses. They're socially conditioned to believe that men's strengths are sex and women's strengths are love. This conditioning makes it easier to judge each other – seeing men as unfeeling, selfish masochists and women as cold-hearted, complaining withholders – than to create loving connection.

We find challenging this belief moves our clients from suffering to healing, bringing each person into a loving, juicy, authentic connection with both themselves and with each other.

Men = Love, Women = Sex

Instead of looking to their partner (whom they can't control) each person needs look *inside of themselves* for what's missing (which they can). In doing so, they become more whole in themselves. The irony is that when our clients do this, they find to their surprise and joy that their partner is automatically more attracted to them, and will often fall over themselves to offer them what they long for.

What do you look inside yourself for?

Men: Your sexual-heart connection

When you feel and own the power of your heart, and you're unafraid to connect it to your sex, you become empowered in yourself. You're no longer driven by your sexual desires; instead, they become a conscious choice. You step out of shame and make love rather than just 'get off'. You no longer feel the need to 'play the game' to get your desires met, so you can be your authentic self.

Sexual rejection becomes less painful because you remain connected to yourself – and meanwhile, rejection paradoxically becomes less likely. Your heart exudes a love that has power far beyond ego, romance or anything commonly seen as love in our current superficial society. You go fearlessly and deep into feeling and lovemaking, focussing on heart-opening pleasure rather than on performance.

Your depth, passion and safety draws your woman close. It may also piss her off at times, as you'll be less manipulated by her agenda, and less likely to tolerate her being anything less than who she's capable of being. You'll have greater ability to take life head on, no matter what it brings.

Women: Your heart-sexual connection

When you own the power of your sexuality and are unafraid to connect it to your heart, you become empowered in yourself. You're no longer driven by a need for intimacy outside of yourself, because you find it within. You can step out of neediness, and embrace pleasure and connection, rather than being controlled by them.

You no longer feel the need to give yourself away in order to get your needs met: instead, you can be your authentic self. Emotional abandonment is less painful because you don't abandon yourself in your vulnerability. Paradoxically, abandonment becomes less likely. You know how to go willingly and joyously into pleasure, focussing on opening your heart to yourself rather than on getting love from your lover.

Your radiance, juiciness and surrender will draw your man close. It may also piss him off, as you'll no longer tolerate anything less than his full presence. You can express yourself clearly and nurture others from a place of inner abundance, rather than need. You too will have an ability to stand up in life and be who you are, no matter what.

Heart-sexual connection brings you home

We see it over and over in our work with couples.

When we talk about heart-sexual connection, we're not talking about the specific actions of love and sex. Instead, we're talking about how you're being inside yourself in that place where love and sex arise from. What you then do with that way of being is up to you.

We're aware that these ideas have stereotypes and limitations of their own, and that each relationship will have their own version of this dynamic. That's why we believe it's worth exploring to find your own core of truth within it. Much is being said these days, due to an oft-repeated quote from the Dalai Lama, about the power of Western women to save the world. We think the world is too complex for the answer to be that simple and believe it will take open-hearted men as well as empowered women. We reveal how in the following pages.

> **Men = Sex / Women = Love Myth Review**
>
> - Take some time to review your response to these ideas. Was your immediate response that it was true for your spouse, but not for you? But if it is true for one, surely it is true for both?
> - Ask yourself what is it that you most want from your partner? And ask them what is it they most want from you?
> - How is it for you when you don't receive what you most want from your partner? And how do you usually go about trying to get it?'
> - Come back to these thoughts again when you've read through the book and see how they sit.

1.3 What Actually IS Intimacy?

Once you've done a bit of myth busting about relationship you can start to look more closely at the intimacy inside of it.

Intimacy. It's a word that brings up desire, longing, fear, hurt and confusion; there aren't generally any neutral responses. Dictionaries use many words to try and explain it: a 'close familiarity or friendship', a 'cosy, private or relaxed atmosphere' or 'the intimacy between a husband and wife'. The term brings to mind words like closeness, sharing, togetherness, attachment, connection, warmth, affection, warm feelings, affinity, understanding and love. Yet intimacy can also bring up fear, and feel fraught with danger and challenge – so for some, it's an experience to be avoided at all costs.

Graeme and I like the tried-and-true New Age meaning of intimacy that is 'in-to-me-see': it's allowing another into your unique little world. It might be sharing your day-to-day happenings, your toothbrush, your body, the depths of your heart, or one of your personal peccadillos, eg the way you like to pick your nose or put your socks on before anything else in the morning.

We've identified a total of 12 different types of intimacy. Notice which kinds of intimacy you instinctively value, and which challenge you and which do the same for your partner.

Types of Intimacy:

1. **Intellectual Intimacy:** Sharing and exploring mutual, or even opposing ideas.

2. **Practical Intimacy**: Sharing physical tasks that require co-operation, being on the same team and working towards a common goal.

3. **Physical Intimacy:** Sharing physical connection between your body and another person's, from holding hands to full sexual union.

4. **Sensual Intimacy:** Sharing connection between your body and another person's through the senses: sight, sound, taste, touch and smell. It may include your genitals, yet is simply feeling and being in the moment without a sexual agenda to arouse.

5. **Sexual/Erotic Intimacy:** Sharing your thoughts, desires and/or physical body, including your genitals with the intent to arouse sexual pleasure, usually to orgasm.

6. **Enmeshed Intimacy:** The sense of there being no separation between yourself and the other person. Their feelings and thoughts become your own, and you as an individual cease to exist. You need the presence of the other person to feel OK in yourself.

7. **Isolated Intimacy**: Minimising the amount you feel by focussing on your thoughts, keeping busy and focussing your attention on things outside of your feeling reality from fear of intimacy with yourself or another. If you do allow yourself to feel, you mostly feel lonely.

8. **Personal Intimacy:** Sharing a mind/body connection with yourself where you learn to listen to your thoughts and feel your body and your feelings fully. Being comfortable with your inner reality and experiencing yourself as separate to, yet not apart from everyone and

everything else. You take ownership of your beliefs, values, needs, desires, actions and their outcomes. This is where self-love lives.

9. **Emotional and Heart-Connected Intimacy:** This is where you share your personal thoughts and feelings about yourself and what you're experiencing internally with another. It's where you start to expose what lies behind your persona's mask and take the chance of being seen in your naked humanity. Here you experience real feelings of connection with the other person and make meaning from it. It's where your ego gets the most messy and is the stage of intimacy most of us love to hate. However the more you remain connected with yourself, the more you can safely enter deep connection with another person.

10. **Soul Intimacy:** A sense of being with another person, or with what we believe to be God or Spirit in a moment of timelessness where our boundaries seem to disappear. It's where the idea of separateness ceases to exist and we merge what is within us with what is around us. Soul intimacy can be experienced in lovemaking, eye gazing, meditation, prayer and other religious experiences, or by simply experiencing an amazing sunset or a moment of total oneness in creative expression of dance, music, art, etc.

11. **Ego-lessness:** Going beyond the boundaries of who you think you are into the experience of being and of oneness with all that is. You still retain awareness in the experience, but without a sense of self. This state can be spontaneous but is most commonly experienced through moments of meditation and sexual ecstasy or orgasm (known as the 'little death' of the ego).

12. **No-thingness:** Going beyond personal awareness into the Infinite. The only way you know you've experienced this is when you come back and understand you've been 'somewhere else'. It has a different quality to sleep: you feel 'altered' by your experience. This state can be spontaneous also, but is more commonly experienced through meditation and more intense orgasm.

1: Setting the Stage for Intimacy

Each level of intimacy is powerful in its own right. One is not better or worse than another, though as individuals we're likely to be attached to some more than others. And even with this huge variety of intimate moments to share with another person, at the end of them we all still have to separate and come back to ourselves. This makes a healthy intimacy with ourselves a vital relationship skill. It also shows that no matter how deep we go with another person, they'll always remain unknowable at some levels – a mystery that keeps us coming back for more.

 Exploring The 12 Different Types of Intimacy

Reflect on your following choices, and what they have to offer you in your relationship.

- Underline the types of intimacy that are most important to you
- Tick the ones you currently engage in and put a cross next to the ones you don't
- Place a star next to those you find, or would find, challenging
- Circle those you'd like to experience more of
- Decide which you'd like to experience more of at the moment. What words best describe how you'd feel with these types of intimacy in your relationship? Imagine ways you could bring more of them into your relationship and consider the steps needed to make it happen
- Discuss what you've found with your partner, ask them about *their* preferred intimacy types and see if you can find common ground, or opposites to explore.

Identifying your intimacy desires will guide you to the most valuable practices for your relationship in the following pages.

1.4 Learning to Feel (and Yes, There's a Reason for It)

One of the main reasons we all avoid intimacy (or find it going pear-shaped) is our inability to connect with, be comfortable with, or understand the value in the feeling parts of ourselves. Graeme and I know this one personally from the inside out, due to the intense nature of our relationship and the life changes we've called in over the last few years. Our emotional intelligence has been invaluable in dealing with this – it's literally been the difference between life and death.

Stop and think for a moment

Connection, love, pleasure, passion, contentment, peace, ease, power, excitement, energy, orgasm, ecstasy, oneness and more are a big part of what we all long for in intimate relationship, and they're all feelings.

> *"Emotions are the stuff of life's inner content and the basis of its richness."*
>
> Aesthetics, Philosopher Nicolai Hartmann

Feelings are not facts, but they *are* an important part of our ability to understand, communicate and connect. Because feelings are stimulated by our older primitive brains, rather than our newer intellectual brains, they form a deep part of our relationship with ourselves. When we know our feelings in a healthy way, we know more of our core selves, and feel more at home there. Feelings are the creative juice in life and relationships.

In relationships more than anywhere else, we get to experience more challenging and less desirable feelings: frustration, anger, anxiety, shame, uncertainty, sadness, jealousy, hurt, rejection, loneliness, abandonment and many more. *All* of these feelings are perfectly normal when two unique individuals get together to create a relationship. Yet we so often make our 'negative' feelings wrong, and want only the 'positive' ones.

Even though you and your partner might believe you're on opposite sides of the fence at times, you actually both want the same thing: to feel good. In fact, this is where we can drop gender associations about feeling: men are generally just as keen to feel as women. It's just that men seek their feelings in sexual intimacy and women in emotional intimacy. And because Graeme and I deal in both types, we're one of the few businesses that have as many men making the first approach for our courses and counselling as we do women.

The reality of feelings is that we either feel, or we don't

Feelings exist in our bodies as energy (we live near Byron Bay so we can use the 'energy' word!) They're like water running through a hose: if we block the hose to one feeling, we do so to all of them. Therefore, to the degree that we close off any of our 'negative' emotions like anger, we close off our 'positive' ones as well. This is what we were referring to in saying men and women close off both sexually and emotionally at the same time.

We can't feel pleasure and not feel our anger, we can't feel joy without feeling our sadness, love without fear, or pleasure without pain.

We might think we're already feeling, but these feelings are a mere shadow of what we're capable of, like a little bit of water leaking around the kink in the hose rather than a full flow. This applies to erotic pleasure and blissful orgasms too. When you drop all the judgements and labels about a feeling, you'll find it's just energy.

You haven't fallen out of love – you've just stopped feeling fully

It's easy to feel the pleasurable feelings that occur in the beginning of relationship. It's more challenging to feel the uncomfortable feelings that inevitably come along later. Sometimes it's even difficult to give yourself permission to feel your *good* feelings (especially your sexual ones) if they weren't valued or respected in your childhood.

The intense and painful feelings that arise when natural differences occur between you, or when your needs or desires aren't met can leave you believing your relationship is going down the toilet. But you haven't so much fallen out of love as simply let your emotional fog get in the way of your loving connection.

A vital part of learning how to 'do' great relationships (and mind-blowing sex) is re-learning how to feel

Emotional Intelligence or EQ is the ability to work positively with your own emotions and those of others. It's a skill that's often valued more, even in business, than IQ. Graeme and I have expanded this definition to include not only your emotions but all of your feelings, including your sexual, sensory and subtle body ones. (Perhaps we should call this OmQ!)

It's vital to learn how to simultaneously feel *and* be in charge of your feelings, because feeling intelligently allows you to be heart-open and available for relationship. Of course, contemplating feeling more of your uncomfortable feelings can be a scary idea. The most helpful thing you can do is develop a willingness to trust in their importance, as dropping this resistance gives you greater power of choice over your feelings.

And take it gently, one step at a time.

Developing feeling awareness

Sensations and feelings

Feeling emotion begins with a physical sensation. Let's take grief, which starts with either a subtle, or more concrete sensation of tightness or heaviness in your chest. In an effort to avoid the feeling, you probably hold your breath and tighten up in your belly and chest. You may feel tears prickling behind your eyes as you attempt to hold yourself together. Perhaps your shoulders and neck also tighten, and your throat might contract with unexpressed words. Your whole body can end up in a state of chronic tension without you even realising it.

Make it a habit of noticing and labelling the concrete physical sensations in your body, then follow up by noticing any feeling that accompanies them. Do so without judging whatever you find, or creating a story about it. Sometimes you've locked feelings away for very good reason – as a form of self-defence or survival. If this is the case, you might like to work with your partner, a friend or a therapist to support you in unlocking these parts of your feeling realm. However you start, this is the way to become more connected with yourself.

 Identifying and Naming Sensations

Sometimes it can be hard to actually feel what's going on in your body if doing so is very unfamiliar to you. For this exercise, pause for a moment, bring your attention to your body, take a breath and let it go, then simply notice what sensations you become aware are there.

Do this regularly. We've included a list of concrete body sensations that can help you better identify what you're experiencing. Once you've identified the body sensation it can be easier to identify the feeling that lies underneath it.

Body Sensations

Sharp Pain	Alive	Warm	Flowing	Faint	Twitchy
Dull Pain	Full	Cool	Sensual	Floating	Calm
Heavy	Open	Hot	Sexual	Disconnected	Buzzy
Sleepy	Expanded	Cold	Tight	Separate	Drained
Tingling	Aching	Drowsy	Breathless	Connected	Exhausted
Numb	Throbbing	Alert	Quivery	Bubbly	Wobbly
Blank	Light	Rigid	Queasy	Blocked	Fluttery
Loving	Stuck	Tentative	Trembling	Ready	Energised
Dizzy	Sweaty	Soft	Enclosed	Surrendered	Hollow
Absent	Aroused	Tender	Trembly	Restless	Home

 ## Identifying & Naming Feelings

Often, we don't have words to describe whatever we're feeling.

Use the Feeling Table below to develop your 'feeling language'. Putting a name to a feeling (without worrying about the mental 'why') can help you to feel it more fully. Find descriptions that intuitively match your feelings, don't worry about getting them 'right'. Whatever you experience them as in the moment is right. Trust this.

Feelings

Accepted	Alive	Amazed	Amused	Animated
At ease	Attracted	Abandoned	Absorbed	Aching
Affected	Afraid	Aggravated	Aggressive	Agonised
Anguished	Alarmed	Alienated	Alone	Angry
Annoyed	Anxious	Apprehensive	Ashamed	Awkward
Bright	Brilliant	Blank	Blessed	Bold
Bashful	Bewildered	Bothered	Brave	Bitter
Bad	Blue	Bored	Calm	Caring

1: Setting the Stage for Intimacy

Cheerful	Courageous	Comfortable	Comforted	Compassionate
Content	Challenged	Close	Cautious	Closed
Cold	Cranky	Cross	Crushed	Delighted
Determined	Dynamic	Drawn to	Depressed	Detached
Disconnected	Diminished	Dissatisfied	Despairing	Dejected
Dependable	Desolate	Desperate	Distressed	Disgusted
Dull	Easy	Eager	Encouraged	Ecstatic
Elated	Eager	Earnest	Empathetic	Energetic
Enthusiastic	Excited	Edgy	Embarrassed	Empty
Enraged	Euphoric	Exasperated	Exhausted	Festive
Free	Easy	Friendly	Frisky	Fed up
Foolish	Forgiving	Funny	Fatigued	Fearful
Flat	Flustered	Frightened	Forced	Guilty
Frustrated	Furious	Gay	Glad	Gleeful
Guilty	Grateful	Great	Greedy	Grieving
Grouchy	Happy	Hard	Hearty	Hilarious
Honoured	Humble	Humorous	Helpless	Heartbroken
Heavy	Hesitant	Hopeless	Horrified	Hot
Hostile	Humiliated	Hurt	Important	Inspired
Ignored	Impatient	Impotent	Incapable	Invalidated
Inflamed	Infuriated	Injured	Insecure	Insensitive
Invalidated	Invisible	Irked	Irresponsible	Irritated
Joyous	Jumpy	Jubilant	Jaded	Jealous
Jinxed	Judgmental	Kinky	Keen	Kind
Laid back	Liberated	Light	Light-hearted	Likeable
Lucky	Longing	Lost	Loved	Loving
Labile	Lazy	Lifeless	Lonely	Loss
Magical	Mellow	Merry	Mad	Manipulated
Melancholy	Mischievous	Miserable	Mixed-up	Moody

Mournful	Lost	Mad	Neutral	Nice
Naughty	Nauseated	Needed	Needy	Neglected
Nervous	Non-attached	Nothing	Okay	Open
Optimistic	Overjoyed	Off	Overpowered	Out-of-control
Outraged	Overloaded	Over-the-top	Overstimulated	Passionate
Playful	Powerful	Panicked	Pained	Paralysed
Pathetic	Peeved	Perplexed	Powerless	Quiet
Quick	Peaceful	Quivery	Quaking	Receptive
Refreshed	Relaxed	Relieved	Restful	Rattled
Rejected	Reluctant	Repugnant	Repulsed	Reserved
Resentful	Restless	Safe	Satisfied	Secure
Sensitive	Serene	Serious	Shy	Spacious
Spirited	Strong	Sad	Scared	Sensual
Sexual	Shaky	Silly	Sore	Sorrowful
Tender	Tickled	Tearful	Tense	Terrified
Threatened	Timid	Tingly	Tired	Unafraid
Up	Unruffled	Uncomfortable	Uneasy	Unhappy
Upset	Useless	Vulnerable	Volatile	Warm
Withdrawn	Woeful	Weary	Wary	Yearning

1.5 Vulnerability: The Blessing and Curse of Intimacy

Vulnerability of the emotional kind deserves a special mention when talking about intimacy. Not only because vulnerability underpins the creation and maintenance of all truly intimate relationships, but because we've all been sold a big, fat lie about it. We've been told that vulnerability is a scary, dangerous place, and a place of weakness. And if you're wondering how Graeme and I know much about vulnerability, try imagining being a middle-aged couple from a traditional rural community who suddenly step into our current roles of relationship and sex therapists, and you'll get a bit of an idea. At times, it's felt like our very skin has been peeled off our bones, leaving us exposed to our core.

But we've learned to see the emotional vulnerability of intimacy as a place of deep openness, availability and even innocence. It's how real connection occurs and it's a vital relationship skill to cultivate. It's also a pathway into self empowerment. Without it, you can share the intimacy of each other's company, have common interests and do things together, but you stay on the surface of each other and of yourselves.

> *"Intimacy hinges on validating yourself rather than trusting your partner to make you feel safe."*
>
> Passionate Marriage, David Schnarch, PhD

Being vulnerable means going a step or two further, by letting your psyche's emotional walls down, either a little or a lot. It means softening your rigid self-protection and being seen, letting your partner in – staying there long enough so that you (and often your partner) feel its impact. It's a beautiful thing. And it's not that difficult, providing you get out of your own way and practice, practice, practice. Vulnerability is not just about sharing your fears and uncertainties. It's also risking reaching out, being willing to be seen and rejected, yet choosing to go there anyway.

It's not possible to love or be loved fully whilst you have your emotional walls up. And yet we all resist the perception of loss of control that letting down our defences brings. We do this even though without true vulnerability, our relationships will die from lack of the real connection and nourishment that most of us long for (whether we're willing to admit it or not).

Coming Together

"Unfortunately, there is no 'get out of vulnerability free' card. We can't opt out of the uncertainty, risk, and emotional exposure that's woven through our daily experiences. Life is vulnerable."

Daring Greatly, Brene Brown.

We want to be clear here that when we talk about vulnerability, we're not automatically talking about being emotional. You can be very emotional and still have your walls right up. You can also feel extremely vulnerable without being obviously emotional at all.

The fear of vulnerability comes from misunderstanding its true nature and the pain this creates, rather than from vulnerability itself. From this fear, people make the seemingly logical choice to keep vulnerability at bay by defending themselves from, or attacking whatever's making them feel vulnerable. When they do this, however, they put their focus outside of themselves and miss out on the awesome potential love, connection and self-understanding that lies on the other side of that vulnerability.

The key to vulnerability is paradoxically in choosing to make it OK, and then just being with it. In doing so, you remain in charge of yourself, your loss of control lessens and your need to protect or defend yourself drops away. You then see your partner's actions with greater clarity and empathy.

If one person consciously takes a risk, shows up and becomes vulnerable instead of choosing defence or attack, downward spirals in your relationship can be stopped and reversed. Graeme and I often see amazing results from this simple little process.

When you make vulnerability OK, choosing to feel it, allow it, even welcome it in, you're in a very powerful place.

As ridiculous as it sounds, focussing on *feeling* your vulnerability, rather than on the exposure you need to protect yourself from, takes you beyond the exposure into connecting with *yourself* more fully. You connect with yourself in a place where you can no longer be abandoned or rejected because YOU are there with yourself. It's the deepest form of self love and self-empowerment, where you no longer feel the need to hide or protect yourself. You go deeply inside yourself and find you're not weak and helpless as you feared. Instead, you're surprisingly vast and powerful. You're also as emotionally open and available as possible in that moment – to yourself, to your partner, and even to love itself.

In this way, you can be deeply in connection with another person whilst remaining fully in connection with yourself. This is the ultimate healthy place in true intimacy: together, yet still individual and the only way to find it is through experience, you cannot think your way into this place.

You can tell when you're connecting with yourself in your vulnerability because you have fewer words and less external 'venting' of emotion. There's less need to defend or attack. You just feel – and the longer you feel, the clearer you become.

If you stop buying into the fear stories of vulnerability and simply learn to be with it, you gain a sense of strength that's like 'Come and get me world! Do your worst, because here I am with no more walls, and nothing more can hurt me! There is no greater gift in intimacy than finding this.'

There will be times when it's too big an ask, but each attempt is a win.

> *"Vulnerability is the centre of difficult emotion. It is also the birthplace of every positive emotion we need in our lives – love, belonging, empathy and joy."*
>
> Floral Notebook, Brene Brown

Going into vulnerability will always be uncomfortable, and it takes both courage and practice. The more willingly you embrace the power of vulnerability, the easier and more rewarding intimacy (including intimate and pleasurable lovemaking) becomes.

> **Challenging Your Mindset About Vulnerability**
>
> Choosing to be vulnerable willingly is a big ask. For now, we suggest you just think about the idea and see what responses it brings up for you.
>
> 1. Grab some paper and write the word 'vulnerability' in the centre. Draw a circle around it, leaving some space inside the circle for later.
> 2. Around the circle, write all the negative responses this word brings up for you. Place the more challenging responses in close, and the easier ones further out.
> 3. Think about the results you gain from these responses. What do they give you?
> 4. Also consider where your responses might limit you.
> 5. Make your responses OK by letting go of any negative judgments and bringing acceptance to them.
> 6. Now, in the centre of the circle, write any positive benefits you can see right now from embracing vulnerability as we've suggested above.
> 7. Notice how willing you are, on a scale of 1-10, to embrace vulnerability at this point in time, with 10 being the most willing and 1 the least. Don't judge yourself for your answer, just be aware of where you're at with it for now.
> 8. You might like to discuss the idea of embracing vulnerability with your partner, or even your friends and family, and comparing your responses about this important topic.

Learning to be OK with Vulnerability

Set an intention to explore your relationship with vulnerability, and see if you can find your power in it. Start with whatever is a low level of vulnerability for you, which will be different for each of us. You can start outside your relationship, if doing this with your partner feels too big.

The next time you're talking about a touchy subject and you feel some vulnerability, see if you can sit with it, just for a moment or two.

- Take a couple of breaths and notice the feeling with as much acceptance as you can manage (in the same way you did when you experienced your body sensations and feelings in the first section).
- Imagine welcoming this feeling deeper into you.
- Notice how when you do this, it becomes more of an OK place to be.
- Acknowledge yourself for going there.
- As you get more familiar with sitting in vulnerability, see if you can stay there a few moments longer. You may even notice that your vulnerability changes into something more comfortable, even something surprising.
- With practice, you'll find you can trust yourself more in your vulnerability and depend less on your partner's response. Over time, you'll notice that your vulnerability isn't as scary as it used to be – and you feel amazingly more powerful in it.

The magic in all of this is that when you take a risk in showing up with your walls down, your partner is more likely to feel drawn towards you, rather than reject you, as you might fear. Genuine exposure (unlike pseudo-vulnerability from behind your walls) invites **attraction to your humanity** rather than the opposite.

And even if your partner does happen to reject you, you're still OK because you're connected fully to yourself and your hurt needs only be temporary. Over the course of this book, we'll reveal how vulnerability is the pathway to what you long for, not only in your relationship, but also within yourself – and we'll give you the tools to make the most of it.

Understanding suffering

Buddha sat under the tree of enlightenment for forty years to discover that life is about suffering. Two unique, separate individuals trying to live together in an intimate relationship *will* experience moments of vulnerability and suffering along with the love, joy and pleasure. Even though you might wish it was different, this is the nature of the beast. It doesn't mean anything is wrong. If you want to avoid pain, avoid relationships. Then again, if you want to avoid pain, you should also avoid being human. Yet there's a difference between hurt that's just plain suffering and hurt that's healing and growing.

> *"Everything worthwhile in life is won through surmounting the associated negative experience"*
>
> The Subtle Art Of Not Giving A Fuck, Mark Manson

Like the best soap operas, suffering pain never has to end. There's always a hook that leaves you breathless for the next episode, caught in your own trap... Healing pain, by contrast, is tolerable because it has an end point. You find healing pain inside your vulnerability, and you can choose your own meaning in it. Choosing healing pain over suffering pain creates safety in your relationship and ends the drama between you and your partner.

It's easier than you think, and is the basis of the ABC practice coming next.

Surrender and Freedom

2.1 The ABC of Coming Together

What *is* 'the ABC of Coming Together'? Does it mean two people scaling the heights of sexual pleasure to reach the ultimate peak of 'coming' at the same time?

Well, no. But we're talking about something that's just as good! And, just like the ABC of 'Airway, Breathing & Circulation', it's also life-sustaining.

This ABC is about your own mind and
body 'coming together' through:

ATTENTION, BREATH & CONNECTION

It's the No. 1 technique to transform your relationship. In fact, it can also transform your life as an individual as it transforms your relationship.

This is because the ABC practice helps you come into greater relationship with yourself, with your partner, with your point of power in the present moment, and with the choices you make as a result.

Modern culture has us all walking around disconnected from ourselves much of the time. We're stressed, half-alive, half available to life and to each other. We're living in our heads, where facts are more highly valued than feelings. In reality though, we're NOT just pieces of meat walking around with a highly intelligent brain on top. We're that highly intelligent brain *and* we're also a feeling/experiencing intelligent body.

The most common ways to experience the connection between these two aspects of ourselves include that moment of stepping out of the ocean tingling all over, having truly great sex, or feeling everything coming together for that one triumphant shot in sports. It involves feeling really alive, connected and in the moment. Less enjoyably, it also happens in emotional discomfort, physical pain or bodily malfunction. But you don't need to limit this embodiment to sex, occasional triumphs or pain. The ABC process will help you find it whenever you want.

But first let's see what stops you from being embodied, ie having a mind-body connection:

- You don't know you can
- You're socially conditioned to live in your limited mind
- You stay too busy, tense and stressed to notice that you're disconnected from your body
- You're used to thinking, or going over the top of, your feelings
- You want to avoid feeling uncomfortable

Living this way, you're disconnected from the full reality of your physical body, your senses, feelings and other subtle realms (whether you believe in them or not) that help to create the magic in your relationship. It's like you're outside of yourself, with your focus facing even further outward without any real connection to what lies within you. This external focus means you're missing half of yourself, a half that is vital to the intimate part of your relationship. Missing this half it's easy for you to feel abdanoned and rejected in your relationship, because you've already abandoned and rejected part of yourself and so the pain becomes a double whammy. This internal disconnection makes it impossible to not only know yourself fully, but also to safely connect with your partner.

> *"One of the clearest lessons from contemporary neuroscience is that our sense of ourselves is anchored in a vital connection with our bodies. Numbing may make life tolerable, [but] the price you pay is that you lose awareness of what is going on inside your body and, with that, the sense of being fully, sensually alive."*
>
> The Body Keeps The Score, Bessel Van Der Kolk, MD

If you regularly check in with your body when there's NO pain or malfunction, you'll get to know more of the amazing feelings it's capable of. This awareness not only feels good, it also strengthens the relationship between you, your mind and body, your sexuality (which lives deep inside your body) and your essence (the part that feels like your centre or truth – your authentic or even soul self). This deeper relationship with yourself will then help you step into, and stay in, a relationship with your partner.

This simple ABC practice is about coming into UNION with YOURSELF

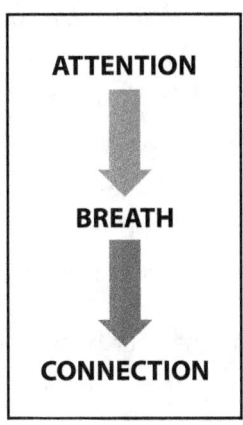

NOTE: the **first** thing you may think about this practice is that it's a waste of time. It isn't.

The **second** thing you might think is that you haven't got time. If it's important enough, you'll find time.

The **third** thing you'll think is that it's too simple to work. It isn't: the simplest things in life are often the most powerful, and like anything worth doing, it takes practice.

To reflect these three very common reactions, we've broken The ABC practice up into three different levels. This will make getting familiar with the process easier. Then, with practice, it will take just a moment or two to do all three levels anywhere, anytime, even with your eyes open.

 The ABC Practice

Level 1: Connect mind and body

1. Pause. Close your eyes.
2. Shift your ATTENTION from your thoughts and the world around you to your body.
3. BREATHE slightly more deeply than normal into your belly and your chest.
4. Use your mind to CONNECT with your body. Notice and experience yourself as a mind *and* a body for a moment.

If this is all you do, it's a good start.

Level 2: Get grounded

5. After Steps 1-4, CONNECT with your pelvis, notice the part of you that lives between your navel and your tailbone (however that part appears in your mind's eye, trust it).

   Breathe deeply. Imagine your body relaxing and sinking into a forest floor; and cool, mossy tree roots from the earth wrapping around your lower body. This is very grounding and reassuring. It sounds weird, but it works.

Level 3: Go deeper

6. CONNECT with the rest of your body. Give your mind the job of scanning your body, observing first any physical sensations of relaxation, tension, heat, cold, tingling, pain, discomfort, etc without judgment (as you did in the last Chapter).

7. Then CONNECT with whatever's happening *inside your body* in your chest, belly and throat. Notice any subtle sensations such as heaviness, lightness, tension, butterflies, anxiety, frustration, pleasure, ease, peace, happiness, blankness, etc. You may experience nothing, yet *this nothing is still something*.

8. Keeping your attention on your feelings, breathe and experience them just as they are *without suppressing or accelerating them with your thoughts*. There's nothing to do here other than drop into the experience with acceptance. As you do this, you'll notice the feelings will shift and change. Stay here for a few moments and keep breathing fully.

9. If you open your eyes here, you might notice that you're looking out of your body, as if through the windows of your 'house'.

Welcome home.

This is you 'coming together' and being in *connection* with yourself. It's being in a relationship *with yourself* in the power of the present moment, where you're most aware and available to life. Comfortable or not, from this place both life and relationships work. This practice is the basis of everything that follows in this book.

And believe it or not, doing this also begins to improve your sex life: for being fully present with yourself is the first step to the sex you long for.

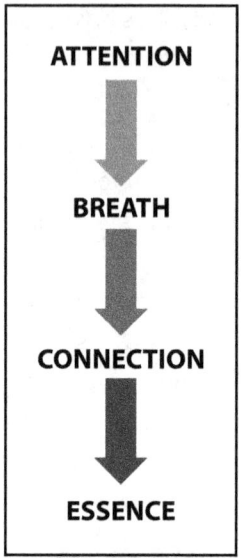

With practice, this process of going within connects you more and more deeply with your essence. If the word 'essence' is too 'woo woo' for you, think of your essence as a place of heightened awareness where your mind is clear, open and focussed, and your body is relaxed. Where there's a sense of greater connection, between 'you' and 'yourself'.

You'll find a variety of feelings here, eg groundedness, inner calm, lightness, clarity, strength, peace, happiness, freedom, spaciousness, pleasure, playfulness, spontaneity, gratitude, compassion, vitality, aliveness, sexuality, creativity, radiance, meaning, or what you might describe as love or spirit (even if your logical mind doesn't believe in this). You'll experience a feeling of greater connection with your partner, and with your subtle realms and with life itself too (again, even if your logical mind doesn't believe in this). You won't lose your more familiar intellectual abilities: instead, you'll add the feeling ones of your intuitive/heart/body mind. This is like having your own internal (Apple Mac) Siri!

You'll learn that while you may experience uncomfortable feelings at times, with your help they'll always shift and change – despite your fears that they won't. You'll learn which feelings to trust and which to ignore. Your ABC practice will also help your mind to clear and make your thoughts easier to see, helping you to know which ones are working for you and which aren't.

If you constantly feel emotionally overwhelmed, this practice will help you become less identified with and controlled by your feelings. If you're unfamiliar with – or resist – feeling, it will help you learn ways to safely navigate your feelings and find the benefits in them.

Connecting with your essence doesn't mean you'll instantly have all the understanding and skills you need for life. You won't suddenly be good at maths, public speaking or communicating if you weren't before. But it does mean you'll be more comfortable in your skin, and more at ease in life no matter what it throws at you. You'll also be more comfortable with people in general, and with your partner in particular – however they're being at the time.

Being in your essence also makes you more attractive, desirable and available to your partner. And from it you'll learn – as Krishnamurti says in The First and Last Freedom, "...not to live an ideal life, but to see things as they are and transform them."

The more regularly and strongly you connect with your essence through this body-centred practice, the more deeply you'll experience it.

You may get just a hint, or you may get something profound. Regardless, the potential is always there. You'll find these otherwise spontaneous moments separate from *any* external sources, they're just waiting there within you. They're worth being alive for, and are a place worth living from.

Practice Regularly

The more you say YES to your mind/body connection, the more its intelligence will say YES to you.

In the beginning, you'll need to stop what you're doing and close your eyes to do this practice. The world won't give you time for this, so you'll have to *take the time for yourself*. With practice, you'll be able to do it with your eyes open, anywhere, any time, *no matter what's happening around you*. You could be in a meeting, on a run, having a shower, in a crisis, making love – and you'll simply trust that it will give you more of whatever inner resources you need.

> *"It is very easy to be compassionate and altruistic when we are sitting comfortably on our seats, but the test of the practice is when we encounter a problem."*
>
> The Essential Dalai Lama, HH The Dalai Lama

There'll be many references to this practice throughout the book to show you how relevant and powerful it is in creating the relationship that will most serve you – and even more, in creating the relationship you'll find you most want.

2.2 Developing Feeling Intelligence

Feelings are part of our human intelligence, communication and survival systems, and are a vital part of our individual and relationship aliveness.

Most people who get stuck in their relationships do so somewhere in their ability to feel. If you're not comfortable with feeling your feelings in a relationship, you'll subtly (or unsubtly) try to manipulate your partner in order to make yourself feel better – a true recipe for relationship disaster.

> *"Given how fundamental our emotions are to our very being and how frequently they arise in us, it is remarkable how little intimacy we may have with them."*
>
> Emotional Intimacy, Robert Augustus Masters, PhD

In this book, you'll find a basic map of how to recognise, understand and benefit from your feelings. This map is like a jetty to dive into the pool of your feelings from, keeping the jetty safely in sight whilst you learn to swim. Otherwise, learning to feel can be a bit like being dumped in the deep end of the lake!

As children, we feel freely and intensely, changing quickly from one feeling to another in response to each moment. As we grow up, however, we internalise messages about how feeling is messy, inappropriate, uncomfortable, and even unnecessary – so we gradually shut our feelings down, becoming less alive.

Feelings can only hurt us if we *don't* feel them. Avoiding or shutting down our feelings has serious consequences for both our relationships and ourselves. Just because we don't feel them doesn't mean they don't exist. In fact, they still do – just below our awareness.

Withheld feelings lead to an inability to concentrate, to think critically, tiredness, stress, physical discomfort and pain, poor health, disease and low self-esteem. We seek relief through unhealthy habits and even emotional or physical partner abuse and violence. Three different ten-year studies showed that emotional stress predicted death from cancer and cardiovascular disease better than smoking.

When we make our feelings wrong we make ourselves wrong at a deep level.

Emotional suppression also leads to lower quality of life and a diminished capacity for intimacy by closing our hearts and keeping us in shame. And – not least important – it vitally reduces our capacity for satisfying lovemaking, because we either feel or we don't. We can't avoid fear and frustration and still feel pleasure. Learning to open up the flow of feelings brings us many benefits.

Knowing *what* we feel is crucial to seeing *why* we might feel a certain way, and to knowing where we stand and what we can do about it. In the West, science shows us that feelings are created in the oldest, most primitive parts of our brains. This means our feelings unconsciously inform our decision-making long before our newer, rational brain even gets involved.

That means we feel our feelings *before* we can rationally think about them. But as illogical as they might seem at times, our feelings aren't *opposed* to reason. In fact, they form our basis for reason by assigning the primary values to our experiences, so it's worth learning how to trust them.

In the East, feelings are thought to exist as energy in motion (e-motion). They're seen as generated by various energy systems in the body – each with their own intelligence – in the form of gut feelings and intuitive wisdom.

There's value in both the Western and Eastern points of view.

Real change in relationships begins when we learn to acknowledge, own and value our emotional experience. So we hope to encourage you to gradually open up your own flow of feeling in a healthy way. This will help you to become happier, more emotionally available, and more vibrant and sexy as well!

Thinking vs Feeling

We *experience* feelings in our bodies. The more familiar and comfortable we are with our feelings, the more accurately our logical brain will interpret the signals it receives from them.

*Thoughts and feelings are separate.
Thoughts happen in the mind. Feelings
mostly happen in the body.
Feelings are NOT thoughts, and you cannot think them.
Feelings and actions can give rise to thoughts, and
thoughts and actions also give rise to feelings.*

 How our thoughts and feelings relate:

Thoughts can create feelings: "Today is Valentine's Day, and I believe I will receive flowers from my lover, therefore I feel happy."

Feelings can also create thoughts: "I feel scared. This means my partner must be going to reject me when I tell her I love her."

Actions can create feelings: "Being cut off in traffic made me mad!"

Feelings can create actions: "Gratitude for my partner had me offer to take her out for dinner."

Triggered feelings can rise from inside of us (usually from our past): "Believing my girlfriend isn't interested in me brings up the same feelings I experienced being with my emotionally unavailable mother."

Most of us try to **think our feelings**

We do this as a logical way to avoid the discomfort of actually feeling them. We also do it because we're so familiar with thinking our way through life and because we're taught that logic is more valuable than feeling. But thinking our feelings isn't helpful: it disconnects us from our bodies and helps us stay numbed out, or in the emotional drama of suffering pain. It also means we miss out on feeling the feelings we want more of, such as happiness. When we drop into our bodies and feel we often find that our actual feelings are quite different from whatever we 'think' we're feeling. Our embodied feelings are usually more helpful than the mentally driven ones.

Ways to find control as you feel

Feelings can give us a sense of being out of control, but we can be greatly reduce this through the thoughts we choose *as* we feel. Actively choosing to acknowledge, accept, understand, resolve and even enjoy our feelings as we feel them helps us to stay in control without avoid having to avoid feeling altogether. Another gift of accepting our feelings is that it vastly reduces our mind's need to over think and complicate things, leaving it freer to get on with what is truly relevant.

If feelings are energy, and you feel them when that energy is moving, the driver of both feelings and energy is your breath. The more you breathe, the more you feel, and vice versa. Imagine trying not to cry, or feeling fear, the first thing you do is stop your breath. So a lot of being emotionally intelligent is simply remembering to breathe.

A Simple Model of Feeling

Dealing with feelings can be complicated, so Graeme and I like to keep it as simple as possible to keep the mind from getting too involved and distracting us away. We use the following model (based on work by Nicholas De Castella) which begins with four main emotions:

Emotions

Molecules of these four main emotions have been found in the earliest forms of life (by Dr Candice Pert and others). Remember: they're part of our human survival system so they deserve a little respect. They are:

- *Anger:* an intense feeling that occurs most commonly in your belly, across the back of your neck, in your jaw, or throughout your whole body that you experience as heat and tension.

  Anger ranges in degree from annoyance through irritation, resentment (collapsed anger), frustration, all the way up to rage. (Note: anger is about you, NOT aggression, which is projecting your anger outwards onto others).

  Anger occurs when you don't get what you want. It is the energy of change, for once you get angry enough about something, you'll change it. Importantly, the flip side of anger is passion, which we'll talk about more later. Despite its power, anger is often a secondary emotion, one that often covers fear, sadness or shame.

- *Fear:* is felt as butterflies, nausea, churning in your solar plexus or coldness/frozenness in your body, which stops you from breathing fully.

  Fear varies in degree from butterflies through anxiety and panic to terror that causes you to freeze, fight or flee.

  Fear is about protection and always relates the future – about what bad things might or might not happen. When you feel fear, you're hypervigilant about your surroundings, seeking to protect yourself and be ready for action. The flip side of fear is excitement, where you believe something good will happen and keep breathing.

- *Sadness:* You feel sadness as a heaviness in your chest, tears in your eyes and a desire to go within.

Sadness ranges in degree from feeling simply sad to melancholy, grieving to depressed. (Be wary of labelling all depression as sadness, however: it can sometimes be suppressed anger).

Sadness is about loss, letting go of the past and moving on – allowing yourself to grieve what you've had, and make room in your life for something new. Not allowing yourself to grieve keeps you stuck in the past and limits future possibilities. This feeling is vital in a relationship, as being stuck in past hurts will destroy the present. A close partner of sadness is love: they both occur around the heart, and feeling your sadness is a great heart opener.

- *Joy:* You feel joy as something good all over. It feels expanded and abundant.

Joy varies in degree from cheerful through delighted and excited to ecstatic. Joy is uplifting, and is motivation for living. When you feel joy, you feel really good about yourself and your life, and you're more likely to get things done.

Sometimes people have difficulty giving themselves permission to feel joy if they were shamed about it or didn't get the chance to feel it as a child. It's easy to lose your joy if you get caught up in the tasks of daily living and forget how life-giving this emotion is.

Emotions are superficial: No matter how intense they become, once you feel them with acceptance and breath (using the ABC) they pass through you and **dissipate**.

Core Heart Feelings

Underneath all of our emotions lie our Core Heart Feelings. These are what we find in our essence through the ABC process. They're feelings such as love, happiness, freedom, gratitude, spaciousness and compassion.

2: Surrender and Freedom

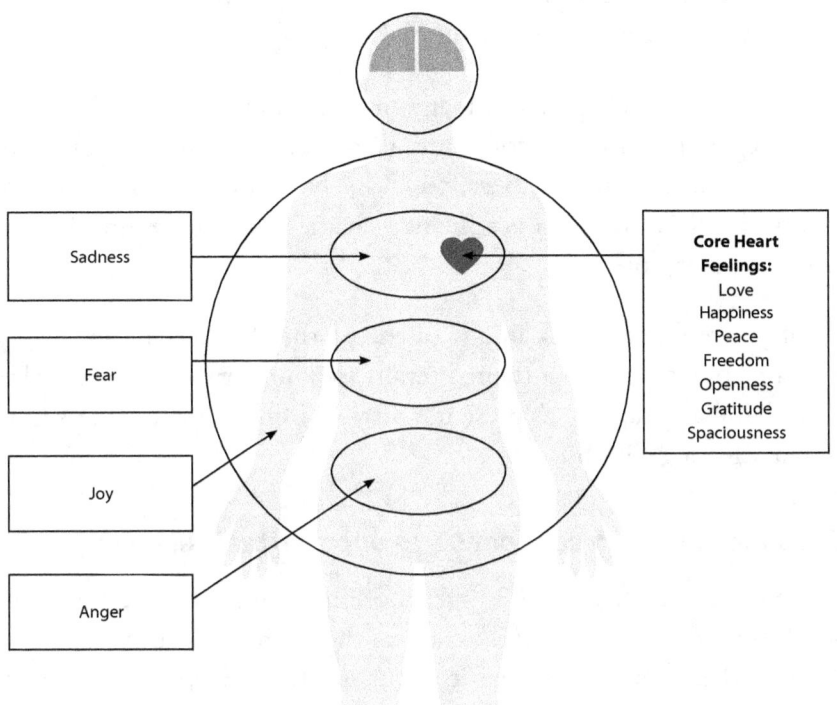

Diagram 2.1 Model of Feeling

*Core Heart Feelings are deeper; the more we feel them, the **stronger** they become.*

So the way to feel more of these desired Core Heart Feelings is to find them *through your emotions*, rather than separate to them. We can experience these feelings separate to emotion yet we don't need to *deny* emotion to feel them. See Diagram 2.1.

Of course, we can experience many more feelings than just these main four – eg guilty, unloved, contempt, disgust, hate or distrust. But if you look underneath each of these, you'll likely find one of the four main emotions. Note: this doesn't include shame – a core feeling in itself, which we'll explore later.

So, if you're feeling stuck in any of these other feelings, rather than go into a mental story about them, literally look underneath them. Feel the underlying emotion that's present, and you'll find your stuckness in the primary feeling will shift.

Our Emotions also connect us to our spiritual selves

As you'll see in Diagram 2.2, our emotional centres also relate to your subtle body energy centres, (chakras) for those who believe in such things. Far from being an impediment to your spiritual self, your emotions are actually a pathway to the intelligence found in the energetic system of your body if you choose to explore them. Feeling your emotions helps to keep your energy centres open, and offers you deeper layers of understanding and connection with yourself and your partner.

Our emotions and our hormonal system

Not only does feeling your emotions keep you physically and emotionally healthier and spiritually connected, it also promotes wellbeing and longevity by de-stressing your body's hormonal glands, as you'll see in Diagram 2.3. Science shows that hormones signficantly influence your motivation for – and satisfaction and connection in – intimacy too.

In Chapter 8, you'll explore the practice of Tantric breathing. For now, Graeme and I just want to let you know that using Tantric breathing

2: Surrender and Freedom

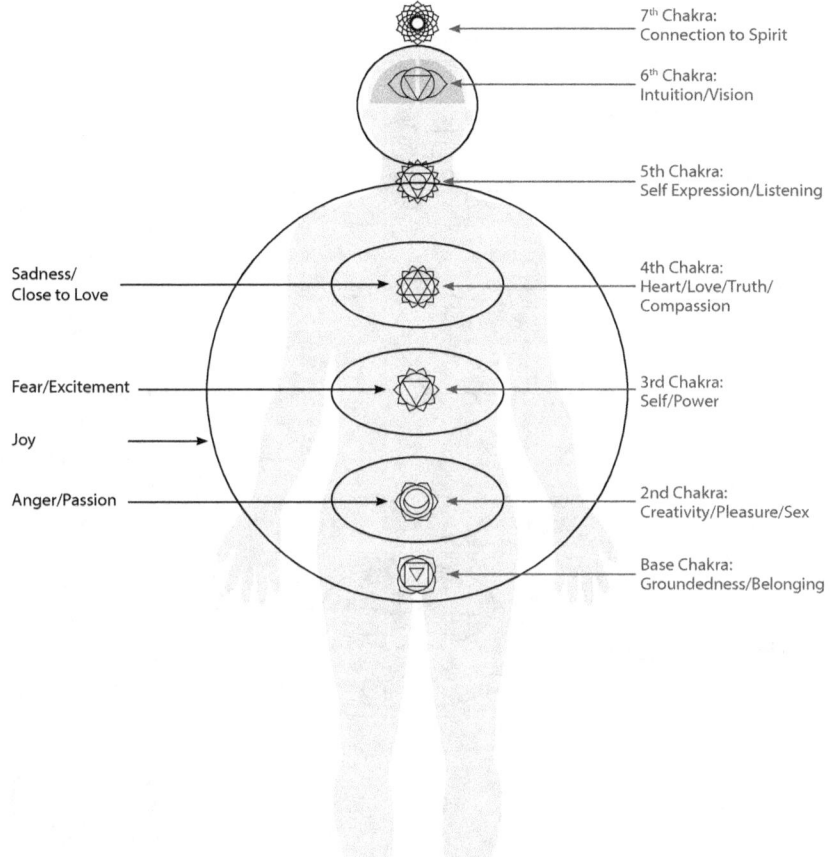

Diagram 2.2 Emotions and the Chakra System

practices in your lovemaking can increase your pleasure, connection and fulfilment, and stimulate your hormonal glands while you're at it! These practices can also help energy to move through up your body, creating full-body nurturing and pleasure and increasing your self awareness whilst reducing the energy you lose through genital orgasm.

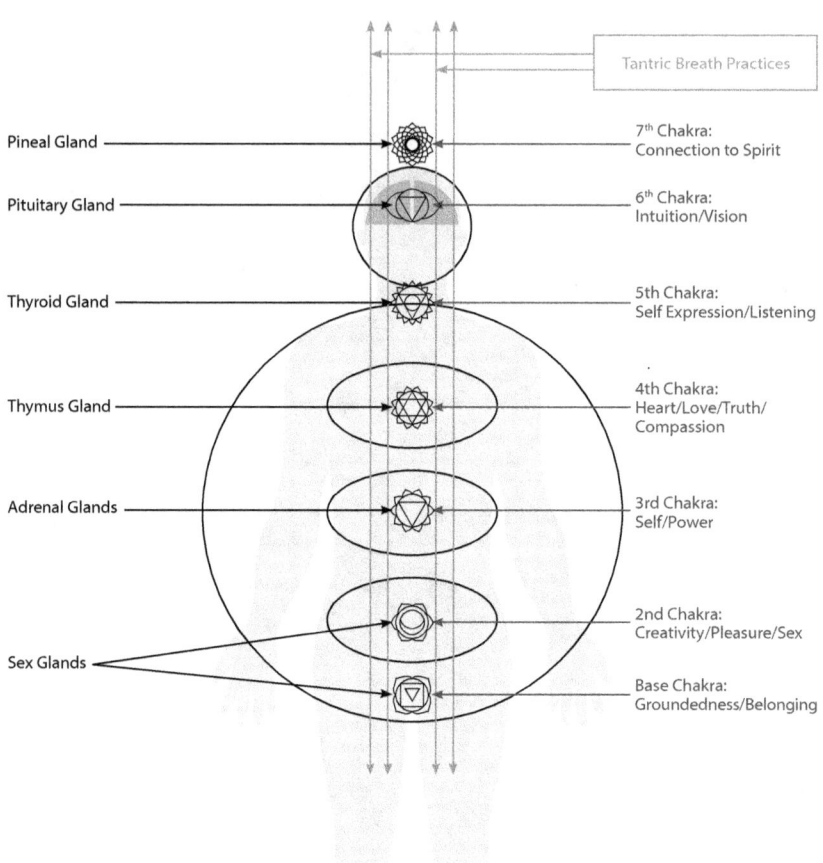

Diagram 2.3 Chakras and the Hormonal System

Real relationship change happens when you learn to acknowledge, own and value your emotional experience. So we hope we've given you lots of reasons to get into greater relationship with your feelings through these slightly left-of-centre understandings about how they work.

Developing Your Emotional Intelligence Skills

Thinking your feelings

Practice noticing whether you're 'thinking' your feelings in your head, or 'feeling' them in your body. If you're thinking them, pause and bring your attention to your body (via your ABC) and notice what physical/emotional sensations you're actually feeling, separate from your thoughts.

Noticing where your feelings come from

Practice noticing whether your thoughts are creating your feelings, or your feelings are creating thoughts; and whether your feeling triggers are external or internal. Noticing this will show you what to do about them:

- ***Thought/action-created feelings:*** If a feeling is untimely or unwelcome, breathe into it (see below) to help move it through your body, so you let go of the stress it causes. Then change your thoughts/actions to inspire more desirable feelings. If a feeling is welcome keep up the thoughts/actions that inspired it!
- ***Feeling-created thoughts/actions:*** If a thought/action is unwelcome, breathe through the feeling attached to it then choose different thoughts/actions. If you like the thought/action simply enjoy them and the feeling underneath.
- ***Externally triggered feelings:*** If a feeling is untimely or unwelcome, again breathe into it to help move it through your body. This will help you to clear your mind and come up with the best response.
- ***Internally triggered (from the past) feelings:*** Accept and feel the feeling fully until it shifts and you gain the insight from it.

 ## *Breathing through your feelings*

Practice controlling your feelings by using your awareness and your breath.

1. Bring your attention to a feeling in your body (as per your ABC).
2. Acknowledge it and breathe into it.

> 3. Notice it shifting into something different.
> 4. Sometimes you will gain awareness of what's behind a feeling, sometimes you can just feel it and let it go as part of your energetic aliveness.
>
> This will help to give you a sense of safety in feeling your feelings, knowing you have a choice in how to feel them. Notice if you access any Core Heart Feelings after feeling your emotions.
>
> We cannot overemphasise the importance of learning to experience and understand the gift of your feelings. It underpins so much of what goes on in intimacy. That's why developing emotional intelligence is the best thing you can do for your relationship.

2.3 The Nature of Mind and the Games that it Plays

This book focusses a lot on feelings, but of course we humans don't live by feelings alone. We all have an equally amazing logical mind that forms a vital part of our relationship picture. This logical, intellectual mind not only gives us the ability to communicate with and understand each other, but it also allows us to share memories, fantasies and desires; solve problems; take action and much, much more.

Yet we can get easily caught up in the games our minds play as they create our 'perceived reality'. In actual reality, however, our logical minds are easily skewed. They 'see' what's most familiar to us – good or bad through something called confirmation bias. This means that you and your partner each have your own experience of 'reality', and that both are equally valid. That's just the beginning.

Like technology, your logical mind is a good servant but a poor master. Seeing more of what your logical brain gets up to is not only incredibly fascinating, but it also puts you more firmly in the driver's seat of the relationship reality your brain creates.

When you own the reality you're creating, you take back your power rather than putting it outside of you by blaming yourself, your partner or your relationship.

Illusion

Eastern mystics say that everything is an illusion of the mind, and quantum science is finding ways to prove this true through experiments such as *John Wheeler's delayed choice-thought experiment at the Australian National University* (see ANU website blog, May 27 2015). This experiment shows that what you perceive as 'life' is what you project onto the screen of your mind's eye, as if you were watching your own individual movie of life.

If this sounds far-fetched, think of the time you saw an old friend walking down the street. As you walked up to him to say hello though, you realised it wasn't him at all. It was just someone similar – but your mind created a strong enough image for him to seem real to you. Or you might be concerned that your partner is not having a good time in lovemaking because you're doing something wrong, when in reality they're just holding back because they need to pee!

The reality movie that your logical mind plays is based on your beliefs, values, needs – both past and present – and your past experiences. It's also based on what you need, fear or fantasise about for the future and what you're thinking and feeling at the time. This means it's a moving target. So no matter how real you think something is, it is to some degree an illusion of your mind. This is true for your partner as well.

The most dangerous illusion in a relationship occurs when you rewrite its past from any current unhappiness. When you're feeling hurt, your mind will conveniently forget all the good times you've shared and recall only the pain points. This slants your view of your future relationship potential, inviting behaviours that create more of the same. Thankfully, the opposite is also true: when you're feeling happily in love, your mind will search its database for good memories you can enjoy, inviting positive behaviours that create more of that.

Graeme and I believe that the clearer you become in yourself through connecting with your authentic essence (through your ABC practice), the more closely your mind movie will match the actual reality around you. So start having some fun with your mind's games by checking them out against 'real' reality (if there is such a thing).

> ***Playing with the idea of illusion***
>
> Consider how your relationship would be different if you saw it from this idea of illusion.

Beliefs

A belief is a thought, idea or principle that you judge to be true, whether it's been proven so or not. Thoughts and beliefs are *not* facts. In fact, you can continue to believe something even after it's been proven patently untrue, because beliefs are often things you *want* to be true. You can find yourself cherry picking evidence that supports your beliefs, and ignoring ideas that contradict them.

> **How Our Beliefs Create Our Reality**
>
> *Mary Ann felt unhappy and believed that her relationship was the cause. Her mind looked for evidence of this belief being true.*
>
> *She saw that her husband George didn't spend time with her on Sundays any more. He also watched TV rather than talked, never complimented her, and criticised her for spending too much*

money. When she added these observations up, they 'confirmed' that she had reason to be unhappy: her relationship was going down the toilet, and George didn't love her anymore.

In the past, when she'd thought George loved her, Mary Ann had felt happy. And – though she hadn't realised it at the time – she'd also felt safe. When she thought now that George didn't love her, she felt not only unhappy, but also an underlying sense of anxiety. When she recognised that her thoughts were creating her anxiety, Mary Ann realised it was similar to the anxiety she'd felt when her family of origin had moved regularly because of her Dad's job. She'd frequently changed schools and had to make new friends – not easy for her with her shy personality.

She also recognised that she could choose to believe that George did love her no matter what (which was George's truth). As she chose this belief, her mind looked for evidence to support it, and saw a completely new picture of George's behaviour.

She realised that she'd started filling up her Sundays with the family, leaving no room for them as a couple. Then, when she talked to George, she heard that his job stress meant he needed to chill out with the TV but he was happy for her to join him. Not only that, but he **had** been complimenting her – she just hadn't heard him through her unhappiness. And his concerns about money weren't criticisms of her, but fears of his own.

 Exploring your reality

Track some of your beliefs to see what actions they lead you to, and what outcomes – both positive and negative – they create in your relationship. Then play with changing them so they work for you!

Mirroring

Mirroring happens when your mind perceives something in someone else as a reflection of what already exists in your unconscious self. It does this to enable you to know yourself better. When your mirror offers you a negative reflection you can either come out fighting, or choose to see the gift it offers. If, for example, you see anger in your partner, you can acknowledge that you're angry somewhere in yourself. If you feel disconnected in your relationship, you're being shown the disconnection in yourself.

What you mirror may or may not be there in you right in that moment, but it's been there at some time because you can only mirror in others *what already exists in yourself.* When you see a mirror be open to looking at your reflection.

Expectations

Expectations are your beliefs about the future. In your expectations, your mind literally creates whatever you expect to see. The trick is to see expectations for what they are: simply thoughts, not yet a reality.

> ### 💬 How Expectations Create Our Reality
>
> *If Ingrid expects Sam to be angry with her for getting home late, she might see him sitting hunched in his chair with an angry expression on his face. Even though Ingrid's expectations about Sam's response aren't comfortable, they feel right because they 'fit' with her beliefs.*
>
> *Sam's reality, on the other hand, was that he was simply tired and relaxing after a hard day's work. He wasn't actually thinking about Ingrid at all. If Ingrid can see her expectations for what they are and checks in with Sam about his reality, a very different outcome will result.*

Play with dropping your expectations

Notice how you experience people and events when you drop your expectations about them. Live in the here and now rather than being attached to the future.

Do you feel less anxiety or disappointment? More energy for yourself and trust in life?

If you can't drop an expectation, just see it as part of your mind's illusion rather than the other person's reality.

Assumptions

Assumptions are what you think (or guess) you 'know' about your partner – eg what they're thinking or doing – without any proof that it's true eg "I assumed you were going to be late so I didn't wait up." Assuming is one of your mind's worst relationship habits. Why? Because it means you put your partner in a box – not really listening to them, or seeing them as they are.

Your assumptions are based on your past experiences of your partner, your beliefs about who they are, and even the unconscious needs of your psyche. Making assumptions about them is not only insulting and havoc creating it's boredom inducing. You can restore the magic by simply dropping your assumptions and seeing your partner (and yourself) as if for the first time, every time: as a dynamic, unique individual who's different in each moment.

 Play with checking out your assumptions

This can be incredibly illuminating, and even hilarious – especially in a man/woman relationship dynamic. Get curious about your assumptions, and make it a habit to regularly check with your partner as to whether they're true. This little step alone will transform your relationship!

Perceptions

Perceptions are your mind's way of seeing, understanding or interpreting something. They're individual to each person, so what's 'common sense' to you might be a foreign language to your partner.

> ### How Perceptions can Create Reality
>
> *Sally grew up on a farm, and from her practical background it made sense that if you had a problem, you took action yourself and got it sorted straight away.*
>
> *To Julius, who'd grown up in the city with an artistic mother and political analyst father, it made sense to explore a situation fully, talk about it and then come to a mutual resolution.*
>
> *Neither of these perceptions are wrong: they're just different. Choosing to learn from each other's 'common sense' brings richness rather than discord.*

Seek greater understanding of your partner's 'common sense'

Compare your partner's common sense to your own. See where you might be misinterpreting each other's behaviour, and find the positives that you can learn from each other.

Comparison

In most parts of the world today, you have more choice in your life than people have ever had before. You can choose who to be; how to be; what to think; where to live; what to wear, eat and drink; and what to work and play at. Unfortunately, choice invites comparison, and comparison invites misery. You might think, "If only I'd chosen xxx, I'd be happy like my neighbour."

Choice also invites uncertainty, and comparison helps it along. You ask, "Will that option make me happier than this?" This is especially true when you've chosen one partner for life and find yourself asking, "Will I want them forever?"

You can have anything you want, but you can't have everything. And even if you compare yourself favourably, you still face the challenge of keeping ahead.

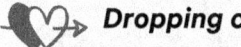 **Dropping comparisons**

Letting go of the need to compare will bring your attention and energy home to use in your own life. Notice the results.

Disconnection/Dissociation

Your mind is very clever at protecting itself (and you) from what it perceives as trauma. Trauma is anything your mind and body experiences as deeply distressing or disturbing – anything that creates severe emotional shock and pain.

To protect you, your logical brain detaches from its awareness of the experience. If the experience is severe enough, your mind will dissociate you from your body so that you don't have to feel the overwhelming pain of it. This is especially true if you experience trauma when you're very young, with limited capacity to understand, control or get away from what's happening to you.

Yet you can also disconnect at more subtle levels from many aspects of everyday life as an adult that are emotionally uncomfortable.

We all carry a degree of shame about sex (even if we think we don't). This makes it rare to be fully present and connected within sex, which is why it's absolutely amazing when we are.

A strong intimate relationship is often the place old blocks surface, simply because you now unconsciously feel safe enough to allow them.

Projection

Another thing your mind does when something is too foreign or uncomfortable to see or own in yourself is to project that thing onto others. For example, a woman who's uncomfortable with vulnerability might complain that her husband is emotionally unavailable to her, or a man experiencing sexual shame might believe that his wife isn't interested in making love.

Projections are your psyche's clever way of giving you the chance to reclaim missing or unfulfilled parts of yourself. By showing you these parts in others, your pysche allows you to see them in yourself. Seeing your projections helps you to own them and free yourself from whatever you've been denying, bringing you to greater wholeness and freedom. You'll explore how to work with projections in the section on Shadows in Chapter 9.

Transference

Transference is where you (unconsciously) redirect feelings and expectations from someone else onto your partner. You then interact with your partner if *they* were the someone you had the feelings or expectations about. And you'll try to hook your partner into your reality by getting them to play along with you.

> ### 💬 Transference in Action
>
> *Annette had a deeply held belief (stemming from something she perceived her mother said to her once) that she needed to work hard in order to be loved. By transferring this belief onto Graeme she 'saw' that he had high expectations of her that she needed to fulfill. So she proceeded to work hard enough to receive his love.*
>
> *Graeme's reality was that he loved Annette the way she was and felt sad that he was living with the projection rather than the woman he loved.*

Again, you transfer in order to heal the past and make new choices for yourself. This is especially true wherever your strongest unresolved feelings lie – usually relating to significant adults from your childhood.

What's Real in Relationships?

As you can see, identifying what's real in relationships (and life) can be very messy and subjective. That's the mystery of them. Occasionally, you and your partner might both be relating to people who aren't even in the room, instead of to each other! All you can do is seek to own the reality you're choosing to show on your personal movie screen and the outcomes you're creating to the best of your ability.

This is where your ABC practice becomes invaluable. It helps you to become grounded, centred and able to see what's happening more clearly. Choosing to own and share with your partner what's happening/happened for you may make you feel vulnerable, but it will ultimately bring you both closer together as they better understand your responses.

> **Showing up in your relationship**
>
> Showing up in your relationship helps to minimise the amount of mind games that occur between you and your partner by letting them see where you're at. It helps you to clear illusions, mirror accurately, own your beliefs, remove assumptions, clarify perceptions, minimise disconnection and illuminate projections. It's about learning to be vulnerable, open and honest. To do this, start with your ABC, then:
>
> 1. Let your partner know where you're at, eg say, "I'm feeling really frustrated, but not at you. The washing machine broke down, the guy was late getting here to fix it, and he made a sleazy pass at me when he did."
> 2. Let them know what your coping strategy is, eg "I just need to vent to get it off my chest," or, "I need to go for a walk before dinner to clear my head."
> 3. Let them know if you need their assistance in any way, eg say, "I just need you to listen" or "Give me some space."
>
> This is a beginning practice that gets you into the habit of showing your partner where you are in your relationship. It will be refined by adding other layers throughout the book.

2.4 The Longest, Most Worthwhile Journey from the Head to the Heart

Your heart is your No.1 feeling tool to support you in seeing the many games that your own, and your partners minds play.

For your heart is not just a mechanical organ that pumps oxygenated blood and nutrients throughout your body to keep you alive. Nor is it just the fluffy pink symbol you see on a Valentine's Day card or at the end of a text message. It's actually an incredibly complex cellular, intuitive and energetic organ. Becoming more embodied and emotionally intelligent will bring you greater access to its many gifts. You'll learn how in the three profound heart practices below, but first a bit of reflection on what your heart has to offer you.

Aristotle, the early Egyptians, and many religions have believed for thousands of years that the heart is the organ of intelligence. Scientific research discovering that 60-65% of the heart's cells are actually neurons (rather than muscle cells) has inspired experiments proving that the heart works similarly to the brain. In some ways, it's even superior: it can generate the strongest electromagnetic field of any organ in your body in response to shifts in your emotions.

> *"Heart intelligence underlies cellular organisation and guides and evolves organisms toward increased order, awareness and coherence of their bodies' systems."*
>
> www.heartmath.com.FAQs

Your heart is:

- the centre of love in your body – home to feelings of fullness, warmth and connection; or equally, of freedom, spaciousness and expansion that casts out fear
- the centre of happiness that makes life worth living
- the centre of courage, wisdom, gratitude and forgiveness, with its own mysterious brand of intelligence and communication
- the centre for resolving hurt in ways that defy description, where judgement and tension melt
- the place of union of your masculine and feminine aspects, where you cease to be male or female and become simply human
- where you can both relate from your humanness rather than from your politically correct or egoic needs

- the home of true desire for your partner, ie when your heart is open you desire them. This is a crucial understanding for relationships.

> *"Love is not blind – it sees more not less. But because it sees more, it is willing to see less."*
>
> Your Sense of Humor, Rabbi Julius Gordon

Cultivating connection with your heart also offers you moments of exquisite tenderness, boundless love, enveloping passion, profound sadness, blissful freedom, generous playfulness and boundless motivation.

Your heart is not just a balm for your hurt, or a dummy for you to suck, it sees a much bigger picture than that. It sees love as more than gratification, sentimentality or obligation. It is without agenda, and it isn't attached to things looking a certain way (unlike your ego). It's not afraid to see things as they are with unflinching clarity and forgiveness is a no brainer.

> *"As you live deeper in your heart, the mirror gets clearer and clearer."*
>
> Collected Poetical Works of Rumi, Rumi

And, as surprising as it may seem, your heart enables greater sexual pleasure. An open heart literally creates more room for sexual energy to flow freely through your whole body, leaving you feeling expanded, desiring, creative and blissful in lovemaking.

Open heart = Desire for sexual connection

Graeme and I see couples getting in touch with their hearts and opening to each other and themselves emotionally and sexually in ways that defy description. If we had to put words to it, we'd call it 'being touched by the mystery of love'.

If you think back to the early days of your own relationship, wasn't that when you had the best sex of your life? This is not only due to the hormonal drive of young (or at least younger!) lust, but also to the openness of your hearts, before there was any real hurt or desire for protection between you. Healing the hurt in your heart allows your desire for sexual connection to flow even better than it did when you were first together and is the key for lasting sexual desire over the years.

Heartbreak is what we all most fear about relationships

Of course, your heart is also, alongside all these good things, a place of pain. Studies have shown that our fear and anxiety play a significant role in how we perceive pain. Yet given a chance, our hearts show us that they're powerful beyond measure in their capacity to heal pain, restore love and rejuvenate us.

Developing a concrete relationship with your heart, and trusting its mysterious ability to heal and support you in your relationship will give you more courage to step into intimacy and connection.

Apart from fearing its pain, we all have a tendency to ignore our hearts

We do this because:

1. We haven't connected with it in this 'intangible feeling' way before.
2. It takes us a moment or two of 'dropping our story' to hear what it has to say.
3. We often don't like what our hearts have to say. Our hearts cut through the bullshit of our ego minds – the part of us conditioned to stay safe – to instead get down to the 'heart' of matters.

What's your current relationship to your heart?

- Do you see your heart as mere mechanics, or are you open to the possibility of it being something more?

- Can you feel your heart? Think of a time when you felt heart-open and grateful towards your partner (for gratitude is a great heart opener). Try to recall the actual physical sensations you experienced.
- Do you trust your heart? Think of that time you 'just knew' something in your heart that you ignored to your later peril. Or a moment when, even though you may have felt like strangling your significant other, you suddenly noticed how cute they looked their favourite old sweater and you fell in love with them all over again in a single moment.

Are you willing to listen to what your heart has to say?

In the beginning, it can be tricky to know what is truly your heart's voice, and what's just your ego's needs masquerading as your heart. How do you tell the difference? You do so by noticing the kind of logic it's offering.

Your intellect (or ego brain) speaks from two-value logic

Your intellect or ego brain focusses on two-value logic: black-and-white or right-and-wrong thinking. It says, "I am this *or* I am that," or, "It is this *or* it is that". It allows for no other possibilities.

Two-value logic often leaves you in a conundrum in your relationship, struggling with win/lose, good/bad choices. For example, two-value logic says that if your partner is in a relationship with you, they can't love, look at, or even think about anyone else.

This logic is driven by your mind's internal programming and your self-identity. Its moral compass about right and wrong comes from your life experience and your external familial, social and cultural environment. Your ego brain speaks in judgements (both positive and negative), self-justifications and an underlying need to be in control.

Your heart (and soul) speak from four-value logic

Your heart focusses on four-value logic, which says, "I am this, I am that, I am both, I am neither," or, "this is right, this is wrong, this is everything, this is nothing" all at the same time and it all makes sense.

Heart talk is limitless with infinite and unrestricted possibilities. It's OK with not knowing. Your heart won't tell you to control or ignore your fear. Instead, given a chance, it will take you beyond it to this place of often-surprising logic.

For example, your heart might say it's OK for your partner to love another person, even though they already love you, because your heart is capable of much greater love than your mind can comprehend. This doesn't mean your partner needs to act out that love, however. It just means you have nothing to fear from the love being there.

Heart-based outcomes are ultimately the most satisfying, because they bring more potential for togetherness.

The heart uses simple language

Unlike your very clever intellect that likes to use many words and complicated arguments your heart speaks in simple 'knowings': those things you just *know*, even though you might not understand *how* you know them. It speaks about letting things be, letting them go, finding compassion, acceptance and understanding. It might also say that it's time for you to get off your butt and have a go at that job, or to be honest and kind even though you don't want to. Or it might tell you stand your ground in a situation and give some tough love. Your heart also has a very good in-built bullshit detector. It will show you the places where you (or others) might be in illusion or avoiding your/their higher truths, or where you're not being authentic you're merely being an arrogant jerk.

Our hearts never seek power over another, but instead offer us power within ourselves.

Whatever heart energy you expend in your life comes back to you either directly or indirectly. That means it's worth putting out there what you really mean from your heart, because that's what you'll get back in kind!

Graeme and I have found this true in our own lives too. The idea that our hearts are more than a muscle started off as a very nebulous, woo woo concept, but it's now a rock-solid part of our self-understanding, and a pathway to connecting with each other. We know that whenever our minds are overly busy with unhelpful thoughts, we're probably out of alignment with our hearts' inbuilt bullshit detectors, so we'd better take a moment to check in and listen…

> **Connecting with your heart**
>
> Take a moment now just to stop and feel your heart.
>
> Close your eyes, do your ABC, feel into your body, and then focus your attention in the centre of your chest.
>
> Is your heart open, closed, tight, full, warm, heavy, light or blank? Is there sadness, love, gratitude, even anger or shame there?
>
> If you have trouble feeling anything, think of something you're grateful for in your life: for gratitude is a great heart opener.
>
> Whatever the feeling is, just be with it exactly as it is for a few moments. Do this as often as you can to start building your relationship with your 'energetic' heart.
>
> The more you connect with it, the more it will speak to you.

Keeping your heart open to love by falling on your sword

There's no doubt about it: feeling your heart can **really hurt** sometimes. But remembering that feelings are just energy in motion, welcoming them in and then literally letting them penetrate your heart helps them to shift almost immediately.

It's a bit like imagining you're falling on the sword of your feelings. The only difference is that, unlike with a sword, being penetrated by your feelings (however painful they may be) won't kill you. It's actually your resistance to feeling your hurt that hurts the most.

Once you allow it to, feeling will free you from the thick walls that most of us build around our hearts. It will crack those walls open in a positive way. It sounds crazy, but if you give it a try, you'll see it really works. It gives you control in an out-of-control place, just like breathing into your emotions in the rest of your body does. It takes more energy to build walls of protection to hold back those unwanted feelings as it does to feel whatever is there in them.

Accessing and letting these feelings in can seem like the most illogical thing in the world, but it's not about being sadistic. It's like the beautiful Buddhist practice of Tonglen, which involves letting go of resistance to suffering and having it transformed into joy or love. The only way to understand the benefit is to try it for yourself.

1. Begin with a small moment of hurt.
2. Rather than contracting against the hurt, take a breath in and imagine it literally penetrating your heart and moving through it. Keep breathing until it passes.
3. You'll find that if you can totally let go of resistance to it, the hurt transforms immediately.
4. Play with this practice in a more painful place, eg when your partner rejects you emotionally or sexually, and notice your results. Its gift is that your vulnerability will invite your partner closer to you rather than pushing them away, creating a deep

intimacy rather than chaos and withdrawal. The intimacy of being with a partner in this depth of process is indescribably beautiful.

Although big hurts, such as betrayal by a partner, job loss, an unexpected financial loss or a spouse's death can create several layers of hurt to move through, the practice is still the same.

As you can see, your heart is a powerful tool to help you see what's real in your relationship, as well as one that offers you qualities that create intimate connection and heal the challenges between you. Not to mention offering you moments of love, happiness, gratitude, peace and more that make your relationship a wonderful place to be. It's a tool that's well worth cultivating.

We trust you now have a newfound (or newly reinforced) appreciation of your heart and its capabilities and an excitement for actively working with it- it can change your life and will definitely change your relationship!

Connection, Separation and Control

3.1 Me, You and Us: The Dance Of Intimacy

"Love rests on two pillars: surrender and autonomy."

Mating In Captivity, Esther Perel

Connection and self don't need to be mutually exclusive in a relationship yet it's so easy to lose sight of in the dance of intimacy between two people. This chapter outlines the ways we lose ourselves in relationship and how to undo the resulting enmeshment that occurs in ways that bring us a healthy balance of individuality and togetherness.

When you first get together with your partner, your focus is usually on the romantic ideal of getting close to each other, and closer to the fantasy of never being alone again. You become infatuated with your partner, finding more and more in common. You entwine yourself in your partner's life, and even feel their feelings, not knowing where one person begins and the other ends.

Being in love with another person who so perfectly fills your life lifts you up into something greater. Loving and feeling loved helps you achieve more than you otherwise might have been capable of. You have more energy, and a sense of abundance and a truly blessed life. Being able to love, give to and support another person nurtures your very soul.

But so does being who *you* are: your unique, individual self with your own beliefs, abilities, talents and boundaries.

This is the dance of intimacy – navigating between being deeply connected with your partner and staying deeply connected with yourself. And the success of your relationship depends upon the success of this dance.

Initially, you're happy to give up everything for the sake of the relationship. You drop friends, commitments and interests because the relationship seems to offer everything you need. But over, time this singular focus begins to feel like boredom, dissatisfaction or even claustrophobia. You feel resentful and restricted by your partner. Or perhaps the intimacy no longer is 'enough', leaving you feeling the exquisitely painful kind of loneliness that occurs inside the relationship that was supposed to 'fix' it.

Resentment and frustration are healthy signs

If this is happening for you, it doesn't mean anything is wrong. It's simply that your individual sense of self – who you are as a unique, individual human being – is seeking to re-assert itself. This is a healthy sign. It's also a vital key to keeping your intimate connection (and your sexual fire) alive and flourishing for the long run. Even the pain of separateness from your partner is a healthy sign that your sense of self could use some attention.

3: Connection, Separation and Control

Maintaining your sense of self: a vital relationship key

> ### ♥ Sense of Self in Action
>
> *Graeme and Annette had been together a year when she gamely hauled him along to their first ever Tantra workshop. It was a couples' retreat called Ecstasy & Intimacy, held near Byron Bay by Oceana & Icarus, the original creators of Oztantra.*
>
> *Annette remembers that it, "...was like going to heaven for a week – all this love and attention opening me like a flower". They stayed on in Byron for an extra few days, basking in the intimacy and pleasure. But after they arrived home, Graeme returned to work and she felt totally abandoned. This made her realise there was something else going on underneath all that heaven.*
>
> *Annette saw that her sense of self had moved totally outside of her, and had become wrapped up in receiving Graeme's love, attention and approval. This was a real shock, as she'd already done a lot of personal development work and felt pretty together. She was about to learn that being in relationship requires skills at a whole new level.*

And seemingly independent, externally successful Graeme had his own little story around intimacy playing out as well.

> *Graeme recalls, "I was reluctant to go to this workshop, and didn't know what to expect. I thought I knew what intimacy was, and I was up for anything in my relatively new relationship with Annette.*
>
> *Oceana and Icarus were the typical Byron Bay hippie couple who really challenged my conservative, Western Victorian rural upbringing. I remember halfway through Day 1, going outside and vomiting in the garden from pure fear.*

During this workshop, I came face to face with one of my deepest fears: the fear of true intimacy. I soon realised that I had simply learned to survive in a relationship, which was very different to how I wanted to be.

It became obvious to me that I was 'thinking intimacy' instead of feeling intimate. I could say the words, but really being intimate at this new and deeper level was a whole new concept, especially with the tantric skills heating things up...

I had no idea in that particular moment, head down and bum up in the shrubbery, that Oztantra would have such a huge impact in my life in the not too distant future. Not only would I learn new skills from this workshop, but Annette and I would eventually be offered this business to place our own unique stamp on it.

This is why we've made connection with the self such a vital part of our work.

Isn't that love?

But aren't you supposed to give up your 'self' in a relationship? Society gives us very conflicting messages on this. It says that all your answers lie in 'a perfect Other'. You hear this message in every romantic song and see it in every popular movie. You're also told that you need to 'be there' for that other person, to give and not be selfish. At the same time, you're told to be and to stand up for yourself and to go after what you want in life. Aaargh!

The truth is that *all* of these answers are true at different times. When you see (with the help of your heart's four value logic) these paradoxical ways of being as different layers of the one whole, you can enjoy them all. This allows you to create a bigger, more flexible space in your relationship for connection *and* for autonomy.

The ways we lose ourselves in intimacy

Becoming enmeshed

In the early dance of intimacy, you often subtly change your behaviours to either get your partner's approval, or to get your needs met. You act 'nice' instead of being real. You might appear to agree when you don't, make promises you can't keep or you focus on meeting your partner's needs thinking it will satisfy your own unexpressed (or unidentified) ones.

You've become other-focused, rather than self-focused. You begin to feel anxious at the thought of saying no to a night snuggling on the couch or speaking up when you feel invalidated. You might put up with things you never would in a friend or co-worker.

This is *normal:* we all become enmeshed in our relationships in one way or another. The point is to see where it happens at the expense of your 'authentic self' and make healthier choices.

> **Enmeshment in Action**
>
> One beautiful couple we worked with met when they were teenagers. They were each the other's first boyfriend/girlfriend and had been together for over 40 years. When we first met them, they seemed like one solid block, with no separation between them. You couldn't tell where one person ended and the other began.
>
> They came to see us because they'd lost the freshness, excitement and meaning in their relationship as they faced retirement and the empty nest syndrome. They wanted to find it again – and this meant rediscovering who they were as individuals.
>
> Several years later, this block no longer exists. They're still very solid as a couple, but their unconscious enmeshment has gone, so they're in a thriving relationship that celebrates their individuality as well as their togetherness.

After enmeshment occurs your forgotten self (or your partner's, or both, as it was for this couple) at some point hopefully starts to push back and 'want' for itself.

Looking outside for answers

The real danger here doesn't come from the situation itself. Instead, it comes from blaming your partner and getting angry when 'Mummy' or 'Daddy' isn't giving you what you want. It comes from criticising the relationship rather than taking responsibility for it yourself.

Then – if you're like most people – you start covertly looking outside of your relationship and yourself for your answers. You might focus on your children for intimacy, bury yourself in work or outside interests, act out with addictions, go online for sex or have an affair – all while continuing to be 'nice' or emotionally shutting down.

These choices result in an 'invisible divorce', where people live together without connecting in any real way. It's often the last step before an actual divorce.

The healthy way to deal with this dynamic is to understand what's happening, to talk about it and find ways to both nurture your sense of self within the relationship and maintain your connection with your partner.

Two halves that make a complete whole

In most couples one person is often great at things that their partner might struggle with - perhaps cooking, organising, doing the finances, removing spiders, driving, finding things, bringing up difficult topics, looking after emotions, being the social director or finding meaning and direction in life. When your partner provides this something, you feel not only loved, but also whole – and vice versa.

Yet too much of this dynamic leaves you incomplete as an individual. This was particularly evident in generations that had more specific gender roles: for example, a man who couldn't cook a meal for himself after his wife died, or a woman who couldn't drive or balance her chequebook.

The way out of this limiting aspect of coupledom is to appreciate the things your partner does in the relationship and to occasionally do them for yourself. This may involve making a bit of extra effort, or even learning a new skill but it will pay off by nurturing your own wholeness. And we can support our partners by encouraging rather than criticizing their efforts to do things we automatically do well!

Becoming who you aren't

There is a part of you that lives according to your unconscious relationship rules, rather than your authentic self. If you're a man, you might automatically become the breadwinner because 'that's what men do'. If you're a woman, you might give up your job to look after your children, or move for your husband's career, because that's what women have always done in your family, culture or society.

You might believe that a good father is one who disciplines his children harshly, while a good wife is one who stays at home rather than goes out with her girlfriends. You might stick together purely because no one in your family is divorced. Or the opposite might be true: your mother or father might have gone through many relationships looking for 'the one', so that seems normal.

If you examine these roles, the beliefs that underpin them, where they've come from and find they're not working for you, can then choose different ones.

The skill in the Dance of Intimacy is looking within

If you can openly acknowledge this dance as a normal part of relationship and address it from within the relationship by examining your beliefs and choices and making healthier ones, your relationship will flourish.

Explore your own Dance of Intimacy Map and discuss it with your partner

- What's the balance of togetherness and individuality like in your relationship?
- Could you benefit from some 'self' time?
- Are you doing too many things for your partner?
- Have you taken on roles about how you should behave that are expected by your spouse or your family, culture or society, and that are no longer working for you?
- Is it time to branch out and try new things for yourself/selves?
- Is it time to put some energy back into your relationship?
- Do you share an activity that challenges you as individuals, yet brings you closer together as a couple? For example, Graeme and I do bootcamp fitness training together.
- How much time do you spend in intimacy with each other?
- Do you cultivate friendships with both the same and different sexes?
- Do you balance the gifts you receive in your relationship by giving to others in the wider community around you?

Once you've got an idea of what might be missing, what you'd like to let go of and what to add in, draw yourself a map of what this would look like. List the elements already there, those you want to include, and the strategies you can use to help manifest them.

Aim to implement one or two strategies each month.

For example: "Our desire is to create more intimacy time together".

So you could:

- Pretend you're having an affair, and schedule two hours per week for each other on a Thursday afternoon
- Clear your diaries to ensure this happens
- Have the kids stay at a friend's after school

- Explore possible ways to spend your time, but keep an open mind on the day.
- Can you feel the excitement building already as the 'shoulds' free up, and the desires build?

There will be as many different maps as there are relationships, and sometimes you may have to move apart a little to come back more enticingly together. If you're doing it together though, it will strengthen your relationship rather than weaken it. Even if you start on your own (letting your partner know what you're doing and why), it will help to create positive change.

No matter what your individual Dance of Intimacy Map looks like, it will be a valuable tool to give you permission to discuss the challenges it raises. It will legitimise the inner pull between connection and autonomy that we all feel and ultimately help to give you freedom *within* your relationship.

Creating this kind of change in relationship takes courage. It's easier to do when you see the fate of your relationship being at stake if you don't. And the more you resist taking these steps (or resist your partner taking them) into greater authenticity, the more important it shows they are.

The Gifts of Dancing with Intimacy

As you learn to Dance with Intimacy you:

- learn to be yourself whilst being with another person
- learn to enjoy moments of being 'at one' with your partner
- can be totally separate and still feel the thread of connection
- avoid minimising yourself for the other person's sake, or caretaking for them
- seek moments of service where you have your partner's back

- know you're still OK where your partner is different from you
- experience and love your partner as they are, not as you need them to be
- see your differences as growth points.

Independence and Authenticity Create Desire

An exciting plus for Dancing with Intimacy in a healthy way is that exploring your authentic self also helps you to remain sexually desirable to your partner. This is because the fire of sexual attraction (this is separate to the desire for sexual connection that arises from your hearts) relies strongly on a sense of 'otherness'. When human beings feel 'separateness', we also find the desire to connect. Looking across the room at your partner and seeing someone just a little unfamiliar, a little unexplored and even unpredictable, can trigger your desire for their juicy 'otherness'.

The gift in an authentic relationship is that this particular 'other' still contains the thread of loving connection from your years together. This gives you the best of both worlds.

A healthy Dance of Intimacy is where relationships stop dying and start to grow new life, it's well worth the effort.

3.2 Using your ABC as a relationship tool

Just as looking within your relationship for answers works in Dancing with Intimacy looking within yourself in moments of challenge also allows you to become more connected with your partner in a deeply loving, yet freeing way.

This happens when you start to actively use your ABC as a relationship tool.

Something wonderful happens when you do your ABC practice regularly. You realise that you have some control over your uncomfortable feelings, that they won't last forever, and that good ones are around the corner. Emotions start to be less of a minefield, and more just something to accept and benefit from. You find yourself becoming more centred with greater clarity in your 'thinking' mind, and a deepening awareness of your 'knowing' mind, bringing the comforts of both to your relationship toolkit.

The duel of two truths

Your ABC practice comes in very handy when you get to a place of 'I'm right, so you must be wrong' in your relationship. Usually, this only ends badly: with each person in opposing corners, pistols drawn and one body about to hit the floor.

A fabulous relationship skill is understanding that there's always **more than one** equally valid truth in relationships. It's not simply a case of right and wrong, but more often a case of there being many truths.

You can **both** be right and wrong, even at the **same time**!

This is because much of the detail in a relationship is subjective, rather than being concrete, black and white facts. It's each person's own internal experience and interpretation (even though it looks like there are only facts on the table). We know the tricks our minds can get up to in perceiving our reality so making your communication goal one of connection and understanding, rather than one of being right, opens up a whole new world of possibilities. It means being more aware and more vulnerable, but it's ultimately more rewarding than the merry-go-round of one-upmanship.

This is where your ABC becomes extremely handy: it helps you stay grounded and present, while listening and participating more clearly and inviting your heart into the discussion. In short, it takes you from duelling to loving.

Being right and wrong at the same time

Humans beings are ultimately logical beings. So no matter how incomprehensible your own – or someone else's – behaviour may initially appear, if you listen clearly enough, and keep any knee-jerk reactions to yourself, it will eventually make sense (even if you don't agree with it).

To be heard, seen and validated is one of our most basic human needs. If you can open yourself to really hearing where your partner is coming from, and then share from your own perspective, you'll find that you can both be right and wrong at the same time – and it won't matter. It's only serious if it stops the sun from shining (and we'll show you how to deal with these moments too). You'll see it's just your individual personalities and life experiences making you see different sides of the same coin. This softening then allows your hearts to open and new ideas, outcomes and possible solutions to arise between you.

You'll start to see each other more clearly than the issue that divides you.

💬 Annie and Roger's Example

Annie was angry that Roger came home from work too late to look after the children so that she could go to her book club meeting. On the surface, the 'facts' showed that he was 'wrong' and she was 'right', making way for a fight.

> **Instead, both chose to get grounded in their bodies with Step 2 of the ABC practice.** *This allowed them to discover the logical understandings behind their individual responses.*
>
> *Annie realised she'd assumed that Roger would know she wanted to go out and would be home in time without her having to remind him. Roger, who was having a busy time at work, realised he was feeling so snowed under he couldn't focus on Annie's needs.*
>
> **Then they used Step 3 of the ABC practice to find deeper understandings though their intuitive/heart/body mind.**
>
> *Annie felt into her anger, breathing through it without venting. This helped her to acknowledge her old pattern of not speaking up for her needs, and then blaming Roger for not 'seeing' her. Owning this pattern allowed her to drop her resentment and re-open her heart. Meanwhile, Roger felt into his emotional closedness and realised he'd been allowing work to take over his personal space, and that he missed the intimacy of his relationship with Annie and the children and wanted more of them again.*
>
> *Because both partners used their intellect AND intuitive insights, the situation ended in a hug instead of a furious argument.*

This is the gift of going within yourself and into your vulnerability; it takes you to a new place of understanding and acceptance. As you see, doing your own work isn't about letting your partner get away with unhealthy behaviours. Instead, it invites them to move closer and join you in looking within themselves. Even if you use the practice alone, it will allow you to get clarity around your own behaviour and reconnect with yourself. This can then invite your partner to do the same – if not at first, then over time.

The Wisdom Comes After

The crucial thing to know about your intuitive/heart/body mind is that, unlike your logical, intellectual mind that can analyse and understand without needing to feel, this mind speaks *only after the feeling has been felt.*

You cannot avoid a feeling and still gain its wisdom.

You'll know your intuitive mind is speaking (through your ABC) when the answers you get are either very simple and straight-to-the-point, or a little more creative than those from your rational mind. When this happens:

- You may just need to feel the feeling, and that's all.

- You may notice the underlying nature of the situation, as Annie and Roger did. If so, be open to having your part in creating the situation revealed to you and be ready to own it. Owning your part gives you power in the situation, helping the feeling to shift and any potential actions to become clear.

- Sometimes you'll become aware that a feeling needs to be expressed outwards rather than just felt. If this is true, trust yourself – and trust that after taking this pause, what comes out will be important.

- If there's nothing to be done and yet the feeling remains, ask yourself (or even better, ask the feeling!) what need isn't being met. Sometimes, it's just something simple: a hug, a smile or a cup of tea. Identifying this need and speaking it – without expecting the other person to give it (though they may choose to) – will shift the feeling into something more easeful. Most times, acknowledging the need behind the feeling is all that's required.

It can seem so much easier to drop into blaming the other person for your hurt than to see what's on your own doorstep, but it *does not serve you* at all. And this doesn't mean you're making the other person right. Instead, you're just seeing yourself (the only person you have control over) and the situation more clearly, so you can take the relevant action.

The more you practise using your ABC this way, the more you'll get a sense of your part and what, if anything, you need to do about it. This turns a potential conflict into an opportunity for connection, rather than a duel of opposing truths. Not only this, but you'll also be developing a greater relationship with your feeling body that will surprise you when you get into the bedroom!

> **Dropping the duel**
>
> When you arrive at a 'right vs. wrong' situation, rather than take out your pistols, use your ABC practice instead.
>
> Going within will help you see the reasons behind your own behaviours and invite your partner to see theirs. It's so much cheaper than cleaning up the damage of a bar-room brawl!

3.3 Dealing with Emotional Triggers

Another use of the ABC practice is in dealing with moments of 'emotional trigger' that commonly occur in intimate relationships. This is when you have an extremely intense and uncomfortable reaction to something that your partner says or does. A reaction that comes out of nowhere and appears to be over the top in response to the situation. We're talking about more intense reactions here than those we covered previously, moments when the sun really does seem to stop shining. Your ABC is a rational process for these very irrational moments.

Coming Together

Get this process right and everything else in your relationship will become easier.

Being willing to explore this process brings even greater self-understanding and a deeper level of connection between you and your partner. The process feels vulnerable, authentic and real, and when you trust each other in it, it becomes one of the foundational building blocks of relationship sustainability.

For intimate relationships are there to trigger us into our own wholeness, and this is one of the ways they do it. This *over-the-top response* is due to a painful past experience (anywhere from last week right back to your childhood) that your brain perceives as reoccurring in the present moment (see the section on Projection in the last chapter). The past experience can be a moment where we've been hurt, closed ourselves down in protection, judged ourselves poorly, or just didn't trust ourselves to be authentic.

Your partner becomes your No. 1 designated button-pusher, not because they don't love you, but because love itself has brought you together for a higher purpose. *It's your partner's role* to unconsciously trigger you into seeing yourself more clearly, helping you to heal pain from your past and to reach your highest potential.

Sometimes they'll just tap your trigger buttons, while at other times, they'll ring them like a bell! And the triggers that impact you most deeply will likely come from their deepest pain (this is how you're perfect for each other). But at other times, they won't be doing anything at all if your triggers are driven by your own projections. They'll simply be standing there wondering what all the fuss is about.

The past is never completely gone

You might believe in leaving the past in the past and 'getting over' things. The trouble with this is that your emotional brain and your body don't work that way. They can't tell the difference between the past and the present moment, so the past can show up as real any time in the present. That means triggers can happen right here, right now, not later when you're comfortable and in control with everything together. That's why it's vital to know how to deal with these minefields in the moments they arise.

Dealing actively with your emotional triggers allows you to simultaneously heal hurts from the past and draw closer to your partner in the present.

Graeme and I have tried using many other more intellectual, supposedly more compassionate and prettier tools for this moment of trigger, including trying to avoid being triggered in the first place. We've discovered, however, that to *really* clear these blocks to intimacy in ways that bring you and your partner closer together, actively dealing with triggers is the only tool that ultimately works, because it makes your triggers a place of growth rather than destruction.

Triggers are SO Uncomfortable

Can you relate to the intense hurt and discomfort of an emotional trigger, where you're trying to place your attention anywhere but on your reaction? With your primal brain going into overdrive and sending adrenaline, neurotransmitters and stress hormones cascading through your body, all you want to do is REACT outwards! Or perhaps you do the opposite and completely shut down.

Psychologically, what you're doing is disconnecting from, rejecting and abandoning yourself.

When you get triggered, you logically probably try to change your external reality (including your partner's behaviour) so you can feel better. This doesn't work though, because you're going outside of yourself to fix an internal problem, and probably pissing your partner off in the process. Whatever lies behind your trigger lies within YOU, not them. Yes, part of your trigger may have a very logical current explanation, eg your partner having done something most people would see as unreasonable. But if you feel hooked into their behaviour with no choice other than an over-the-top emotional reaction that feels totally out of your control, something deeper within you is looking to be explored.

With practice, the ABC tool will allow you to press the hold button on your reaction, and instead let you RESPOND in your moment of trigger (or recover more quickly if you did react). And it does this in a way that keeps you open and available, both to yourself and to your partner.

Use the Feeling to Bring You Home and Find the Gold

Rather than looking for answers in your rational mind's story of who did what to whom, use your ABC and *stay present with the feeling*. Something happened once – whether it was last week or 20 years ago – that made you feel limited, wounded or unloved. If you stay with the feeling, you'll come back into connection with yourself and no longer feel disconnected, rejected or abandoned. You'll not only clear your wounding, but you'll also see your story of limitation isn't true. Instead, you'll see that in reality you're an infinitely lovable, powerful and unlimited being. This is the gift of your trigger, and the relationship that provided it.

Tim and Patricia's Emotional Trigger Situation

When Tim walks away from Patricia's emotional intensity, it triggers feelings of abandonment for Patricia. Without the ABC process, this little moment could end up causing days of suffering for them both.

Even though it feels so right to lash out angrily at Tim for abandoning her, Patricia's challenge is to not abandon herself by projecting her hurt outside of herself onto him. Instead, she comes back into presence with herself by doing her ABC.

Staying connected to herself allows Patricia to intuitively understand that although part of her discomfort is with Tim in the here and now, the depth of it is about her dad, who wasn't emotionally available to her when she was a child. As she feels this with her ABC, she not only frees herself from her frustration with Tim but from the lifelong fears from her past that have lived in her body.

Without Tim's trigger, she wouldn't be able to access the depth of this place in order to heal it. It's not about excusing Tim's behaviour, but instead getting to the gift in it.

Using his own ABC, Tim isn't overwhelmed by Patricia's emotional intensity and manipulated by her fears and insecurities into feeling guilty, as he was with his mother. He realises it's OK for him to step back and look after himself instead, so he remains grounded, present and heart-open. This is Patricia's gift to Tim – and she gets the emotional space she needs to see her own limiting behaviour without Tim needing to step back from her.

Irrationally Rational

The ABC process works because it gives your rational mind a job to do in an irrational situation. This means your mind and your feelings work *with* you rather than *against* you.

It's a simple thing to do, but it's not easy. This is why it's essential to make your ABC a regular practice, so that in moments of trigger, it becomes your default setting. It's like a soldier who spends hours practising drills so that when they step into the chaos of battle, their actions become instinctive.

Find the safety to feel in your mind/body connection

"The healing is in the feeling."

Keys To Emotional Mastery, Nicholas De Castella

Problems occur when you make what's happening wrong, or try to resist or control it. Understand instead that nothing is actually wrong: it's just an opportunity for growth.

The breathing and allowing in the ABC process redirects the flight/fight response of your primal brain and allows you to ground and reconnect with yourself. When your mind sees that your body has enough room to breathe fully, it receives a message of safety: that things are OK. This then puts you back in control so you don't need to react outwards or shut down.

Dealing with your trigger is a moment of vulnerability and 'being', rather than of doing:

- Get grounded then drop *inside* your feeling and *be* with it.
- You might not understand it or agree with it, but simply accept it and trust that you'll be OK.

- Remember that your feelings are just energy-in-motion and you're bigger than they are. Your body is the hose and your feelings are the water running through it.

- As you connect with the feeling, keep breathing consciously and drop through the layers of feeling in your body, ending in your heart.

- This allows the feeling to move through you and dissolve, leaving you lighter and in the freedom of your essence, often with an intuitive understanding of where your trigger came from.

You've been able to deal with your emotional trigger without creating chaos in your relationship. Now you can see what, if any, action you need to take.

If the feeling doesn't pass...

If the feeling remains, you might be still thinking it, or resisting your vulnerability. Gently keep dropping further into it, rather than moving away from it. You may need to focus more on the grounding part of your ABC practice first to feel safe enough to do this.

Looking for hints to go deeper

Your intuitive mind can help your feeling to process. Ask it for a word or an image about the feeling that will take you underneath to deeper layers of feeling and awareness.

Be gentle with yourself

Sometimes you won't be able to go IN to yourself, so you'll go OUTWARD instead into reaction. Be gentle with yourself: this is part of being human. The most valuable thing you can do is OWN what you're doing without making it wrong. This will ground you and help your partner to feel safe enough to stay present with you.

If not now, then later...

Sometimes it won't be appropriate to fully experience your feelings if they're too intense, eg if you're at work or a family event. In those cases, just acknowledge the feelings and move away from them back into your head. Then make the time to explore them later when you can through your ABC. They'll still be there if they're important.

Maybe you're not ready

Sometimes, a feeling is just too scary or intense to be with in this way at your level of experience. If this is the case, just acknowledge the feeling to yourself (and your partner if appropriate) and move away from it back into your head. Decide to come back to it when you feel ready, or when you have support from your partner, friend or therapist.

Dealing with resistance

If you find you keep getting triggered into the same feeling and resisting it, there's usually a good reason. Often, your psyche has put a barrier in place to protect you. Reflect on the ways that this resistance could be positive for you, and acknowledge it for keeping you safe. Let it know you respect it by not trying to crash through it. Instead, imagine holding it in your hand like an ice block, and allowing it to melt a little at a time. Really old feelings can take a few hours, days or even weeks to shift and just allowing them to be there is still the way to resolve them.

Despite your best intentions

Occasionally, you can try your best with the process of ABC and still feel like you haven't gotten anywhere. If this is the case, rather than continuing, we suggest you step back from it and do one of the many activities suggested in *Activities of State Change* in Chapter 6.

Some hurts have layers

The ABC process works with both big hurts and little ones. As we mentioned in Chapter 2 when talking about healing the heart, big hurts can contain several layers of hurt that need to be moved through.

The practice is the same with each layer, no matter how long the overall process takes. It can feel like you're going over the same ground whilst you're in the intensity of the feeling, but once you step through it, you can see the different layers in the one situation.

Maybe you DON'T get triggered

If this is you, nothing your partner does or says appears to trigger you in any way. You're completely above it all. A question to ask yourself in this situation is how much you're feeling in general. Is your lack of triggers a lack of awareness of your feelings, or an active avoidance of them?

Nobody wants to be triggered into emotional intensity, but seen in a positive light, triggers add to your ability to feel joy, love and other positive feelings. Use your ABC practice to come into greater relationship with your feelings: your partner will be happy if you do!

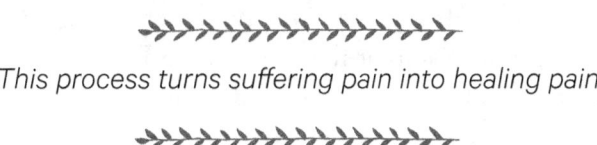

This process turns suffering pain into healing pain

This is Not Analysis

Don't be tempted to overthink this and go on an endless merry-go-round of analysis. Analysis feels better because it's less vulnerable, but it won't fully clear your issue. The more time you spend in your rational mind trying to work your trigger out (and the smarter you are, the more time and effort you're likely to put into trying to figure it out), the harder it will be. Intellectual tools can never fully resolve emotional challenges.

Graeme and I know this from years of personal suffering, so you don't have to make the same mistakes!

Yes, alluding to things like your body's intuitive wisdom and your heart's capacity for truth can sound like bullshit if you're not used to this kind of thing. Yet there's more and more science coming out in support of this way of being as we get smart enough to understand and measure it.

The ABC tool keeps you grounded in your body and moving through your life experience without getting stuck in the feeling or over-analysing it. You have too much life to live and too much relationship to share to spend much time here. The better you get at this process, the faster it happens, and then you can move on.

You'll know from your results that it's working, as you find yourself more comfortable and resilient in situations that used to trigger you.

3.4 Ending The Power Play

Until you learn to dance together in intimacy, it's easy for your relationship to become a power struggle – one where love turns into a commodity to be bartered in an endless game of point scoring or tit-for-tat. It can become a place of conditional love where, rather than giving from sheer generosity, it's 'I'll only do that for you if you do this for me' and loving becomes a transaction.

This closed-hearted giving leaves you feeling resentful and closed-hearted in return, diminishing your genuine desire to give. You start to feel love only when you've received something and focus on what you're missing out on, rather than on what you're already receiving. You start controlling or manipulating your partner to get what you want. You focus on what your partner's not getting right, making it easy to blame them instead of what you really want to do, which is love them.

This is especially true during the times when your relationship is in one of its natural ebbs or flat places, for nobody lives in 'wedded bliss' the whole time. Your self-protective emotional brain starts incorrectly interpreting your partners words, actions and even facial expressions and body language; predicting danger rather than pleasure.

What can you do to end your power play?

Even when you don't feel loving, you can still *choose* to act in *unconditionally loving ways* towards your partner. This helps you to access the love inside yourself that you desire to feel. It tricks your brain out of its victim status, giving you a sense of your own empowerment and allowing your heart to re-open.

Receiving unconditional love or attention meets one of our deepest human desires – to receive just because we *are*, not because we've done anything to deserve it, just like we (hopefully) did when we were children. Giving your partner (or yourself) the gift of a loving action when it's unexpected or least deserved works because it feels like an act of Grace, a gift of God or Spirit.

Below are a few creative options that will help you to step out of victimhood, out of power plays and back into love. Plus the many practices in this book are aimed at helping you find your power within yourself, rather than needing you to have power over your partner.

> **Centre into the love within you through your ABC practice**
>
> The ABC practice will get you back into your body, and connected with yourself, the warmth and openness of your heart, and your mental clarity. This will allow you to see the power struggle for what it is: a pointless, never-ending cycle that only takes you away from what you want.
>
> Once you're there, find gratitude for something you already have – or you may find that just reconnecting with yourself may be enough for you to move forward.

Nurture yourself with an act of unconditional love and acceptance

This is especially powerful when you feel most unworthy of receiving love or most resist giving it to yourself. Do something for yourself that would be a real treat.

Tip: Stay away from treats that involve significant amounts of money here. Needing to spend money you don't have can have other consequences and is more likely to be ego-driven: the heart doesn't care about the financial value of its gifts.

If you're not sure what treat to give yourself, take a few minutes to do your ABC, then centre into your heart and ask it what you desire. It might be something obvious like a long bath, a walk in the park, or chilling on the veranda. Or it might be something less obvious, like giving that friend a call, exercising, cleaning your desk, or doing your BAS statement (or getting someone else to do it for you).

Keep an open mind about what your answer might be.

 See your partner's love more clearly

In a long-term relationship, it's easy to get into a place of complacency where you literally cannot 'see' how your loved one is there for you. You don't feel their presence as you speak, you criticise their efforts rather than seeing the love in them, and you see them as selfish rather than loving.

Most often, the love that brings couples together remains – so if you look hard enough for acts of love from your partner, you'll probably find them. Remember that your mind projects whatever movie suits it, so if you want a movie that lets love in, simply choose it. Then cement the movie by expressing your gratitude to your partner for whatever you find.

Nurture your partner with an act of unconditional love and acceptance

Love is a vast and mysterious ocean. Yet it can also be found through a simple act.

This one takes a bit of pre-planning. When we humans do something for someone else, we often think of things that we'd enjoy ourselves. But actually, our deepest desires are a bit more personal and unique than that.

So if you want to give your partner something that really hits the spot, ask them what **they'd** most like to receive and give them this, even though it might seem insignificant or even pointless to you. It's how your gift impacts **them** that counts.

Try both separately writing out a list of the things you'd each most love to receive from each other. Again, use your ABC practice to connect more clearly with your heart's desires. What exactly would 'loving you more' look like? Be specific.

To keep it clean avoid suggestions with any existing hostility around them.

Remember that desire sharing is quite a vulnerable thing so share your desire list and receive your partners **without passing judgement**, just ask for clarification where needed. See your different desires as gifts to explore rather than a problem. Exchange lists without expectation too, as this manipulates the energy of giving. Keep the suggestions handy, and when you'd like to create love in your relationship, do one of these loving actions for your partner.

This can be:

- from a moment of openness in yourself
- to lift a flat spot in your relationship
- to create a shift in yourself when you feel closed off.

It's especially powerful to do when you feel the least like it, or when you believe your partner least deserves it.

It works because you're meeting ***your partner's*** deepest desire unconditionally, literally touching their hearts. It's vital to do this without obligation or expectation of anything in return, as this will put you straight back into the barter system you're trying to escape.

And as a bonus, you also get to learn about your partner's desires as you share your own.

As you can see, love isn't only a mysterious force that operates outside of your control. Sometimes you can choose to create it through loving actions, thus maximising the moments of love in your life and relationship.

Self, Self and Self

4.1 Know Thyself First: Acceptance is the Key

You have your own unique personal story. What you bring to your relationship is a totally unique set of strengths and challenges. There's no one exactly like you in the whole world: nobody who's had exactly the same geographical, cultural, societal, familial, financial and personal life experience as you. Your story holds the key to the person your spouse or partner fell in love with. That means it's important to really get to know and accept all parts of yourself so that you continue to have a never-ending supply of YOU to bring to your relationship.

Who you are is made up of many layers: the way you were born, cared for, nurtured, taught, encouraged, protected, loved, valued and inspired have all impacted the person you've become and will continue to do so. This means your family of origin, early caretakers and friends have a particularly powerful role in helping to form this part of you, as have your early life experiences. They all shape how you respond to life's opportunities, dreams and challenges.

For example, take Stuart Diver: the sole survivor of the 1997 Thredbo landslide that killed 18 people. He survived 65 hours in sub-zero temperatures in a water-filled space with only two inches of breathing space and his wife dying beside him. Apart from his obvious physical fitness, the fact that he'd had many adventures travelling extensively with his parents as a child, including climbing to Mt Everest base camp at age nine, no doubt influenced his mental and emotional ability to cope with such an extreme situation.

Most of us can recall only small parts of our lives at any one time – as little as 10%. You might think that this edited version of yourself is who you actually are, but the reality is much more extensive than that. Defining your story is about not limiting yourself to the small part currently on the surface but remembering you are much more than that. It's also about having enough perspective to not be attached to any particular part: not limiting yourself to being the dumb one, the betrayed one, the rebel, the sufferer or the high achiever or whatever mental script you carry about yourself.

And this is the other point of your story – it's also about who you've been in the past. Who you choose to be now or in the future is up to you. The point of power is ALWAYS in the present moment.

Taking a little time to reflect on who you are, to understand yourself, how you got to where you are in life and where you might be going will give you a strong, wholistic (but unattached) sense of yourself to share with your loved one. It will help you gain a deeper appreciation of yourself, of your flaws and your inadequacies as well as your skills and your successes.

It will also help you to be less attached to your 'story' when you're communicating. In turn, this means it's easier to see when you're caught up in drama and step back, take a breath, and remember you're much more than the story you're trying to tell. This enables you to start again from a grounded, open place.

Life Review

Take some time to reflect back over your life story: allow a minimum of one hour, or longer if you have it.

- Find a place where you won't be disturbed, preferably out in nature, and sit comfortably upright (not lying down: you want to remain awake for this!).
- Get yourself into a receptive state using your ABC practice.
- Bring to awareness various moments in your life. Start with today, then move to this week, last week, last month, last year and every year (or couple of years if you're older) of your life as far back as you can remember.
- Notice important life events (even if they were only important to you).
- Notice where your strengths were and what you learned from your failures.
- See where you chose from love, and where from fear.
- Find yourself acknowledging, understanding and accepting any choices you've made.
- Finish when the process feels complete for you.

You might do this review a few times to get to know yourself, and then make it an annual practice, perhaps on your holidays. You'll find you experience yourself and your life differently and gain new insights each time, because *you'll* be different.

- Take the opportunity to share what you've found with your partner and ask them questions about themselves. Acknowledge what you see and respect in your partner as a result of their life's journey.
- Take the time to share your dreams about the future, your ideas about what you want to build, create or manifest in your life, for yourself, your family or your world.

These activities and practices will deepen your understanding of and connection with yourselves and each other, activating feelings of love and desire whilst making it easier to choose positive behaviours in times of challenge.

 Connecting with your soul self

Take a really good look at yourself in the mirror. Who do you see? Can you see the one who has lived out your stories? If you keep looking, can you see the part of you that lies beyond them?

Can you sense the part of YOU that is timeless and unchanging? That perhaps even feels like love? This is the part of you that's connected to your soul or essence. Spend a few moments here.

When you get this larger sense of yourself and your life, it's easier to find appreciation, gratitude, compassion and even awe for yourself and for those around you, including your partner. It's easier to let go of any over indulgence in self judgement and start living from your magnificence

4.2 Your Relationship Begins with You

Being this totally unique individual means you have the power to create your reality through your thoughts, the choices you make, the beliefs you take on, the values you live by, and the actions you choose. And of course, you can also do it through the way you manage your feelings.

It's not so much what you're doing in your relationship that matters, but where in yourself you're doing it from.

Make it a practice to notice yourself and how you're being during your day. Don't do this from a neurotic, narcissistic viewpoint, instead just simply notice. This will, with practice, allow you to see yourself more clearly and make healthier choices as you go along.

Who am I Being?

Taking a step back from yourself and becoming aware of the choices you make means becoming responsible for them – and seeing the impacts and the results on both yourself and those around you. This doesn't mean taking responsibility for other people's choices, but instead owning and making the most of your own.

Pause for a moment throughout your day and ask yourself the following questions:

- What am I choosing right now?
- How is how I am being serving me and/or my partner?

 Reality Check

It's easy to live in the glow of your own little world at times, thinking you're doing much better (or much worse) at something than others experience, or than results show. Every now and again, it's worth checking out how your inner reality stacks up in the outside world. Try viewing yourself objectively as if you truly were a fly on the wall – separate from yourself and just watching you from the outside. See what you notice about yourself and the results you're creating.

Occasionally, ask your partner, a friend, or even a range of different people for feedback on how they see you. Although their points of view do reflect themselves, it can still help you see places where you might be deluding yourself.

4.3 Trust Your Essence

The tantalising suggestion about relationships is that once you've found your life partner, you'll never again have to feel lonely and that abandonment and rejection will be a thing of the past. If you're like most people, you carry a belief that somehow your significant other will give you permanent relief from your aloneness through their love and desire (or through accepting your love and desire for them).

The reality, of course, is quite different and something you need to face to be truly at peace with yourself within your relationship. Your partner *can* be there to share a hug, kiss and an "I love you," or to make love with all their heart, but they won't always be. Sometimes, they'll have their own lives to attend to.

In fact, ultimately even their love for you is about *them*, it's nothing to do with you, just as *your* love is nothing to do with them, it's about you. Understanding this is freedom from being controlled by love.

You might understand this at a rational level, but a part of you just doesn't get it. This is the ego part of you that your partner can *never* fill, no matter how perfect they are or how hard they try. It can feel filled at times of deep intimacy or in lovemaking where you feel totally at one with them – yet after these experiences, you still need to come 'home' to yourself.

The 'self' you come home to here is your essence. It's the part of you that's totally fulfilled in being alone no matter what. It enjoys and loves connecting with others but is also complete in itself if connection isn't possible. This part of you can look into the abyss of loneliness, neediness, loss and pain that lies within each of us, and feel it without being controlled, overwhelmed or destroyed by it. It's freedom. In your essence, you can be in a relationship with your partner, yet allow them to retain their unique identity. You can be interdependent rather than co-dependent or totally independent.

You can only truly find this part of yourself through the uncertainty of moments where you must face not getting what you deeply desire (and, at some level, believe you should be entitled to).

It's a scary part to look at, because doing so means looking right into the chasm of darkness that lies within you, rather than resorting to:

- manipulating your partner to supply love
- playing the victim when you can't get it
- emotionally shutting down

- numbing yourself with any number of attractive addictions to avoid it.

This is the paradox of relationship: it offers you something from outside yourself that you ultimately need to find within. But it's worth it, for this part of you is *always* there, reliable, unchanging and a part of life's inherent mystery. You can find it through your ABC practice. It can be both a huge solace to the part of you that suffers, and enlightening to the part of you that sleeps. And the more often you choose to experience it, the more easily it will happen – and the less drama and suffering you'll create for yourself and the one you're in your relationship with.

4.4 Yes, You are Fascinating: Your Beliefs, Values, Needs and Desires

Part of what makes up your individuality is your particular combination of beliefs and values as well as your universal human needs and individual desires. In this section, you'll find exercises that help you explore, understand and get clearer about who you are, what's important to you and how to negotiate this in your relationship.

It's amazing how many couples go along from day to day never really knowing each other (and unsurprising how many then drift apart). Sharing with your partner what you find as you do the following exercises will give you years of conversations to come. You can do them as formally or informally as you like.

You'll also find suggestions of how to ask for what you need and desire without shooting yourself in the foot or getting your partner's back up. And you'll learn how, much like your triggers, your deepest needs and desires are part of what drew you and your partner together in the first place. Your answers here will reveal even more surprisingly why you were both made for each other.

Your ABC tool will help you to find what's true for you here, it's one of the benefits of building a greater connection with your body-mind. When you hit on something that's true for you, it will 'feel right' to you – like a 'yes' inside you, with your body softening and opening. If something isn't right, the 'no' might feel like a tightness or tension, a pain in your heart, a resistance in your gut, or perhaps a numbness or 'nothing' feeling. If you don't feel a clear 'yes' for something, stay connected with the process until you feel it for something else.

Identifying Your Beliefs

As we said earlier, a belief is an idea or principle that you want to be true, whether it's been proven so or not. Beliefs help to form your reality. They come from your logical mind making sense of your experiences, and they can be conscious or unconscious, helpful and unhelpful.

The beliefs that are both hardest to see and your strongest influences come from your earliest experiences. Imagine the common real-life scenario of a child who tries to get his mother's attention but sees her turn away from him to catch something on the stove. He might take on the logical but untrue belief that he's unimportant to her, which then impacts his adult relationships with the women in his life (true story).

The beliefs that give you the most headaches are likely the limiting ones *you take on about yourself as a result of your painful experiences*. Even very traumatic experiences themselves aren't as painful as the years of suffering you create from the limiting beliefs you then find yourself living from. You can never change what's happened to you, but you can change the beliefs you take on as a result and the impact they have on your life and relationships. Beliefs such as 'I'm not good enough', 'my sexuality is wrong', 'men/women are untrustworthy', or 'I'm not capable of creating what I need in my life'.

Exploring Your Beliefs

Without censoring them, write a list of some of your beliefs about yourself, your partner or your relationship, both positive and negative. Take one belief to explore here.

Get centred with the ABC practice, then notice the following:

- What feeling lies within this belief? Allow it to be there as you ask yourself the following questions and observe when it shifts.
- What's your evidence for this belief? Is it true? What stories are attached to it?
- How do you treat yourself and/or your partner when you hold this belief?
- What benefit does it give you to hold onto this belief? (Even negative beliefs bring you something that works for you – eg believing it keeps you safe, lets you hide, etc.)
- What does your life look like with this belief going forward?
- If you see that the belief no longer serves you, how willing are you on a scale of 1-10 to drop it? What belief could you choose instead? How would that belief make your life look? What practical steps could you take going forward with this new belief?

The *Activities of State Change* in Chapter 6 can help here. So can looking inside your emotional triggers. Once identifying your beliefs (either through this formal process, or as a result of your ABC practice) has become normal, you'll find yourself becoming less attached to your unhelpful beliefs and no longer allowing them to control your life.

If you still can't identify an underlying belief that's leading you astray, body-centred therapies eg breathwork, focussing, somatic therapy, kinesiology and counselling will help.

Identifying Your Core Values

Your values are part of your essential self. They're based on what's important to you, who you are and the way you choose to live, and living from them makes you feel good about yourself.

Values determine your standards and priorities, and they're the measures you use to make decisions that honour yourself and tell you if your life is turning out the way you want it to. In times of challenge, your core values are what you keep coming back to, they're the 'bottom line' that you create your reality from. There are no right or wrong core values, only the ones you choose.

Your core values are the ones that stay in place for long periods of time, enduring even when other aspects of your life change. Partners who share core values find their relationship easier to deal with in difficult times.

A few examples of core values:

- Complete honesty is best at all times
- Work/life balance is important
- Infidelity is a deal-breaker
- My partner needs to share my political/religious/spiritual beliefs.

 Identifying Your Core Values

Centre with your ABC and write a list of your core values. Start with what's most obvious, keep your mind open as you work your way through to ones that may surprise you. Ask yourself:

- What do you believe these values offer you and your relationship?
- Are you living your core values? Are there any changes you can make so you're living in a place of more integrity with yourself?

Pick a time to share some of these values with your partner. Take the time to show them who you are, then invite them to do the same.

> Feel the increased level of connection, safety and love that can arise from having clarity in your shared values. If you have differing values, explore how they impact on your relationship.

Identifying Your Needs

We all have needs. It's human. Life is too complex to do it all ourselves, and love creates the desire to help and support our partner, so it's a perfect system, right? Yet needs remain one of the most difficult areas to confront in a relationship.

In a society that highly values selfhood, we can even feel shame about admitting we have needs.

If you grew up in a family where your needs weren't valued, you might not even know you have any. On the opposite side, it's becoming more common to grow up with a high degree of entitlement, believing your needs should be consistently met over other people's – a poor combination for a relationship.

In fact, we're 'entitled' to absolutely nothing, not even our next breath.

Most often though, you just get caught up in the busyness of life, where your needs take a back seat to your shoulds until they start screaming to be met. As a creature with a strong innate will to survive, it's VITAL for you to acknowledge your needs. For if you don't, your psyche will go about getting them met covertly. This covertness will see you acting out in all sorts of unhelpful ways that your relationship can do without, so as challenging as it can be it's much better to get your needs up front.

Most partners love to help and support each other wherever they can. This is a deeply satisfying part of what love is. But it's essential to keep in mind that:

It's not automatically our partner's responsibility to meet our individual needs.

Your partner can certainly choose to meet your needs – and in a healthy relationship, they'll often desire to in many loving and creative ways. Yet the reality is that another person can't *always* be there for you and we can forget this. Continually putting your needs onto your partner and demanding they be met is entering into a child-parent relationship with your partner, rather than an adult-to-adult one.

Over time, this will create resentment on the part of the 'parent' and place the 'child' in a victim status. Of course, there will be times when this dynamic is required temporarily, eg during illness, one partner's lack of skill, knowledge or experience. But *both of you* need to let go of the dynamic when the inherent situation is resolved.

If you respect your partner's boundaries during times when they're just not up for meeting your needs, they'll repay you in spades by becoming 'up for it' again soon.

Here's a list of common human needs:

- ***Physical Wellbeing:*** Air, food, exercise/movement, rest/sleep, safety, shelter, sexual expression, touch, water.
- ***Connection:*** Acceptance, affection, appreciation, attention, belonging, cooperation, communication, closeness, community,

4: Self, Self and Self

companionship, compassion, consideration, consistency, empathy, inclusion, intimacy, love, mutuality, nurturing, respect/self respect, safety, security, stability, support, to know and be known, to see and be seen, to understand and be understood, to like and be liked, to need and be needed, trust, warmth.

- *Honesty:* Authenticity, integrity, certainty, presence.
- *Play:* Adventure, diversity, fun, excitement, challenge, risk, joy, humour.
- *Peace:* Beauty, communion, ease, equality, balance, harmony, inspiration, predictability, order.
- *Autonomy:* Choice, freedom, independence, space, spontaneity.
- *Meaning:* Significance, awareness, celebration of life, challenge, clarity, competence, consciousness, contribution, creativity, discovery, efficacy, effectiveness, growth, hope, learning, mourning, participation, purpose, self expression, stimulation, to matter, understanding.

(c) 2005 by Center for Nonviolent Communication (with a couple of our own added) Website: www.cnvc.org

---

 Knowing Your Needs (Use the list above as a guide)

- Centre yourself with your ABC. Circle any needs in the above list that you require to have met to be fully who you are. The list covers all human needs, and you as a unique individual will rate some needs higher than others. Then rate the five most important ones to explore. Your partner will have their own unique combination of priorities.
- Imagine and feel what having the most important need being met would be like. What would it give you? How would your life be significantly less without it? Keep going underneath each layer until you reach what feels like the core reason behind this need. When you reach this layer, your body will feel relaxed, at ease, heart-open, in peace or similar.

- Repeat for each of your three most important needs. Then do the same for your three least important, as these may surprise you.
- Explore which needs are currently not being met in your relationship.
- Examine the ways you might be covertly trying to get these needs met, either inside or outside your relationship.
- Explore which of these needs you can healthily meet yourself if your partner can't (or asking someone else to help).
- Ask yourself which needs you need help with and ask. Remember: there's no shame in needing help – it's part of being a complex and lovable human being. Whether you get that need met or not has nothing to do with your inherent self-worth.
- Ask yourself whether you're over-caring for your partner's needs. For example, are you regularly doing things for them that they could be doing for themselves? You're their partner, not their parent or caretaker – being seen as the latter is not only unsexy, it also invites powerlessness in them. If you answer yes here, a further worthwhile question to ask yourself is what does doing so give you, or what can you avoid in behaving like this?
- Then ask yourself whether you care *enough* about your partner's needs, or whether you're busy off living in your own reality. If you're not sure how you might be supporting your partner in meeting their needs, take the easy way and ask them! The benefits are worth the risk.

 ### Discuss Your Needs Upfront

Rather than waiting until things aren't working, make a point of discussing your needs with your partner and invite them to share theirs on a regular basis. Share too how it is for you to ask for things, and how you can best help meet each other's needs.

Having this conversation outside of the heat of the moment can allow surprising solutions to arise. This also takes your needs out of the

> shadows and into a place of healthy recognition, reducing the emotional intensity that can build around them.
>
> Remember that life is about change – ebb and flow – and humans are no different. There'll be times when you'll have more needs, or more intense needs than your partner and vice versa. Normalising them will help you both move through these changes.

Desperation is a Key

Graeme and I have found that the more desperate your need feels, and the more attached you are to getting your partner to fulfil it *exactly* how you want it, the more likely it is that there's something in it for you to learn. And that 'something' is likely to be to giving what you need (or at least an aspect of it) to yourself, to grow your own wholeness, rather than getting it from your partner.

The urgency is your psyche's way of screaming at you to see yourself more clearly, and to listen to your heart more than your ego. For wherever there's attachment, you can be sure your ego's playing a part. So do yourself a favour and look deeper: you can experience profound shifts in both yourself and your relationship as a result.

For example:

- If you want more love, love yourself more.
- If you want to be seen, see yourself more (and you might see where you're not seeing your partner).
- If you want more sex, be more comfortable in your own sexual feelings.
- If you want more desire from your partner, find the desire in yourself.
- And if you want more intimacy, be willing to go first in being vulnerable.

If you find your needs are continually going unmet, first review whether you've attempted to meet them yourself. Then review the section on 'How to ask for what you want' to check whether the way you're asking for what you want is getting in your way of receiving it. If you're clear that you're not shooting yourself in the foot, it's vital to discuss what's happening with your partner, as this is not a viable long-term situation.

People often ask us "What's the point of being in a relationship if the other person isn't there to fill our needs and we can meet our own?" What's left is simply desire to be together...

Identifying Your Individual Desires

If your needs reflect your humanity, your desires more often reflect your uniqueness. Human desires can range from enjoying an occasional fresh lamington with cream, to anal sex hanging upside down in a sling, or saving the world from hunger. You can survive without your desires being fulfilled, but life is much less inspiring, for your desires are an important aspect of how you experience and express yourself.

Desires are the place in a relationship where most people find both opportunity and challenge. Again, it's not your *obligation* to fulfil your partner's desires, but it can be immensely rewarding. It can be as delightful as your partner introducing you to a new hobby you learn to love (like bootcamp for Annette), an adventure holiday, an evening stroll, a healthier diet, a new way of understanding the world, or even the joys of football. And in turn, you might enjoy supporting your partner in their desire to take up a challenge that's right for them like going back to university, trying BDSM, travelling overseas for work or healing an old wound in their family.

> **Owning Your Desires**
>
> - Start with doing your ABC practice so that you identify your desires from your most open and free self. Start this separately from your partner.
> - Write out a list of your desires without censoring them, starting out with small desires, then going deeper. Really feel into your desires, flesh them out in your imagination and feel them fully.
> - Identify the desires you could fulfil for yourself. Then identify the ones you'd like to share with your partner, and the ones you think might be challenging in your relationship.
> - Lastly, pick a time to share your lists with each other using the *Embodied Communication* technique you'll learn in Chapter 5, and see which ones you could bring to life in your relationship. Leave aside any that you disagree on for now, and set aside time to play with the rest.
>
> You'll be surprised at the energy that actively exploring each of your desires will bring. And once you've both built up a layer of trust in your exploration, you can look at the more challenging desires.

The Gift of your Deepest Needs and Desires

Your partner's deepest needs or desires (or your own) will likely deeply challenge the status quo in your relationship, bringing up judgement, fear and resistance. Graeme and I believe, and have found in our own relationship and through our work with couples, that these deepest needs and desires are part of the reason we all unconsciously chose to be in a relationship with each other in the first place. They're an opportunity to grow beyond anything you might have imagined for yourself.

This is because the deepest needs and desires in you somehow match your partner's deepest fears, and vice versa. For example, one of my deepest needs was to feel loved, and my desires often centred around having time with Graeme. Meanwhile, one of Graeme's deepest desires was to honour his need for freedom, which often clashed with my need for closeness. Out of this clash, which could easily have seen the end of our relationship, came some of its greatest gifts, which you'll read about more fully in Chapter 9 on Shadows.

You can choose to shut down in this place and limit the love in your relationship, or you can look at your fears and resistance and see how they might be a growth point for your own limitations and an incredible gift for your partner. This is where a *Relationship Agreement* (Chapter 11) and *Embodied Communication* skills (Chapter 5) come in handy.

Finding your Gifts from Each Other

Stuart was sure that Marcie had 'stuff' she needed to look at in relation to her sexuality, because she was never really 'there' when they made love. As a result, he didn't know what to do with his sexual intensity, which he believed was too much for her. He could feel a need in Marcie for something more from him, but believed she was looking for something that he couldn't give. And he believed that it was up to her find the answer within herself. All he could do was limit himself to his own isolated experience, without the intimacy he longed for or the pleasure he suspected was possible.

Stuart was correct in believing that Marcie's first point of call was to look at her own stuff. But it was equally true that Marcie was calling Stuart on something in him: something that would not only support her, but would take him to a whole new place in himself. In fact, this second layer was one of the unconscious reasons they got together in the first place – a deeper layer of polishing their diamond inner selves.

Marcie had always seen Stuart as her rock – someone she could rely on when things got tough. And he could be her rock without even trying as it was a core part of who he was: strong, generous and powerful. But she was looking for more than that in him. She was also looking for his vulnerability – the part of him that would help her feel safe enough to open even more into her own feelings in a sexual space.

This part of Stuart was his heart connection to himself and to his balls. This was the part of him that so far, was there for everybody else, but that he didn't trust in himself. It showed up in his not going for the next level of management at work, and in his fear of opening deeply (despite his desires to) in lovemaking. This was the part of himself that Stuart couldn't 'see' whilst he needed Marcie to do her stuff.

This was her gift to him: to not be put off in asking for what she wanted (whilst also doing her own work) and challenging him to look deeper. And Stuart's surprising gift to Marcie was that in being disconnected from this part of himself, he gave Marcie the opportunity to be her own rock at times, to stand up for her own truth, and not be put off by his 'strong man' mask.

See where your deepest places are challenging each other to grow.

How to Ask for What You Need/Want

Below, you'll find some simple but powerful tips on how to go about asking for what you want or desire in your relationship as clearly as possible, without getting in your own way and literally preventing your partner from supporting you.

If this list looks a little daunting, just try a couple of things at a time and build on them... knowing how sad it would be if you never asked at all!

- Believe absolutely in your right to *ask*. The getting is separate to the asking, and does not relate to your self-worth.

- Identify clearly what it is that you need/desire (see above).
- Ask without any attachment to getting what you want in the way that you want it. Being attached to an outcome or having an agenda creates limitation so make the asking the most important part.

This literally keeps your energy inside you, rather than focussing it all on your partner's response, leaving you exposed and unnecessarily vulnerable. This also prevents you from unconsciously trying to manipulate your partner, leaving them free to respond authentically.

- Be willing to receive a 'no' before you ask the question. Imagine it happening and you being OK with it.
- Avoid hinting, implying, suggesting, or any other covert methods of asking for what you want. Just be clear, open and direct so the other person can hear you (especially if you're asking your man for something).
- Never make a demand, as it leaves your partner with one of three unhealthy responses: to give in, resist or fight back. None of these end up anywhere you want to go.
- Avoid asking from the negative, eg saying, "You're never here on time when I want it. Get it right, can't you?" This is not very inviting, but it's *very* common.

It's a lot easier to criticise your partner than it is to be vulnerable in yourself and ask for what you want/need.

- Make it clear the outcome that getting what you want will create for you. This inspires your partner to help you manifest it. For example, "If you put the kids to bed for me tonight, I'll feel really cared about and close to you," or "If you send me a sexy text whilst I'm at work today, I'll feel seen and validated by you."

- Ask if there's anything they need to help you achieve what you want, eg, "Would it make it easier if I put the kids' PJs out on the bed for you?" or, "Would it make it easier if I gave you a melting hug and kiss before I left for work?" This allows your partner to feel like you're both on the same team.

- If your partner says, "no," hear it without judgement. And don't stay in the 'no'. Instead, make space for something else to arise. Be willing to negotiate in ways that might surprise you.

- If your need has a big 'empty tank', you'll have less flexibility in negotiation. In this case, can you partially fill it in other ways? For example, if you find yourself desperate for intimacy with your partner, can you spend some time sharing intimacy with a friend? Once your intimacy tank has been filled up a little, you'll feel a lot safer about asking for intimacy with your partner from a place of vulnerability, without blame or shame.

NB. It's important not to whinge about your partner or share things you've hidden from them when you're sharing intimacy with your friend, as this creates a divide and leaks energy from your relationship.

- If your partner can't meet your need, meet it yourself, eg by giving yourself a hug, a cuppa or self-pleasuring.

- If you're finding it difficult to identify your need, let the other person know this before you start. Invite them (or someone else if appropriate) to help you explore what the need might be. Just be clear that this is a separate conversation to the one where you actually ask for it.

- If you have difficulty asking for what you want, explore your 'stuff' around asking with your ABC. Do you have a fear of not being worthy, resentment that it won't happen, past pain from being rejected, or beliefs that asking is wrong? Identify and acknowledge what drives your resistance and choose to not let it control you.

- If your partner consistently rejects your request, ask them their reason in a non-judgemental way. Be prepared to listen, and you'll probably learn something useful.

Receiving Your Partner's Request

If your partner asks something of you that you're not able to give you can say no by saying no to the request but not to them eg "I'm going to be away that day but I can spare some time on Friday, would that work?" or "Even though I can't do this I'm still glad you were willing to ask me as it makes me feel part of your life."

Creative Need and Desire Fulfilment

How can you embrace your needs and desires during times when your partner can't meet them (much as they might like to)? You can do this by using your creative or higher intelligence. Your mind doesn't know the difference between imagination and reality, so you can often experience having your need or desire met by simply using the power of your mind and body.

 Creative Need and Desire Fulfilment

This actually works!

- Centre yourself with your ABC, and imagine yourself experiencing your need or desire fully. Fill it out in your imagination as clearly as you can, noting how you would feel.
- Then ask for help in meeting this need or desire from your higher creative self, your heart or your higher power – whatever this might mean to you.
- Allow your imagination to fulfil your need or desire in the most creative way possible, feeling your response in your heart and body if this is helpful. Fully embrace the moment, as this will change how you feel about the real situation.

> You can simply enjoy what you've received without needing anything more. Or use the creative solutions you found to fulfil your need or desire in the real world.
>
> Equally, however, feel like you can ask for what you need or desire without manipulation or shame. Standing on top of your solid foundation of supportive beliefs and values, you can step forward in this area of your relationship with clarity and purpose.

4.5 Surviving Letting Another Person in Close: The Importance of Boundaries

Personal boundaries are tools for protecting and getting to know your essential self. They also show your partner who you are. Your personal boundaries, just like everyone else's, are unique to you as a result of your individual personality and life experiences. Because boundaries are so personal, you don't need to justify them to anyone else, they're a sign that you're maintaining your essential self.

Getting clear on boundaries is a vulnerable-yet-essential part of relating. Boundaries aren't just ways to protect yourself from hurt. Boundaries are where you learn to say a healthy 'Yes' and 'No' in your relationship. Setting boundaries helps you to feel safe and respected enough to fully *engage in* your relationship rather than pull away from it, allowing you to get really close to your partner (and them to you) without either of you losing yourselves. Let's now look at how to identify, clarify, express and maintain boundaries as clear and flexible signposts, and pathways to getting healthily closer.

Boundaries are there to teach yourself and your partner about how you wish to be treated.

You have boundaries in all areas of your life, from saying no to another committee in order to have more rest during your week, to saying no to a particular sexual practice that doesn't feel right for you. Graeme has a particular boundary around his toilet bag (leave it alone) whilst Annette has one around her nipples (start gently). You also have boundaries within yourself, ie 'Is this a good moment for me to allow myself to be vulnerable?'

A boundary may be a solid brick wall at the far edges of yourself, or a gentle fence as close to you as you can put it. The one thing healthy boundaries *aren't* is permanently fixed. They're always open to review and change as you become more comfortable in yourself. Healthy boundaries can even show up unhealthy ones.

It can initially feel like setting boundaries is pulling you away from your partner, but the opposite is actually true. So let's get started exploring this very powerful part of your relationship.

Other Things Boundaries AREN'T

Boundaries are NOT about avoiding your relationship

When you set a boundary, you don't use it to protect yourself from engaging with your partner just to avoid being uncomfortable. This is simply avoidance with a covert, manipulative label. Instead, set a healthy boundary by requesting a delay until:

- you have more time or energy
- you have more information
- you feel clearer in yourself and more willingness to be vulnerable.

Then offer a time when you'll be willing to have the conversation or interaction your partner wants, and follow through with it. This is saying 'no' to look after yourself without rejecting your partner.

Boundaries are NOT about controlling your partner's behaviour

Your boundaries are about you, they're not about trying to impose your standards of behaviour onto your partner. Attempting to do this is both manipulating and invalidating who your partner is. It's effectively saying that you need them to be different from who they essentially are for you to love them.

This is a very unloving thing to do.

Your boundaries are about you rather than your partner.

Reasons for Difficulties with Boundaries

Having your boundaries regularly crossed as a child can create difficulties with boundaries as an adult. This crossing can range from a well-meaning parent getting you to kiss a loved aunt or uncle when you didn't really want to, not allowing you to close your bedroom door, all the way through to sexual abuse.

You can also experience boundary crosses as an adult, but your childhood experiences remain the primary determiners of your sense of self. This is why bringing them to light is so powerful. If you have difficulty with your own boundaries, (which is very common) you're more likely to have difficulty in seeing and respecting the boundaries of others.

Identifying Your Boundaries

The most direct way to explore your boundaries is through feeling them:

- **No** = a contraction in your body, or something feeling icky or off in your gut that feels like you'd lose something of yourself if you overrode it.

- **Yes** = an expansion, lightness, relaxation or opening in your body that feels like you'd maintain or expand in yourself if you respected it.

If you have difficulties feeling an embodied response keep practicing your ABC until it gets easier. And in the meantime think about your boundaries intellectually using the following ideas.

How to Set Boundaries

You can communicate your boundaries in various ways:

- *Vague:* I need peace and quiet when I come home from work.
- *Manipulative:* I need a space of peace and quiet after work, so you have to turn your music off when I walk into the room.
- *Healthy:* I need peace and quiet when I come home from work for about half an hour, so I'll move somewhere else to decompress till I'm ready to engage again.

A healthy boundary lets you express your desire without imposing limitations on the other person. This leaves your partner free to hear and feel your reality, and invites a helpful response, eg them choosing to use headphones for this period of time.

A good question to ask yourself when you're setting a boundary is whether you're making the boundary about you or them.

Using your boundaries cleanly

Boundaries don't work unless you're willing to identify, state and then stand up for them.

Remember too that they're *your* boundaries. And if it's your boundary, it's up to you to maintain it. So whilst it can be challenging at times for you to remain aware of them, think about how much harder it is for your partner. They have a totally different set of boundaries to yours, and they won't necessarily automatically understand or remember yours (or you theirs). Sharing (not justifying) what's behind your boundary helps.

This means you'll need to talk about boundaries often, and sometimes reinforce them more than once, before either of you 'gets' them. This isn't a show of disrespect – it's just a reminder that you're different.

Understanding The Other Person's Reality

If, once they've become aware of your boundary, your partner chooses to keep crossing it, seek to understand what's happening for them and what the need behind their actions is. Between you, you may be able to find another way to meet this need.

Sometimes, particularly in an intimate relationship, the other person is unable to hear your boundary, even though you've stated it clearly and tried to understand where they're coming from. This is usually because it's hitting some unconscious hurt or need that's beyond their current reality, they're not doing it deliberately.

In this case, you'll need to continue to enforce your boundary until they can see themselves more clearly. The gift for you in having to do this is that it invites you to strengthen a part yourself that needs attention, eg self-awareness, self-respect or the ability to speak up for yourself.

Enforcing a Boundary

Even though your boundaries are about you, you may need to set some kind of consequences for your partner's actions for them to 'get' your boundary. Start with a soft consequence from the most grounded and heart-open place in yourself that you can manage. If you're still not being heard, make sure your partner knows you're not rejecting *them,* but instead taking care of *yourself.* Then set firmer consequences.

Here are three different examples with varying degrees of consequence.

a. *Your partner keeps making you late for appointments by not being organised.*

- *Soft:* Let them feel your hurt and frustration at not being heard.
- *Firmer:* Let them know that if they're not ready, you'll leave them to make their own way.
- *Firm:* If they're consistently not ready, travel to the event separately and make sure they know why.

b. *Your partner touches you genitally in lovemaking before you're ready.*

- *Soft:* Take their hand away and place it on a more ready part of your body.
- *Firmer:* Take their hand and hold it still for a period.
- *Firm:* Say no to sex whilst this behaviour continues. Let them know how it impacts you, and that you'll be open to sex again if they can hear you and meet you in this.

c. *Your partner continually dumps their emotional garbage onto you without owning it.*

- *Soft:* Staying grounded and heart-open, let your partner know you're willing to listen but tell them how their behaviour is impacting you. Use this time to practice not being drawn into your partner's stuff, whilst checking to see what your own stuff might be.
- *Firmer:* If nothing happens after a reasonable period of time, again state that you're willing to listen but not be disrespected or take on what's not yours. Let your partner know you're not deserting them but respecting yourself, and that the choice in how to continue is up to them.

- *Firm:* State that you're willing to listen to them when they're willing to connect with themselves and own what they're doing, but until then you won't be emotionally available. Respect yourself by walking away after letting your partner know why, and that you'll be willing to try again later.

In this way, each time you leave your partner with a choice in how they respond, rather than making them feel as though they're wrong. (If they choose to feel wrong, this is their choice and a different thing).

What if you offend your partner by saying "no"?

When your boundary is a clear "no" for you without manipulation or avoidance, it's important to look after yourself first. Your partner's response is then their business.

They may feel hurt or pissed off, and if so, have compassion for them. If you're genuine, they'll eventually feel it and respect you for it (although, if your boundaries touch deep places in them, this can take some time).

If your partner really wants the best for you and their relationship, then even if they don't understand your boundary, they'll support you in maintaining it. If not, there's some shadow operating somewhere, and you have bigger questions to ask yourself about your relationship.

Boundaries can shift

It's important to regularly review your boundaries, as they can change from time to time, and even moment by moment. Sometimes just expressing a boundary and feeling the safety it brings can allow it to shift. For example, if your partner has been willing to discuss and set sexual boundaries with you, you might feel more adventurous or willing to move closer to them in the bedroom.

Sometimes, you can get caught in 'protecting your protection'. Having a lot of fear around a boundary can cause you to protect it more than is ultimately helpful, so it's good to check how relevant your fear still is, or whether it's just fear of fear itself.

And, as with your needs and desires, you and your partner have boundaries that unconsciously attracted you to each other in order to heal them. Think back to Stuart and Marcie's relationship dynamic: both of them could have chosen to protect their boundaries. Stuart could have believed that Marcie was crossing his boundary in asking for something more from him and stayed closed. Marcie could have believed she was staying safe in disconnecting from herself in lovemaking and being limited by her fear of her sexual power.

As always, see opportunities to learn rather than something being wrong, and use your ABC practice to grow through them.

 Reviewing Your Boundaries

Healthy boundaries are flexible and open to change, so it's a good idea to review them regularly. Consider a couple of your personal boundaries and ask yourself whether anything has changed from when you first set each boundary, then ask:

- Is it working? If not, are you maintaining it?
- Is it about protecting yourself, or about controlling your partner in some way?
- Is it still required, or does it limit you now that you've outgrown it?

If removing it feels like too big a step, is there a smaller step you *could* take?

If you can't think of any boundaries you have it's a good idea to find some for yourself so you can find more of you!

 Sharing Your Boundaries

Talk with your partner about the idea of boundaries and what they mean to each of you. Share one or two of yours, explain how you're

> currently managing them, and – if needed – how you might do so in a healthier way. Ask them about a couple of theirs.
>
> Discussing the idea of boundaries and their importance upfront makes it easier to understand them when they're put into place. It can help you to not take your partner's boundaries personally – to remember that their boundaries are about them, not you.
>
> Also remember that healthy boundaries are as much an essential part of keeping you together as those moments of divine boundary-lessness you find in lovemaking.

4.5 The Importance of Inter-Generational Boundaries

Inter-generational boundaries refer to the healthy separation between couples and their children or parents. Without clear boundaries, couples easily become enmeshed with their children, or stay enmeshed with their parents, draining energy from their own intimate connection. Enmeshment is being overly involved in each other's lives and feelings without clear boundaries or any sense of each person's own independent selves, needs and desires.

> *"From the time we're first wrapped in a blanket, family members encourage us to be our authentic selves, while they unconsciously encourage us to express certain traits, qualities, or behaviours and to deny or inhibit others to suit them. People need us to be a certain way for their own sake."*
>
> The Dance of Intimacy, Harriet Learner, PhD

The relationships between individuals and even the best of families are complex ones.

Coming Together

Clear and managed boundaries make relationships healthy for everyone.

Enmeshment DOWN the Generations

Jane and Tim have been together for 17 years in a solid relationship. But both would admit that some distance has developed between them as Tim has worked away quite a bit, and Jane is stressed about money when he's home.

> ### ♥ Jane's Enmeshment with Brad
>
> *Jane has unexpressed resentment about Tim's absences, but tolerates it for the income and lifestyle his job provides. However, her resentment has crossed an intergenerational boundary into her relationship with her 13 year old son Brad through her consistent complaints to him about Tim.*
>
> *She complains about Tim not earning enough for her and not contributing at home, including the odd reference to her sexual frustration about what Tim might be up to when he's away so much. She finds Brad a softer target for her frustrations than she fears Tim would be. But this gives Brad the subtle message that men are uncaring and irresponsible, leaving him unconsciously reluctant to grow up and turn into one. Brad then puts an emotional barrier up around his father who he really still longs for approval from.*
>
> *Jane would be much better off sharing her frustrations with Tim (the source of them), and finding other ways to release them without involving Brad. This would leave him free to grow up into a man he can admire.*

> ### ❤️ *Tim's Enmeshment with Jacinta*
>
> *Tim, on the other hand, has unconsciously transferred his need for emotional intimacy from his unhappy wife Jane to his soft and smiling 10 year old daughter Jacinta.*
>
> *Jacinta always rushes up with her arms out and a big smile for him when he arrives home, unlike his less-than-certain greeting from Jane. As a result, he allows her to stay up past her bedtime, sit on his lap and be his 'little girl' whilst Jane looks on with a subtle discomfort she doesn't realise is envy.*
>
> *Tim has also crossed an inter-generational boundary, getting his need for emotional closeness from Jacinta, rather than the harder target of Jane. This gives Jacinta the subtle message that she's a little princess with power over men, who can get her needs met by manipulating them in their emotional vulnerability.*
>
> *Tim would be better off learning to navigate the emotional distance that has arisen between Jane and himself, and then enjoying his time with Jacinta free of underlying emotional agenda. This frees Jacinta to grow up feeling safe enough around men to be herself, rather than being there for their needs and manipulating them for her own.*

Enmeshment UP the Generations

> ### ❤️ *Kerry's Enmeshment with Her Parents*
>
> *Kerry loves her dad. As a child she found him a hard-but-fair disciplinarian whom she never answered back. Kerry felt she could go to him for answers, even if she didn't always like his rules. Her mum was always there for her as well, being supportive and caring. Kerry knew she was blessed in her upbringing.*

Her problem is that she keeps looking to her Dad for approval in her decisions, even after she married Jeff. She also has a deep underlying fear about the death of her parents and being left alone with no grownups to refer her decisions to.

Even worse, she sometimes feels she can't speak up in her relationship to Jeff for fear of his disapproval, just like she did with her Dad when she was little. She loves Jeff and they have a great relationship with two kids, but a part of her is always in fear, trying to control things and getting angry when she can't. Jeff's own underlying anxiety doesn't help, as Kerry wants him to be the strong man her dad is for her.

Kerry's challenge is to learn to trust her own authority. She needs to acknowledge that her fears and her anger are about her own lack of self, rather than anything to do with Jeff. She also needs to let go of judging Jeff against her dad and let him be his own man.

Jeff's Enmeshment with His Family

Jeff is one of a large and very close family that gets together regularly, and is always participating in unique family traditions. He's always felt like he could talk to his parents about most things and has a special place in his heart for his kid sister Jill.

As he gets older, however, he has a sense that their closeness depends on him staying within a certain set of parameters. When he mentions his new interest in the Greens party or his new permaculture friend Austin, either uncomfortable silence or negative judgement comes his way. He knows his parents aren't too fond of Kerry either, believing that she's a bit 'full of herself'.

This results in him feeling slightly anxious about what he's doing and who he's being, no matter how well he's doing in his life. He **is**

> *doing well, with his own gardening business, five employees and plans for expansion. And his family never misses an opportunity to tap him for a loan when they want one, which he somehow never feels he can refuse. This isn't helped by Kerry running off to her dad for advice, leaving Jeff feeling that his is never quite good enough.*
>
> *Jeff's challenge is to understand that his anxieties around not feeling good enough are part of his family's enmeshment with him and with a certain way of being in life. Anything outside of this brings fear and judgements to maintain the status quo.*
>
> *Jeff has to learn to trust in his own authority and his choices in life, letting his family and Kerry get used to the change in him, and trust that they're capable.*

Moving from a Child to an Adult Relationship

We all need to become fully fledged adults who are capable of our own adult-to-adult relationships. Growing up on the inside can happen long after our 21st birthday. It can happen through recognising where you still behave with your partner as the child you once were around your parents, needing their approval or your needs to be met at your partner's expense without recognising they have needs of their own. This is OK when you're two, but not when you're 42.

Growing up can also happen where you see that you're attempting to engage your partner in recreating feelings familiar in your past, be they good or bad. For example, if you spent a lot of time feeling uncertain in your childhood, you might constantly (unknowingly) challenge your partner's decisions, making them feel uncertain so you can then feel uncertain too.

This is definitely not about parent-bashing. It's simply acknowledging the truth of your past experiences in order to be clearer in your present relationship. In fact, you can also take the time to understand your parents' reality and learn why they made the choices they did, developing empathy and connection (where possible) as you do so. However, it's important to know the difference between understanding your parents' reality and invalidating yourself by making excuses for their behaviour. This difference then allows you to step from being a wounded child into a self-empowered adult.

Another simple question to help you explore the impact of your childhood conditioning is 'What is it in you that you had to give up to survive your family and how can you give it to yourself now?'

Reflecting on your patterns of relating and making more empowering behaviour choices also helps you see your parents as they really are – fallible human beings doing the best they can, just like you. And to see your children as independent beings you're blessed to help get started in life.

The Fine Art of Communication

5.1 Known as the Finer Art of the Shit Fight

Problems in communication are usually seen as the No.1 issue in relationships. If effective communication in an intimate relationship was easy, everybody would be doing it. But it isn't so don't beat yourself up if it's a mass of misunderstanding for you too. Graeme and I have been doing it with awareness for years now and we still get caught up in domestics at times! It's particularly difficult because communication here isn't just an exchange of information and ideas, it's the one place we can't avoid the messiness of feelings, emotions and deep human need. Not to mention that we're communicating with someone who is extremely important to us that we don't want to lose.

Rather than providing a quick fix solution that won't last, this chapter offers you a way to navigate through your many layers of communication – layers which have the potential to bring you closer together rather than push you apart, no matter how intense the communication may become.

For mostly what happens in moments of painful communication is that we make our partner (or ourselves) wrong and put up walls around the discomfort that occurs inside of us. Making our partner wrong makes them close down or retaliate and then we miss learning the truth of what they were actually saying, ending up feeling isolated and alone.

This chapter is about Embodied Communication – which is being present and aware in yourself using – you guessed it – your feelings, as well as your intellect and your heart/body-mind as you communicate. You'll use your ABC practice to be inside yourself in the here and now, and in your point of power - the present moment. Being present inside yourself in the here-and-now will allow you to see and connect with your partner in ways that will amaze you. It will help you make healthier communication choices and turn your partner (and yourself) into a fascinating new being each time you communicate with them at this level.

What's going on when communication gets messy?

Messiness might look like 'something being wrong', yet despite appearances, it's actually part of your relationship growth cycle. Much relationship conflict and messiness comes from losing connection with yourself. When you lose this connection, your partner becomes the enemy and you drop into drama and strategies of defensiveness and protection. You seek control, rather than connection and understanding.

> *"Almost 90% of all human communication comes from the (usually unconscious) need to control."*
>
> Saying What's Real, 7 Keys To Authentic Communication, Susan Campbell, PhD

Part of this is due to gender differences, which are covered later in this chapter. The other part is due to feeling unfamiliar or uncomfortable in your feelings. This is why getting comfortable with your feelings and staying present in yourself through *Embodied Communication* transforms the way you communicate.

Creative defence strategies

Some of the very creative strategies we all implement to defend ourselves when we communicate (through both protecting and attacking) include:

Protection strategies

- Detaching from or avoiding/denying the feeling
- Emotionally or physically withdrawing/shutting down
- Intellectualising, rationalising, working out 'why', using black/white thinking
- Denial, dishonesty, allowing shadow behaviour
- Being nice and playing it safe, or staying cool and not engaging
- Not wanting to hurt the other person's feelings
- Hyper-protection – being unwilling to enter discussion and denying resolution
- Shame/invalidation – making yourself unnecessarily wrong
- Resentment (collapsing of anger)
- Forgetfulness, compartmentalising (separating the bits you don't like and disowning them), repressing (blocking)
- Regressing – refusing to engage in normal activities (sulking)
- Undoing – trying to take back thoughts or actions
- Altruism – meeting your partner's needs whilst ignoring your own
- Compensating – counterbalancing your perceived weaknesses by emphasising your strengths, eg ignoring your anger and being over-compassionate
- Forming reactions – converting dangerous feelings into their opposite safe ones, eg convincing yourself you feel loved when you're actually afraid
- Suppressing – totally avoiding your own internal experience.

Attacking Strategies

- Blaming/demanding – making your partner responsible for your reality
- Speaking more and more loudly in an attempt to get your partner to agree with you
- Telling them how they should be, so you don't have to feel
- Being dismissive or minimising your partner's feelings
- Shaming/invalidating – making your partner wrong, being negative
- Criticising, complaining, interrupting, interrogating, sarcasm
- Hijacking what your partner says and making it about you
- Assuming you 'know' where your partner is at or jumping to conclusions, rather than being in uncertainty
- Projection – putting your undesired thoughts, impulses and feelings onto your partner
- Focussing your full attention on your partner's thoughts, feelings and behaviour to avoid your own
- Focussing on your own thoughts and feelings to avoid your partner's, leaving them unheard
- Trying to pull your partner into your drama so they lose themselves
- Triggering your partner into negative behaviours so you can make them wrong and avoid your own stuff
- Displacement – dumping your own unrelated thoughts or emotions onto your innocent partner, ie 'kicking the cat' syndrome
- Drama/acting out – expressing feelings/thoughts that you can't otherwise express by performing in an extreme way
- Passive aggression – covertly expressing aggression towards your partner whilst appearing to cooperate, eg. regularly being late whilst always having excuses.

5: The Fine Art of Communication

Can you recognise yourself here?
Congratulations, that makes you human!

This is why communication isn't easy. These tactics are definitely unattractive, but they're readily understandable when you recognise that you're just seeking to protect yourself. However, they also leave you emotionally cut off from yourself and your loved one, often confused and literally fighting for your emotional life.

It's more productive to use the ABC practice instead to get grounded and safe in your body, learning to respect and feel your discomfort and save all the potential drama. This leaves you present with your partner and available in the conversation. Sometimes, of course, you don't get a choice: you're over the emotional edge before you know it. But with practice, stepping back from the edge will become easier.

> **Embodied Communication**
>
> We all have our favourite go to protection and attacking strategies when the heat is on. Review these lists and reflect honestly on what your own might be.
>
> Share them with your partner and ask which ones they also notice in you. Then invite your partner to share about theirs.
>
> Agree to acknowledge it when you notice yourself using either a protection or attacking strategy and choose to pause and do your ABC instead. This will bring you back into connection with both yourself and your partner. It takes practice but it will happen.

Remember: it's All About You!

Remembering that you're creating your own reality helps you make healthier choices in your communication. So does seeing that *what you choose* and *how you respond* has nothing to do with your partner. Instead, know your actions, reactions and responses are about you. Your partner might trigger you into a response by their words or actions, but your responses are definitely *yours.*

For example, if your partner asks, "Why are you so out of sorts today?" you have a multitude of possible reactions, including but not limited to:

1. "I'm out of sorts because my boss gave me a really hard time today."
2. "I'm out of sorts because my boss gave me a really hard time today. And don't you start!"
3. "I'm out of sorts because my boss gave me a really hard time today. Thank you for asking – it makes me feel cared about. Would you like to share a cup of tea and I'll tell you about it?"
4. "If I am out of sorts, what's it to you?"
5. "I'm not out of sorts!"
6. "Yeah? I bet my day was much worse than yours!"
7. Giving no response apart from a scowl as you stomp past to the TV.

Your response is about *you,* regardless of what's said. Where you're at in that moment, your background, beliefs, life experience and skillset will all determine whether you speak up, open up, shut down, reach out, attack, defend, compete and more. Of course, your choice of response might be an unconscious reaction that you can't stop, but you *can* own it afterwards and then choose what to do about it.

And it's also NOT About You!

If what *you* share and how *you* respond is all about you, it's extremely helpful to remember that when your beloved is speaking – even if they're talking about you – what they're sharing is NOT about you: it's about *them*.

Even if they're using the word 'you', whatever they reveal is still more about them. This definitely doesn't mean that your words and actions don't impact your partner, it's that the response they choose is about them.

So taking something your partner says personally only makes things messy. Seeing it as about THEM will help you to stay present, open and able to respond rather than react. Not getting in their way will also make it easier for them to see, hear and own what they're saying for themselves.

And it's about both of you

You're both responsible for how you choose to speak, act and respond in your relationship. It's good to remember these choices and the impacts associated with them are what creates the landscape of your togetherness.

Exploiting the truth

In our human messiness, our logical minds try to help out by rationalising our behaviour and exploiting elements of the truth to get us off the hook of hurt, and avoid feeling our discomfort. Speaking from our unfelt emotion, we go to elaborate, illogical efforts to justify our position, getting very convoluted and irrational in our story-telling.

Our logical minds are compartmentalised, and their separate parts come up with different, even opposing, points of view at the same time, which we argue as if they all make sense. We take something that's 10% true and elaborate it with 90% bullshit to make ourselves feel 'right' (ie safe), often making our partner wrong using one of the defences listed above.

All this story-telling creates further mind-generated feelings that are mostly irrelevant to the original feeling that was triggered. So feeling your feelings up front can save lots of heartache later on!

Protecting ourselves takes us further and further away from ourselves and into our 90% bullshit.

Going down the rabbit hole

All couples have places in communication where their favourite emotional triggers instantly take them into an oh-so-familiar downward spiral of emotional drama, whilst each person holds tightly to their chosen 10% truth/90% bullshit story.

Graeme and I call this 'going down the rabbit hole'. We've known couples who'd get into near-relationship-ending fights over who didn't empty the kitty litter, who didn't turn off the garden hose, or the right way to stack the dishwasher.

The ABC process helps couples like these to get to present with themselves, and with what they're saying and hearing. This makes it easier for them to each change what they're saying into something useful, and to listen more clearly. They get honest in their 10% truth and see that it usually involves owning something imperfect and vulnerable about themselves that they want to hide.

Change happens over time

Using your ABC and being embodied helps you to choose your response and own it, keeping you more present, engaged and authentic in your communication. You cease having to come up with 'nice' responses, instead *owning* the ones you *do* choose.

As vulnerable and untidy as it might be at times, this realness brings a solidness and safety in your communication. Over the long run, you'll experience fewer so-called negative feelings and exchanges. Your anger, sadness and fear will feel more real, and so will your moments of happiness, love and connection. Rather than taking you down the rabbit hole, communication will trigger opportunities to connect with yourself, to be vulnerable and to create greater intimacy and closeness in your relationship.

Hints For Loving Communication

- Make nothing wrong, including your feelings. Remember there are always two truths occurring- yours and your partners.
- Fight fair where possible. If you slip up, own it and stop it.
- Start gently so you've got somewhere to go.
- Be curious about your partner's experience, and your also your own.
- Be courageous, honest, and willing to engage and talk about the hard things.
- Slip in statements of humour, affection or respect to keep the communication open hearted.

"It's not that couples don't get mad and disagree. It's that when they disagree, they're able to stay connected and engaged with one another. Rather than becoming defensive and hurtful, they pepper their disputes with flashes of affection, intense interest and mutual respect."

The Relationship Cure, John Gottman

Embodied Communication

Avoid getting into 'the drone zone' where you're both flying around in circles focussing outside of yourselves on the other and what they're doing wrong. Come into land inside yourselves, get vulnerable and you'll find a way through.

Rather than communicating to be right, win or seek agreement, communicate with the intention of better understanding and connecting with yourself and each other. The following steps in Embodied Communication might feel awkward and challenging in the beginning; but like anything, with practice they'll become easier. Of course, it's not necessary to talk at this depth all the time, but the moments you do will become like gold in your relationship.

Your No. 1 goal in communication is to stay in connection with yourself.

Begin by talking about something with a low level of emotional heat to it. Then, next time, try something a bit 'hotter'. Finally, with practice, build up to your 'biggies' – those two or three topics that usually take you down the rabbit hole – trying the skills in your new toolkit to create a different outcome.

Introduce one or two of the following tips at time. Then, with practice, add more until they become automatic.

Before you start:

1. Rather than simply launching into an intimate conversation whenever *you* feel like it, respect the quality of what you're trying to create. Check in with your partner about whether they're in a space to have such a discussion first. If not, set a time for when they are.

2. Let your partner know the topic you want to discuss and your desired outcome, eg:

   - I just want to be heard
   - I want to understand something better
   - I'd like resolution on something
   - I'd like your advice
   - I want to explore a new solution or possibility
   - I just want to feel more connected with you.

3. Sit, stand or lie directly opposite your partner, where your energies can align and you can make eye contact more often. This helps you get more authentic, seen and heard. If this is too much in the beginning, work up to it slowly.

4. Believe it or not, the power of touch can help to open (or keep open) your hearts by making a connection beyond the level of the mind. The touch can be from just a hand, leg, foot or even finger resting – (but not stroking, which is distracting) – somewhere on your partner's body, or theirs on yours. Again, if this is too far out of your relationship comfort zone at the moment, either drop it or work towards it

Make communication an exploration of each other by creating a space for love to enter.

Getting started: Being the speaker

1. ***Begin with naming what's up for you.*** This can be, "I'm feeling really excited about telling you this," "I feel scared to talk to you right now," "I fear you might reject me if I share this with you," or "I feel so angry that I really want to leave the room right now." Naming your feelings helps you to stay connected with yourself and lets your partner see where you are before getting into the details. It creates an opening through its realness and vulnerability.

2. ***Listen to yourself as you're speaking.*** Hear what you're actually saying and how you're saying it. This will help you to experience how you might be coming across and allow you to adjust as you go along – remembering that you're creating your reality.

    Are you vulnerably expressing what you have to say without attachment to an outcome? Or are you putting up a wall with a protection strategy, lashing out with an attacking strategy, or 'hooking' your partner in, in some way? If you're doing any of these, pause, take a breath, drop into your body, get safe and start again.

    Keep choosing connection, staying grounded, breathing and owning your truth, eg, "I don't know where I'm at right now. I just need to keep talking," or "I'm not feeling connected with you, and my heart feels closed."

3. ***As you're speaking, notice what you're feeling.*** Notice whether the feeling is in your head (thinking it) or in your body (feeling it). If you sense it's in your head, shift your attention to your body, scan it and see what you're *actually* feeling.

    Any time you're connected with a body feeling, trust and express what it wants to say, eg, "I feel sad when I see you turn away from me and I notice that I'd really like to talk to you some more."

5: The Fine Art of Communication

When you speak from a place of being connected with yourself, it has a more tangible impact

4. ***To help you stay inside yourself and connected to your own your experience, use 'I' language.*** This lets your partner hear you without feeling attacked or threatened. To help keep you focussed on yourself, imagine you're sitting in a hula hoop and talk about only what's inside your hoop, which is your half of any situation. If you notice yourself outside of your hoop, bring yourself back in.

5. ***If you find yourself using terms like 'You never' or 'I always' to make your point, recognise that you're probably speaking from your wounded child self.*** Absolutes in human behaviour are unlikely to be true. Let go of this one and give a specific example instead.

6. ***If it's important to know that you partner has heard you clearly ask them to feed what they heard back to you.*** This doesn't mean getting them to repeat what you've said exactly. They just need to let you know what they've understood through the screen of their perceptions, assumptions and expectations. Acknowledge what they've heard – and if they're not clear, try to say things in a different way.

7. ***If you need to clear something painful use the following steps:***
    - State what you experienced
    - Own what you felt as a result (use feeling words here such as sad, angry, unwanted etc)
    - Share what you believed your partner was intending (own this as your own reality that may not be theirs)

This might look like: "When I was left at the café waiting I chose to feel rejected and believed you didn't care for me."

- Share if there is anything you need now or would like them to do differently next time, e.g. "Next time you're running late I'd like you to text me and let me know. Right now a hug would be great."

8. ***If the heat gets turned up and you're drawn into a familiar toxic spiral, don't be afraid to say, "I need to stop here".*** Take a breath and mentally step back. Recognise you've gone away from the issue and into your 10% truth/90% bullshit story. Do your ABC, ground and go underneath your story into the feeling.

   Use your ABC to follow the feeling, bring you back into connection with yourself and gain insight into what's going on for you. Remember that wisdom comes *after* the feeling, not before it.

   You might even need to take some time out and come back later when you've had a chance to see what's going on for you, or if you need to do the trigger practice outlined in Chapter 3.

   Reconnect with your partner by having a laugh at how you've moved into your shit despite your best intentions. Once the heat has cleared, acknowledge anything more that needs to be explored.

9. ***Thank your partner for listening.*** Recognise that they've given you their valuable time and attention, which is truly a gift of love. Then ask them if they have anything they'd like to share.

As the Listener

1. ***As the listener, be willing to just listen and hear the other person.*** Be fully present, and open with your ABC, rather than thinking about what you have to say next. Remember your partner's intention for the communication. Ignore the need to express your point of view (unless they ask you for it). Recognise that the gift here is in *being heard*: your attention is a loving power that invites greater authenticity.

5: The Fine Art of Communication

2. ***As the listener, it's important to have a healthy empathic wall.*** This is a sense of your own boundaries, where the other person ends and you begin. Imagine you're sitting in your own separate hula hoop. Allow yourself to feel a little of what your partner is feeling then come back to yourself. This helps you to notice your own authentic response and find some empathy without getting lost in your partner's issues.

    If you notice your partner is projecting their stuff across into your hoop, let them know you're feeling pushed away and gently remind them to return to their own hoop.

3. ***Seek to validate the speaker in some way.*** This helps them to not only feel heard, but also to feel safe. You don't need to *agree with* what they're saying but validating them speaks more than words. Try, "I can see that it's difficult for you to bring up something like this", or "I like the way you said that because..."

4. ***Notice any words the speaker uses that have 'energy'.*** You can sometimes ask them a question about those words, helping them to go deeper into their topic eg you might say "Can you tell me more about...?" But mostly, just stay present and listen, allowing your partner to feel heard.

5. ***If the other person says something that brings intensity up inside you:*** *Rather than getting caught in the right/wrong of what they're saying, choose to feel instead*. Use your mind to notice the feeling, get grounded, drop all resistance, breathe and welcome it in. Own that it's *your* feeling. It's only a feeling and can't hurt you. This will allow you to come home to yourself, stay present, get curious and listen long enough to get the full story and find an authentic response.

6. ***Give feedback, suggestions or advice only if invited.*** When your partner has finished, share your own response and what lies underneath it, taking your own understanding and connection deeper. Ask your partner if they would like any suggestions or advice before giving it.

Once the first person is finished, swap roles if desired, and repeat as above.

 ### Identifying your 10%

Rather than getting caught up in the messiness of your 90% bullshit and trying to understand it, try something different the next time you're going down the rabbit hole.

See if you can identify the strongest negative point you're trying to make (it's usually about your partner). This is where the gold is. When you've identified it, counter-intuitive though it may appear, simply notice the response in your body that it creates, eg tensing your shoulders, contracting in fear, churning in your gut, or wanting to attack, pull away, go blank or disappear.

Use your ABC to take a breath in and slowly let it out again, getting grounded in your body. Taking this deep breath helps to soften your reaction. Your body will intuitively begin to feel safe, allowing you to thoughtfully respond rather than react. Any emotional discomfort will then pass more quickly because you're not resisting it or escalating it through drama.

Ask yourself what you're avoiding in yourself by pushing this point? This will help you intuitively identify your 10% truth in the situation. Most likely, you'll find a useful thread within the point that can unravel your bullshit and let you see it for what it really is.

 ### Deflating your partner's 90%

If you sense that your partner is disconnected from themselves, getting lost in their mind's 90% bullshit and trying to hook you into its drama, identify and own your part in the 10% truth (because it will be there). If your partner can hear it, the truth in you will help them to reconnect with what is true in themselves.

> ***Embodied Communication***
>
> Practice a few of the Embodied Communication steps above, adding in more as you feel comfortable with them.
>
> You can practice these yourself even if your partner isn't comfortable to use them, as they mostly focus on how you are being, and it will still have an impact on your mutual relating.

Your Communication Toolkit

If you combine your *Embodied Communication* and *Identifying Your 10%* above with *Dealing with Emotional Triggers* from Chapter 3, and the *Finding the Passion* and *Speaking the Unspoken Practices* from later in this chapter, you'll have a relationship toolkit that will take you a long way towards a happy, fulfilled intimate relationship.

Despite your best intentions however, the occasional shit fight *will* happen. See this as something that clears the space, and be gentle on yourself and your partner when this happens. Own that it was messy and that it's not really where you're at, but you just needed to get it out. You can always clean up afterwards using the more eloquent hints above and probably learn something new along the way.

Shit fights only become a problem when they're a constant occurrence with one or both sides getting battered and nothing ever being resolved. This is when you need some expert help. Otherwise, using these suggestions over time, you'll find your communications becoming clearer, gentler and more rewarding, with less drama and more enjoyment.

5.2 Finding the Passion

Passion is that feeling of almost uncontrollable emotional intensity. It's part of our vitality and energy for living. It's also part of our longing and desire for our partner.

Most people believe that passion – and our hunger for it – is one of the things that automatically die in a long-term relationship.

How do you maintain passion whilst it's flourishing, and how do you find it again once it's gone? Graeme and I find that in most couples, the passion hasn't died. Instead, it's more likely just hiding. And the most likely place you'll find it is lying inside your anger, because anger and passion arise from the same place.

This is, of course, the same anger you probably tell yourself that you're wrong for feeling. It's the same anger you suppress by stifling the words in your throat, finding rational ways to avoid it, or venting unconsciously onto your loved one creating shame and fracture. Blocking this anger is also blocking the energy of heat, desire and passion in your body, making it unavailable when you really want it – in the bedroom.

One of the things we always ask the couples we work with is, "What do you do with your anger?" The answer to this question often largely determines how they find their way forward – more relationships die from a lack of anger than from too much of it. (Remember though that when we mention anger here, we're not talking about aggression or drama – see the *Emotional Intelligence* section in Chapter 3.)

You may be thinking that trying to be a good partner means controlling or even transcending your anger. Or perhaps you believe you don't have any? If so, Graeme and I might ask, "Really? None at all?"

Perhaps you actually stifle your anger by being 'nice', not noticing it leaking out in criticism, sarcasm, cynicism, resentment, bitterness or passive-aggressiveness around your partner? Or maybe you use it as a weapon, seeing it as a method for gaining control? Perhaps it's only evident in your high blood pressure, heart disease, teeth grinding, arthritis or many other stress-related diseases?

5: The Fine Art of Communication

"Women believe their aggression results from a loss of self-control, while men see their behaviour as a means of gaining control over others."

Men, Women & Aggression, by Anne Campbell

We're two of the rare 'spiritual' teachers who don't see anger, or passion for that matter, as anti-spiritual. We see it as a natural force within you that you can make healthy or unhealthy choices about. Anger is so universally shamed that finding your authentic anger voice in a positive way is an incredible boost to your self-worth. Remember that wonderful scene in *The King's Speech* when George VI finds his freedom through his anger after years of stuttering?

Anger is a force that can open new ground in old relationships, breaking through a callus that keeps you stuck. When you clear anger in an open hearted way, you find the love, passion and desire that still lives underneath it. And you'll resolve any underlying resentment, contempt, sadness, lack of compassion and more that often lies within it.

We encourage you to take charge of your anger. If you don't, it will take charge of you. Saying 'yes' to your anger and owning it in a healthy way is an act of love. And when you give yourself permission to really feel it, you'll find your anger is not as scary, or as endless as you fear.

The following practices are challenging. As a human being, you crave certainty and control. You want to feel indestructible. Yet our clients have shown us over and over again that meaning in a relationship comes from being willing to embrace the unknown. The more the unknown, the greater the growth. The following practices offer both.

> **Safely Releasing Anger**
>
> This practice invites you to embrace your anger in a healthy way whenever you feel stuck or blocked or have unexpressed anger to release. Done regularly, in a way that works for you, it will free up

your energy and passion and keep your anger where it belongs. If you believe you don't have anger, just play with the idea of freeing up your passion and vitality instead. You'll likely feel very silly, rather than angry at the beginning, just ignore this and do it anyway.

Anger is released by breath, movement and sound.

The level of practice required depends on the intensity of your anger (which can be about anything).

Level One Anger:

- Bring your attention to the physical sensation of anger in your body, without making it wrong in any way for being there.
- Breathe deeply and fully, feeling the anger move through and out of your body. Remember to stay focussed on feeling the anger *in your body* release, rather than on the angry thoughts in your head. Otherwise you'll just be venting and not fully resolving it.

This may be all that's needed.

Level Two Anger:

- You'll need to find time and space for this one. Move your anger out of you by moving your body. Literally jump up and down, do vigorous gym or sport, dance wildly or bash a pillow on the bed.
- Anger is a very powerful emotion that can need to be given a voice. Make the sound of your anger. When you've connected with the feeling in your body, speak from it. Say (loudly if you're alone) in as few words as possible what you've been unable to say. Don't beg, plead or ask why, get to the core of what it is you don't/didn't want in the situation. "I didn't want to be ignored." Then express what you do/did want. "I wanted to be loved." If you can't find the words, just make sounds.
- If your anger doesn't shift, you may be thinking rather than feeling it. Concentrate on finding the anger in your body. Or you may not be getting angry about what's really going on, so look

- deeper into the situation and see what else is there. Or you may simply not be getting angry enough – if so, keep going.
- You'll know your anger is resolved when you feel a tingling, lightness and softness spread through your body. You may also find the sadness, regret, compassion, etc that's lived underneath your anger that you've so far been unable to access. You may even end up laughing at the things you were once so pissed off about.
- If you need to talk to your partner about what made you angry, you can now do so safely without it boiling over out of control into the conversation.

NB. If you have fear about anger – either other peoples or your own – the best way to move beyond it is to feel it in a safe way *within yourself* as we've described above. Breathe through any fear that may arise and see the anger for what it is: just intensity that can be managed safely.

The more you do this practice, the more quickly and easily you'll access and move through your anger. What would have previously taken you days or weeks of gnashing your teeth will be over in a few moments. You'll also find it easier to move through anger when it arises in a conversation, without having to do it later by yourself.

You'll even see the times that your anger is futile, and choose to understand instead, leaving the anger behind. However, you first need to get into a deeper relationship with it and make what you do with it a conscious choice. Anything else is just avoidance.

Speaking The Unspoken: the Passion Game-Changer

Just like you might avoid your anger, if you're like most people you probably avoid saying what's really going on for you. You try to be loving, respectful, responsible and giving. Inside your head, you deny your inner truths or make them wrong. In doing so, you choke off what's real, denying who you are and giving away your power. You also deny the parts that are scared and vulnerable, that hurt, hate, want to blame, are closed to love, and that indeed feel unlovable.

Your unspoken areas may feel messy, but they're an equally valuable part of who you are, and as such they're NOT WRONG. In fact, they may be amazingly insightful and authentic. Orphaning your 'bad' parts leaves only the voice of your inner critic, which is only too happy to make you wrong.

> *"No relationship can truly grow if you go on holding back. If you remain clever and go on safeguarding and protecting yourself, only personalities meet and the essential centre remains alone"*
>
> Being In Love, Osho

This exercise offers you the chance to bring your 'unspoken' safely out of the closet: to own it and bring it to a place of ease. Most people avoid being honest like this by telling themselves they'll hurt our partners with their truths. More often, you hurt them by not being real, or by closing your heart and disappearing out the door instead. More likely, your partner will appreciate you for being so courageous and open in return. Even if your truth is painful hearing, its reality helps to diminish fear and makes room for you to deal with it, for truth has its own power to heal.

This is not about trying to fix anything. It's about being seen and heard. Doing this practice in an authentic way allows new insights and surprising outcomes to arise.

5: The Fine Art of Communication

 Speaking The Unspoken 5+5 minutes

This very rewarding practice is challenging because it probably goes against the grain of all you've been taught. You and your partner will both give yourselves permission to speak whatever lies unspoken between you in an unfiltered way, directly to each other. Rather than being nice, you're going to be authentic. You'll also own what you share as yours, and about you.

Surprisingly, this practice is known to bring trust, passion and unexpected solutions back into a relationship through the heartfelt clarity it offers. It's the willingness to go there that creates the safety. The main thing is for the partner who's not speaking to be in listening – rather than judgement – mode.

NB. This is NOT a dialogue. It's is a chance for each of you to speak and be heard without interruption. The listener stays grounded in their body with one hand on their heart.

1. ***Both agree to the practice.*** Partners do this one at a time, but both must participate, even if one feels they don't have anything to share. Once given permission, things tend to arise. Trust that if you've got this far, you'll be OK.
2. ***Set your phone timer for five minutes, then decide who's going first.*** Sit opposite each other, far enough apart to feel safe in your own hula hoops, as in *Embodied Communication*.
3. ***As the receiver, remain open as you receive your partner in this very vulnerable way***. If there's any feeling intensity in what the sharer has to say, imagine it simply passing through you like water, rather than taking it in. Remember what your partner is sharing is about them.
4. ***Before you begin, each share two things you honestly like or appreciate about your partner.*** This helps you both get used to the process and builds a zone of safety and connection.
5. ***In the second round, the person expressing their 'unspoken' speaks unfiltered for five minutes.*** They speak whatever

has been dammed up in them without having to be nice, understanding or even coherent. They just need to be real without anything being wrong – to just feel, express and *own* their reality. As scary as this sounds, it's a very liberating experience.

At the end of the five minutes, the person receiving says only, "Thank you," and then you swap over. Be clear with your time boundaries.

Completion: Pat yourselves on the back for taking up the challenge, and then share a melting hug for 30 seconds, relaxing and breathing together.

This helps to clear any shame you might carry about having been so honest. Don't process any triggers that feel unresolved at this time. Instead, take a break and come back later – this practice is for sharing only.

Sometimes, people are so used to stuffing down their truth that that don't even know what truth they're hiding. In this case, their lack of honesty or truthfulness isn't avoidance, it's a lack of knowledge about themselves. When you get used to speaking your truth though, you'll feel safe enough to get clear on what your 'unspoken' is, and this activity will give you a place to go with it.

If this activity has worked for you, follow it up by agreeing to make it part of your relationship. Agree to always ask the listener's permission before sharing, and if one person shares, then so does the other. *You can even use this practice for sharing about your sex life.*

Positively dealing with this heavy material creates understanding and feelings of lightness and freedom between you, as well as trust as you move forward. You'll find that the more space and validation you give anger and truth in your relationship, the less angst you'll have between each other (and within yourselves). As you become more comfortable with truth-telling, you won't need to do it in this formal way but it's a great place to start to both feel heard.

> Regularly including the *Safely Releasing Anger* and *Speaking The Unspoken* practices in your relationship will make anger a safer place and create more authenticity, clarity, connection and passion and silence your inner critic. It's worth the risk!

5.3 Men and Woman are Different

Have you ever noticed how a man who's not particularly good looking (maybe slightly balding with a paunch) can walk down the street thinking he's God's gift to women, whereas a woman who looks like Elle McPherson can be riddled with self-criticism? These inconsistencies might leave you thinking that maybe women really might be from Venus and men from Mars.

Or can you relate to the frustration of feeling totally misunderstood, or unseen by your partner no matter how hard you're trying? Maybe you answer your partner in a way you think is perfectly clear, only to have them have go on at you as if you hadn't spoken? Or perhaps you have to remind your loved one over and over to do something, but even though they say they care, it doesn't get done?

As you've probably noticed, men and women generally ARE different; and even though there's a greater appreciation of gender diversity these days, some general differences still remain. As human beings, we all have common threads of experience that help us relate to each other, but it seems when it comes to man/woman relating, certain difficulties just keep showing up. Behind these difficulties lie the misleading *perceptions* we have of each other, which drive what it is we actually hear.

Seeing your perceptions for what they are means you can see each other more clearly and reduce the angst that lies between male/female relating.

For example:

Graeme and I often hear from women that a man should be 'more feminine' in his communication, ie more sensitive and wordy, and they judge him as inadequate when he isn't. We also hear from men that a woman would be better off being 'more masculine', ie more straightforward and direct. And they, in turn, judge the woman as too emotional when she isn't. This is seeing each other through our own filters, instead of appreciating and learning from each other's differences.

Not understanding creates powerlessness

As we mentioned in Chapter 5, feeling heard is vital to our wellbeing in relationship. Not understanding these and other gender differences in perception leaves each partner feeling unheard, and repeated experiences of feeling unheard leave both partners feeling disconnected, frustrated, powerless and alone. From this place of hurt, they try to get their power back by taking the offensive, actively attacking, withdrawing or covertly criticising their partner. This gives them a few moments of powerfulness over the other, temporarily relieving their suffering. Can you relate to this?

The downside is that this also leaves the attacked person in protection mode, where it's extremely difficult for them to defend themselves and do what the other person is looking for, which is to reach out to them. In effect, they sabotage themselves.

From here, it's only a small step to further frustration, attacks and cycles of domestic abuse by both men or women (men usually overtly, and women usually more covertly), when both are just trying to be seen and heard.

So how are men and women different in communication?

Here's a little look at how Graeme and I see how men and women experience difficulties in intimacy from their inherent (or conditioned, depending on your viewpoint) differences. These differences won't be true for all people, but in our experience they're common. We offer an understanding and appreciation of these differences that give power to both men and women in relating, rather than only to one. For either BOTH partners are empowered, or neither are.

Communicating differences:

Men will more often *self-reference* in communication, sharing about themselves. They do this in order to be seen and loved. Women tend to be *other referenced*, seeking and giving empathetic responses in order to feel connected. Women can see men's communication as selfish yet it's quite vulnerable to put yourself out there and risk rejection as men do. Men commonly don't understand what women are looking for from them and miss the connection their woman is looking for.

Feeling Differences:

Despite common beliefs to the contrary, we find that *both* men and women have feelings. However, because of their conditioning, they each tend to manage those feelings differently.

We find that women are generally comfortable feeling their emotions *externally* –talking about them and expressing them – partly because this is how women 'are' and also because talking about feelings has become the socially accepted way of dealing them.

Meanwhile, men will generally feel their feelings *internally* and directly, simply because they're not as familiar with talking about them. And because men have been conditioned to think they *don't* feel, they'll miss their feelings and avoid communicating about them for fear of being unseen or judged.

Women have been taught that they have the moral high ground when it comes to feeling. Our experience is that given the right context and support most men will go deeply and rapidly into their most unfathomable feeling places – places that hold just as much challenge for women as for men.

Here's how we see these communication differences play out between Sallie and Joel, and how to make the most of them if this is you:

 Sallie's Challenges:

- *In expecting Joel to communicate with her like she does, Sallie misses his attempts to communicate. Joel speaks and feels directly – so for him, something's often already been said (and felt) whilst Sallie's waiting for it to happen.*
- *Sallie is comfortable thinking, talking about and expressing her feelings externally, without realising she's less comfortable feeling them vulnerably within her just like Joel is.*
- *This external way of processing her feelings pushes Joel away, as he experiences her intensity as an impenetrable barrier, or an overwhelming pressure. Sallie is left believing her feelings have no place in the relationship.*
- *Sallie often does Joel's feeling work for him, feeling what she perceives his feelings should be, which lets him off the feeling hook.*
- *Sallie constantly tries to draw Joel's feelings out from him, usually getting a one word response.*
- *When Joel does talk he often talks about himself, rather than ask anything about her, leaving Sallie feeling unseen.*
- *If Joel does become emotionally vulnerable, Sallie – who's been conditioned to expect a man to be strong like a rock – feels fear, and unconsciously shuts him down to feel safe.*

5: The Fine Art of Communication

 Sallie's Solutions:

- Sallie can drop her expectations about the way Joel should communicate, and instead trust that he IS communicating. This allows her to really listen and feel him. (Ironically this is just what she most wants to receive from Joel.) This will allow Joel to trust that he'll be heard, leaving him more willing to communicate from his feelings and his heart.
- This receptivity doesn't mean Sallie can't debate or disagree with Joel. She merely receives him by giving him the space to speak.
- Sallie can embrace the vulnerability of embodied feeling via her ABC rather than just talking her feelings, which leaves Joel safe in her emotions and draws him closer.
- Sallie can try giving herself permission to speak more directly. Because she's used to using lots of details being direct can feel a little bossy and even scary to her, but it can also be liberating and a breath of fresh air for Joel.
- Instead of doing Joel's emotional work for him, Sallie can stay grounded in herself. She can invite Joel to share and be ready to listen if he chooses to go there, but otherwise stay comfortably in herself. The space gives Joel room to feel himself.
- Rather than trying to pull Joel's feelings from him Sallie can instead share her own in an embodied way. Her authentic vulnerability will help invite Joel into his own.
- Sallie can understand that Joel talking about himself IS his way of seeking to connect with her. It's different to her way, but it's not wrong.
- Sallie's willingness to feel and own her own fear in Joel's vulnerability will help him to feel supported and stay emotionally open.

Joel's Challenges:

- Joel will check out of Sallie's conversation when she's using more words than he can handle and misses what she's trying to say.
- Joel's way of feeling is more internal (apart from anger which he occasionally vents) so he doesn't understand her need to 'talk' her feelings out.
- He fears Sallie's emotional intensity, as it feels directed at him rather than remaining within her, so he pulls away.
- In rejecting Sallie's emotion, he safely avoids his own.
- Joel feels manipulated into somewhere he doesn't want to go by Sallie constantly asking him about his feelings and he shuts her out.
- When Joel does try to communicate with Sallie he feels wrong and frustrated that she's trying to get something from him he doesn't know how to give.
- Not knowing how to trust or handle his own feelings, he shuts them down and offers an intellectual solution focussed approach to Sallie's emotions. This invalidates Sallie's feelings.

 Joel's Solutions:

- Joel can understand that Sallie's way of dealing with her emotion is different to his and all he needs to do is hear her.
- Joel will find that simply grounding himself and listening to Sallie with presence while her emotional intensity runs, without taking it personally or needing to fix it, is a deeply loving space for him to hold for her.
- If Sallie's dialogue runs on, instead of collapsing or disappearing, from his groundedness Joel can ask her what's going on for her, what she's actually feeling under the surface. This invites her into her vulnerability where he can really feel her.

- *Instead of listening to Sallie's details, Joel can tune into her key words and her body language, sensing where she's coming from rather than needing to get all the details, and responding to her from here.*
- *Joel can understand that Sallie's beauty and attractiveness comes from her energetic intensity and enjoy it without needing to understand it. His enjoyment will be reflected in Sallie's responsiveness to him.*
- *Joel can allow Sallie's safe use of her emotions to invite him into his own, trusting in his own capacity to feel in his own way, and choosing to risk sharing this part of himself with Sallie.*
- *Joel can understand what Sallie is looking for in her communication is reciprocity. And that taking the time to ask her a question about herself, or what she's talking about, will allow her to feel connected to him.*
- *Joel can develop a more emotionally intelligent language that would help him feel more comfortable communicating with Sallie in this area. There are plenty of suggestions in this book*

 Undoing Your Gender Conditioning

Underneath our gender, all of us humans are just looking to be heard, loved and accepted – and in this, we're definitely equal AND the same.

Use this viewpoint to explore where gender conditioning might be operating in your communication, remembering to see differences as opportunities rather than suffering.

Talk to each other about your respective beliefs about how men and women 'are' in their communications. Share where you feel any limitations on yourself or your partner as a result. Seeing these beliefs as coming from your conditioning rather than being 'permanent' helps to loosen your attachment to them.

> This is a large and complex topic, and this list is by no means exhaustive, but beginning with these simple understandings can allow huge shifts to happen in your relationship with the 'opposite' sex.
>
> Graeme and I take this further in the sections on men and women in love in Chapter 10, where it makes even more sense in how each operates.

Further communication resource: http://www.queenscode.com/

5.4 So, Let's Talk About Sex, Baby!

Now we move on to an even more challenging and potentially more fulfilling conversation – about sex. Even in this supposedly open era, few couples feel comfortable talking about what's happening in their bedrooms, even with each other. In our culture, sex purely for pleasure and intimacy is a pretty recent invention, so it makes sense that we're all still learning how to talk about it.

It's confusing too that in Western culture, sex is used to market everything from alcohol to shampoo, yet we can't talk about it honestly with the people we actually do it with. It's hard to talk about something we feel ashamed, scared, rejected, frustrated, insecure or sad about. So if this is you, you're not alone. Yet if you want a better sex life, finding a way to talk about it is absolutely essential.

This is because there's no one right way for sex to look. It's totally up to you (and your partner, of course) to decide for yourselves what to do with it and talking about it is the first step. Actively embracing your sexuality – and your partner's – in ways that offer you a place of pleasurable intimacy, freedom, power and fulfilment will keep both you and your relationship energised for decades.

Tips to help THAT conversation

Know that yes, the conversation may be uncomfortable, embarrassing, icky and scary, but take some deep breaths and gently jump in. Use

5: The Fine Art of Communication

your ABC and the communication tools (*Asking For What You Want, Embodied Communication* and *Speaking The Unspoken*) to help you stay present and grounded.

- Pick a time and place with some space and privacy, but not during sex.
- Simply owning your fear and embarrassment is a good start. Have no doubt that your partner will be just as scared and embarrassed as you, you make this OK by admitting your own.
- Be willing to share first and take a level of risk that feels doable for you and your partner. Just discuss a little at a time, if this is easier.
- Keep the conversation as light as possible. There may be moments of challenge but you can also enjoy it.
- Begin with a compliment.

Never underestimate the power of appreciation in this vulnerable place.

- Seek to explore, understand, be curious and non-judgemental.
- Speak more about what you DO want than about what you don't.
- Absolutely avoid trying to get your partner to better meet your needs through criticism! Imagine how you'd feel if you were on the receiving end.
- It's not easy, but don't take your partner's comments or desires personally. Again, remember that your partner's comments are about them not you. Breathe into what you feel and stay present.

Going about this the right way can mean that simply having a conversation about sex can itself be a fulfilling sexual experience.

Topics to Explore

What is sex for you?

Starting with a look at the bigger picture of sex may help because it's less confronting. See the *Acknowledgement of what lies at our core* exercise in Chapter 7 to explore your own beliefs about sexuality and share what you've found with your partner. Exploring it yourself beforehand will give you more clarity and confidence when you speak with them.

Do you see sex as one or more of these:

- A source of love and connection?
- Relief of stress and tension?
- Unconditional giving and receiving?
- Seeking excitement and pleasure, being on your edge?
- Fantasy fulfilment?
- Fulfilment of a spiritual hunger to merge and be at one with all that is?
- Maintenance sex, enjoying what works, keeping it easy without lots of effort?
- An inner exploration where you learn something new about yourself?
- A healing of unmet intimacy needs, sexual shame or conditioning?

Discuss what you each mean by your answers, and try to be as specific as you can to help your partner understand where you're coming from. Try not to force any outcomes, just make it an exploration of where you're both at. Have the mindset that taking a step back to see things more clearly may take you forward in ways beyond your wildest imagination.

Getting specific about your sex together:

- If you have any concerns, sandwich them between a layer of positives and offer a replacement suggestion so your partner has somewhere to go with your concern.
- Discuss what you'd like more of/less of. If you're partner asks for something you have resistance to, feel into your resistance and see what lies within it. Then you will have a clearer, more loving 'no', or maybe your 'no' will turn into a 'yes'.
- If you don't know what you want for yourself, *make that OK*. Sit with it, do your ABC, and allow whatever's under the surface to come out, rather than covering it up with something you think you should want.
- Get clear on what your/your partner's signals are for wanting sex, and what is NOT a signal.
- Share your 'quickie turn-on's. What fills up your sexy tank if you're starting out a bit flat? We each have our own unique ones: find ones you can share.
- Are there any times when your body is simply not available? Sharing these upfront reduces rejection.
- What's your end game? How do you each like to finish? Can you combine them or alternate?

Asking for sex:

Yes, it's both scary and challenging to ask for sex, and it can be easier (and sadder) not to. Hopefully, this book has inspired you enough to want to go there – if so, here are some helpful tips:

- Ask from a place of being already there rather than one of trying to hook your partner into giving you something. Allow yourself to feel your desire, enjoying the feeling, and breathing it through your body in a way that relaxes and opens you, then approach your partner from this place. This way, if you get a 'no', you're less devastated as you're already feeling pretty good.

- Don't ever assume or covertly hint, eg come to bed without your PJ pants on, or ask for a neck massage hoping for more. Manipulation is not sexy.

- A great way to approach your lover is whichever way works for them, so ask them what this is.

- If they're not sure, the direct approach is simply to look them in the eye with a smile and say, "I'd really like to ....with you. Would you like to join me?" If you get a 'no', ask whether there's anything they need that would make your invitation possible.

Conversations For Getting Started

Before having sex, check in with yourselves via your ABC to see where you're each at. Rather than judge where you're at, use it as a starting place.

- Are you feeling keen and excited, or resistant and needing to take it slowly?
- Do you need some nurturing first?
- Do you feel creative and like exploring?
- Are you feeling kinky?
- Or are you ready for a cuddle?

When you can start out by being real with your desires, it brings an openness to working together to create a mutually agreeable outcome. And starting gently often allows desire to arise if it's not there at the beginning.

Sharing your fears, boundaries and desires

This can be another way of getting started.

- ***Sharing fears:*** It's good to share any fears that come up for you about sex, as this allows them to be heard and let go of.
- ***Sharing boundaries:*** Don't automatically assume you have the right to do something just because it's with your partner, or because they were into it last time. Equally, don't assume they're ready for something new because you are. Instead, make boundary setting a regular part of your love-play.

As funny as it might sound, boundaries are still important in relationship sex. They not only protect and maintain your essential self, they help you to avoid taking your partner for granted. Boundaries also allow you to feel respected and safe enough to trust and open more deeply to loving pleasure.

- ***Sharing desires:*** What is it you're up for? If one of you isn't open to full sex right now, are you open to exploring anything else? For example, could you lie together and share sexual energy or mutual pleasuring, or could they be present with you whilst you self-pleasure, etc?

Talking About Sex During Sex

Talking during sex doesn't have to be dirty talk (although this can add spice if you're willing to risk it). Simply letting your partner know you're loving what's happening for you is a great way to build the intensity and deepen your connection. We all love being affirmed, and this is a very powerful place to be affirmed in.

Your affirmation can be as simple as, "I'm loving that thing you're doing with your tongue right now. It feels AMAZING!". Oohs and Aahs are a good start but being specific (when you can engage your thoughts) is even better.

Talking when it's not working during sex:
- When you're actually in the moment, keep your communication simple and direct.

- Many people fear speaking up about what they want, but if you do it in a non-shaming way, most partners will love you for it.

- Most of us fear criticism in this tender place, however. So rather than focussing on what's not working, ask for what you want instead. If you want a change, say, "This is nice, and a little to the left would be even better!" or "I'd love it if you could go a bit slower so I can feel it more. That's great – can you go even slower?" or even "I love it when you do... Could you do it now?"

- Don't expect your partner to remember what you want every time. Just make a habit of asking for it. (Ironically, this takes the fear and frustration out of it for your partner so they're more likely to remember.)

- If nothing's working, it's OK to pause, breathe, do your ABC and take the time to come back to a place of connection with yourself and see what emerges from there.

Don't make it, or your partner wrong. Instead, focus on what IS happening for you and share it, eg, "I'm feeling distracted," "I'm not really present," "I'm disconnected from myself," etc. Own this as *your* feeling, and nothing to do with your partner (even the best technique in the world won't get you there if you're not available).

And if your partner is feeling something less than perfect, don't make it about you. As scary as it sounds, stating what is and allowing it to be OK can empower things to shift and for you to see what is needed.

Talking After Sex

Just a simple 'that was wonderful' or 'I love you' can suffice immediately afterwards.

A little later, there's great benefit in sharing about what you experienced. For even when you're feeling totally connected with each other, you each still have your own uniquely personal perspective.

Talking about sex afterwards is a great way to learn more for next time, although it's definitely a time to be gentle and leave criticism behind. Sharing can include what you learned, what worked for you, and what challenged or didn't work for you – always owning your comments and speaking from your heart.

Sex = Children = No Sex

It's funny how the gift of children that come from the act of sex seems to be the reason many people stop having it after those same children arrive. This is partly due to the place we keep sex in our minds: that it's private, embarrassing, naughty, dirty, or just noisy, and that kids shouldn't know we're doing it.

However, it's important to normalise sex, to make it a healthy part of family life, and to make your relationship intimacy equally important as caring for your children's needs. There's no reason that kids can't be in the house whilst you're making love. Open-hearted pleasure that leaves you feeling great will nurture and uplift those around you as well (although do keep the really noisy times for when you're alone).

With young children, talk about 'parent time' for loving each other or having cuddles. Set them up with an activity to keep them occupied; and if they happen to interrupt, just tend to their needs and come back, rather than give up or let your child get into bed with you.

If your children are old enough to be up without supervision, let them know you're going to have some 'connection time' (no details needed). If you clearly hold sex in a place of importance and sacredness in yourself, your kids will do the same. Even if they roll their eyes and say, "Yuck!" they'll highly value the positive role modelling you offer.

Reassess Your Sexual Map

Lastly, reassess your sexual map regularly, as your sexual desires will change over time just like you do. And even if talking about sex doesn't go well the first time, keep trying: the gifts of lovemaking are too big to ignore.

The couples Graeme and I see find that the benefits of getting to an open and loving place in communicating about sex make communicating easier in all other areas of their relationship too. We trust it will be the same for you.

Stuckness and State Change

6.1 Activities to Shift Your State When You Get Stuck

When two unique individuals try to bond together, tough spots are only to be expected. And when you're in one of these spots, it can feel frustrating – like being 'stuck'. No matter how much you might desire stability in your relationship, you have an equally strong drive for change and ease that makes this stuckness feel wrong.

The stuck feeling can merely be the boredom of over-familiarity in the relationship itself. Or it might come from not being able to 'make' your partner be (or give you) what you need or desire. It can also be about something in your own life that's separate to your relationship. Regardless, feeling stuck equals feeling powerless.

If you're like most people – a creature of habit – when you're stuck, you usually just try harder at whatever you were already doing: nagging, resenting, annoying, detaching or avoiding. And, not surprisingly, you probably get the same results. While it may feel hard at the time, taking ownership of your stuckness will immediately give you back your sense of self-empowerment and self-efficacy, allowing you to move through it.

This is where the art of State Change comes in. Instead of trying to change your partner or the situation, try changing your internal state of stuckness instead. Creating this change by shifting yourself into a different energetic state allows you to come back to your relationship (or your life) with fresh eyes.

NB: Don't do this with the intention of avoiding your situation, or of letting your partner get away with unhealthy behaviour. Do it to help you reconnect with yourself and find your power within, while at the same time gaining a new – and often broader – perspective.

The internal shift in you will also energetically impact on your partner. They'll see and feel you being different, which will potentially create a change in them as well. Either way, it will allow you to respond to their behaviour from a clear place.

Positive State Change

During stressful situations, most of us change our state with less healthy things like electronic devices, junk food, smoking, alcohol, drugs, overworking, gossiping or dumping on the cat (unconscious anger). These options all drain your energy and make you unavailable in your relationship. Instead, try some of the following mind/body-focussed suggestions, which will energise you, ground you and more easily bring you back to a state of openness.

Begin with identifying your current state

Using your ABC practice, identify what state you're currently in. This will help you to identify what kind of activity will serve you best.

38 Simple State Changing Practices

Do these practices mindfully. Not only will they help to change your state, but they'll also support your wellbeing.

1. Breathing: deep and slow relaxes, short and fast energises.
2. Practicing your ABC.
3. Shifting your energy by doing some kind of physical exercise, eg walking, jogging, bootcamp, cycling, yoga, heavy gardening or chopping wood. Osho's active meditations are also great. (Download them free from osho.com.)
4. Safely expressing your anger with movement, breath and sound. (See the Anger section in Chapter 5.)
5. Getting out in nature. Try the local park or nearby bush, the back lawn in your bare feet, or sit on the ground with your back against a tree trunk. You can also just use your imagination if your environment doesn't allow these options.
6. Meditating.
7. Journaling/Free Writing: write what you feel without judgement.
8. Practising mindfulness.
9. Walking to your local cafe for a coffee.
10. Doing some housework or gardening.
11. Having a shower or bath.
12. Sitting in front of the TV or movie with the intention of chilling out (for a set time).
13. Listening to relaxing, expressive or uplifting music.
14. Watching a movie that has meaning for you.
15. Doing familiar things in a new way.
16. Preparing yourself some nourishing, fresh food.
17. Using affirmations.

18. Putting on some aromatherapy oils.
19. Dancing freestyle to your favourite music.
20. Going for a swim.
21. Preparing and eating a nutritious meal.
22. Getting out and talking to someone new.
23. Self-pleasuring.
24. Making love.
25. Exercising whilst consciously releasing anger through your breath or voice.
26. Getting professional help from a counsellor or coach.
27. Having a massage or exchanging one with a friend.
28. Snuggling up under a blanket, either in the dark or maybe next to a candle, and just being with yourself.
29. Reaching out and speaking to a stranger, connecting with your humanity.
30. Sleeping alone.
31. Finding a place where you can feel totally safe and filling yourself up with it.
32. Doing some art or craft.
33. Performing an act of service for someone. Giving freely to another person is a great heart opener.
34. Doing something you've been procrastinating about.
35. Singing, playing music, chanting or just making sounds.
36. Creating a ritual for whatever's troubling you. For example, you could light a candle, write a letter about your pain, and then release it by burning it

37. Sharing your challenge with a friend or support group, and just asking to be heard rather than seeking advice. Talk about yourself using 'I' language, and focus on hearing and feeling yourself fully.

38. Experiencing something beautiful: a sunset, a starry night sky, a church, a flower, a painting, a young child, or even just the amazing complexity of your own hand. Beauty can be very transformative.

Notice how you feel after changing your state

- Did you receive any insights?
- Do you feel refreshed and ready for life again?
- Was it worth taking responsibility for yourself?

For some delicious meditations to suit your every need, see www.oztantra.com/meditations/.

6.2 Dealing With the Great Debilitator – Shame

One of the most uncomfortable states we confront in relationship (and in life) is that of shame. You wouldn't think that a relationship built on love would have anything to do with shame – the most icky and uncomfortable feeling you're emotionally capable of. Yet it does, and this is particularly true in your sexual relationship.

Shame is one of the great 'unspokens' in the world (though Brene Brown is having a good go at getting it out there.) You might not realise it, but shame is alive and well under your shiny, all-together surface to one degree or another, as it is for each of us.

It is this belief in our innate wrongness or inadequacy that creates our deepest blocks to real intimacy.

Intimacy and the potential for shame coexist. To create intimacy, you need to expose yourself to your partner and risk rejection and invalidation. This leaves you open to feeling shame as you seek to be seen, understood, respected and loved. Fear of shame can keep you from seeking the intimate connection you crave, and even prevent you from surrendering fully to pleasure.

But what actually IS shame? It's feeling wrong or not good enough – a sense of going blank or numb, wanting to curl up inside, hide, disappear and even cease to exist. Yuk!

*The joke is that **all** of us are wrong in some way.*

Humans are about as imperfect a species as you can get. Yet it's in your imperfections that your perfections lie, where you can find even more of a meeting place between yourself and your partner than you do in the love and perfections you strive for.

Some shame is healthy, of course. It's important to feel your shame when you've actually *done something wrong*, eg hurt someone else or yourself. What we're referring to here however, is the toxic shame where you feel you *ARE something wrong*. Toxic shame has been unconsciously, and occasionally consciously, put onto you by those around you – perhaps by the society, religion or culture you live in as much as your family, friends and society. Or it's shame you've taken on through your life experiences eg masturbating. It's shame that serves no real purpose apart from separating

6: Stuckness and State Change

you from every facet of who you are. Shame also stops you from letting love in- effectively not allowing yourself to be loved.

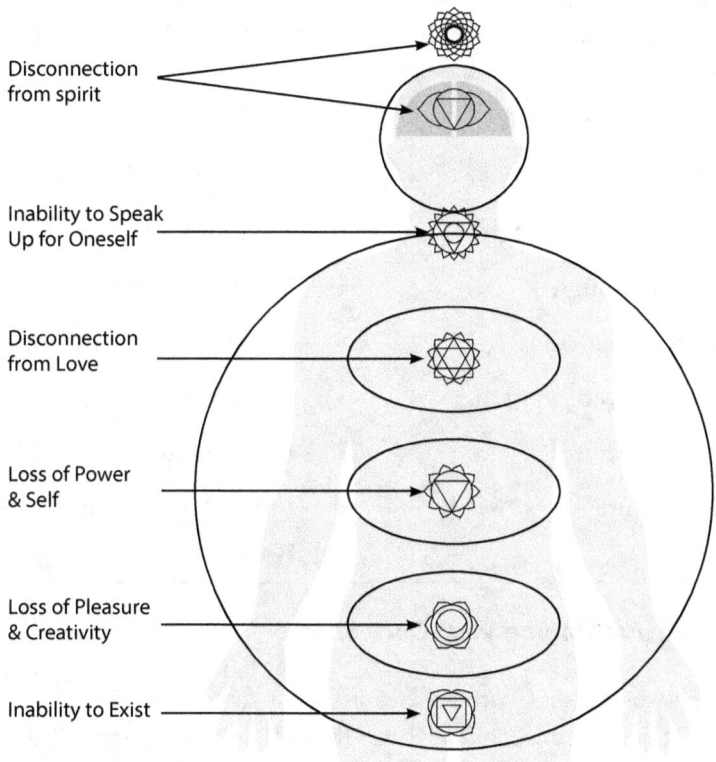

Diagram 6.1 How Shame Impacts Us

Toxic shame comes from your externally taken on shame-based beliefs, even if you might rather die than admit to them. For you, toxic shame just might be a blip on the radar. Or it could be a daily nightmare but it will be there somewhere. You'll find it in your core shame beliefs.

Core shame beliefs:

- I'm wrong/bad
- I'm not good enough
- I'm not enough
- I'm not important
- I'm not loved/wanted
- I don't matter
- I'm a failure
- I'm invisible/I don't exist
- I'm unworthy/worthless
- I'm powerless/unsafe
- I'm alone/don't belong
- I'm different/crazy
- I'm too much
- I'm bad for wanting to be sexual

 Identifying your Core Shame

Notice which belief in the above list most resonates with you. You'll likely feel a response in your body that will help you decide. If there's more than one, pick whichever has the most energy for you.

- Reflect on how this core shame belief shows up in your life, and where it might have come from.
- Notice how you behave when you hit on this belief, and how it limits you.
- Decide how willing you are to take control of shame by using the Shame Busting Practices below instead of letting it control you. Then, when you're ready, read on!

In your desire to avoid the incredible discomfort of shame, you've understandably developed an armoury of strategies to keep you safe from it. Unfortunately, these strategies not only keep you separate from your

6: Stuckness and State Change

partner and yourself, but they also compound your shame by making you feel bad about yourself.

Your shame avoidance strategies might include:

- intellectualising (staying safely in your head)
- judging yourself negatively and compounding your shame
- tensing up and disconnecting from your body
- distracting or numbing yourself with addictions
- covering up your shame with a secondary emotion, such as anger
- dumping your shame on your partner (or others) to avoid feeling it
- seeking perfection where shame cannot exist (unfortunately, perfection doesn't exist either!)
- avoiding reaching out to your partner or trusting them
- keeping yourself small and not taking risks in opening up and being seen
- avoiding being sexual.

These avoidance techniques all make you extremely normal!

 Shame Busting:

1. **Play with becoming empowered in shame.** The next time you feel embarrassed or ashamed, rather than making it wrong, turn it around and make it OK. Using your ABC, connect with the feeling and move towards it. Remember: it's a feeling and it can't hurt you, no matter how uncomfortable it is.

   Say to yourself, "It's OK to feel shame. Feeling shame does not mean that I *am* wrong. I'm bigger than it is." Take a few deep breaths and let the shame flow out of you. If you can stay present with it – even just for a few moments – you'll find compassion for yourself, indeed you'll see that your shame is connecting you with your humanity.

If you can let your shame be there for long enough without needing it to go away you'll come to see that the belief attached to it is not true, eg by feeling through the shame that carries the belief 'I don't exist,' you'll see that you actually do. It takes great courage to do this but in this way your shame will shift into love.

2. **When you catch yourself about to go into a shame avoidance strategy, feel into the shame underneath it.** This shame may feel like a vague uneasiness, a numbness or nothingness that's easy to miss. If you feel into it however it will shift. Then you'll see your need for avoidance disappear, and your ability to reconnect freely with yourself (and your partner) return.
3. **Share your shame story with your partner (or a trusted friend).** A powerful way to resolve shame is through connecting with another person in a healthy way. Shame is about wanting to hide, so it makes sense that the opposite – sharing it – will heal it. You don't necessarily have to share whatever triggered your shame (though this works beautifully if you feel safe enough to go there), but just reconnecting to your humanity by acknowledging your shame with another will help.
4. **If your partner seeks to shame you, take control by agreeing with them!** Say, "Yes, sometimes I *can* be a loser!" or whatever they're attempting to lay on you. Own it and find the freedom in it, knowing that this label isn't all you are. The power lies with whoever can laugh at and accept themselves as they truly are (which is a bit of everything). Mentally give the shame back to the person needing to shame you and find compassion for them, for their shaming of you comes from the unacknowledged shame inside them..
5. **Heal sexual shame by claiming yourself as a self-empowered, sexual being who's willing to honour and take responsibility for your own sexual pleasure.** Because our culture layers a

> HUGE amount of shame upon sexuality, being willing to own your own sexuality is a huge shame buster.
>
> How do you do this? By believing that sexuality is beautiful, giving yourself permission to experience pleasure, being willing to create your own pleasure and believe you're worthy of receiving it from another. And by being willing to feel the shame that arises when you're being sexual without making it wrong, allowing it to leave.
>
> Shame busting will make it easier to reduce shame-avoidance strategies and increase your level of self- and partner-compassion. It will also help to minimise the shaming behaviours you lay on your partner (and yes, we all have them!), because you'll know directly how bad shame feels and the negative impact it carries in a very personal way.
>
> Reducing shaming behaviours in your relationship will then make it a happier, more respectful and loving place to be.

6.3 The Ultimate Art of State Change: Dissolving Your Ego

We're going to get a little Zen here so you might want to get yourself a cuppa and bikkie before diving in…this is one of those sections that may take a few reads to actually get it, this is because your ego will put up resistance to you doing so in order to protect itself.

Here we look into how intimacy can leave you in a magnificently devious double-bind, where what you most long for leaves you at risk of what you most fear.

Seeing this bind for what it is can support you in instantly shifting from being rigid, contracted and unavailable in your relationship to its opposite: flexible, loving and open. It's the ultimate art of state change!

You'll see how the places of deepest struggle in your relationship aren't personal – they're human and the same for everyone. You'll also see how this struggle is ultimately not with your partner, but with yourself and the love that lives inside of you. And you'll better understand the gift of choosing to be vulnerable as a relationship practice.

This is the big-picture thinking behind the benefits of the ABC process in your relationship.

Let's Start by Looking a Little More Closely at Your Ego Self

Your ego is the part of you that can be *most challenged in intimacy*. So better understanding your ego helps you to see the paradoxical gift it offers as a pathway *to deep intimacy* rather than a limitation of it.

*Your ego is only part of who you are, not all
(even if it likes you to think it is).*

Your ego is who your intellectual mind 'thinks' you are, it forms your socially acceptable personality or 'mask' you present to the world. It's your 'I', the part of you that is individual, separate and unique and gives you your sense of self. You're 'I' is heavily influenced by the conditioning of your family, gender, culture, community and society. It's also where your socially unacceptable shadows you try to keep hidden reside.

Ego is often judged as selfishness, but you need to have enough sense of yourself to be in a healthy relationship with another. The unhealthy aspect is when your ego's needs and fears (of which it has plenty) run amok.

> *"The most common ego identifications have to do with possessions, the work you do, status and social recognition, knowledge and recognition, physical appearance, special abilities, relationships, person and family history, belief systems, and often nationalist, racial, religious and other collective identifications. None of these is you."*
>
> The Power of Now, Eckhart Tolle

Ironically, it's your ego that drives you to seek a relationship with another person in the first place, for in the ego's belief in its separateness, it feels incomplete and imperfect alone. As much as you might want to be an individual, you also have an equally strong drive to fill the empty space inside of you which you can't outrun- the space where your wholeness, and your magnificence lives.

You get a taste of this wholeness when you're with someone you love and who loves you. You feel magically complete. Yet it's only a taste, because it relies on something *outside of you*. And within this intimate closeness with another person lies your ego-based fear of your imperfect – and therefore unlovable – self being exposed and rejected.

Tricks of the Ego's Trade

Your ego tries to keep you (itself) safe at all costs. Instead it mostly creates suffering by:

- Believing that its fears and stories of suffering is all that you are
- Believing that it's separate, and seeking attachment in order to be safe
- Believing that receiving love and approval are conditional on your behaviour
- Being rigid in its thinking, needing to judge and be right
- Seeing everything (including its suffering) as a problem so it can be useful in solving them

- Holding on to its intellectual concepts rather than risking experience
- Thinking in the past or the future, rather than the point of power: the now
- Continually desiring newness, stimulation and gratification to distract itself from its suffering
- Seeking power through power over others rather than in its own surrender.

> *"The ego is the false self- born out of fear and defensiveness"*
> Anam Cara: A Book of Celtic Wisdom, John O'Donohue

As you go about your daily relationship, your ego self continually offers you opportunities to challenge its fears about itself. These opportunities come in the form of:

- Negotiating boundaries
- Making the first move
- Dealing with differences
- Talking about money
- Planning the future
- Expressing fears
- Offering sex
- Potentially apologising, rather than defending
- Believing your spouse still loves you when they're grumpy and irritable
- Above all, being seen in your fully open heart. Especially in sex.

How you manage these challenges determines both the quality and longevity of your relationship.

Clearly seeing ego in your relationship

The challenge of intimacy is letting go of your attachment to the reality your ego self perceives and seeing that your ego – with its limited strategies of fear and struggle – is simply a *part* of you, rather than all.

When you see your ego for what it is and identify it, you no longer ARE it, you see your wholeness. You can still choose to enjoy this part of you, but its games no longer control you.

What lies beyond your ego self?

Beyond your ego self lies your mind, body, feeling, and heart and soul connection – that part of you that you long for even more than your partner. This is the part of you that fills the hollow place inside you without needing anything from outside, and gives you access to your expanded, extraordinary potential.

Your ego self is not separate to your whole self but is contained within it. As you access what follows, loneliness disappears, trust arises and struggles become challenges. You open to more heart-connected moments of ease and freedom, and a have more creative response to life. Sound too good to be true? The hard part is going there.

Annette's Practical Experience with Ego Fears

Annette had somehow followed Graeme and his three teenage children (all adrenaline junkies) on an adventure tour to New Zealand, even though she was afraid of heights.

Wanting to challenge her fears she stood, totally terrified, on the side of a mountain, all suited up in a parachute harness with three hot adventure guides, each doing their best to convince her that jumping wasn't just safe, but it could be great fun too. Meanwhile, her egoic mind was bringing out all its big guns in order to keep her safely on the mountain:

Fear 1: *Being In The Unknown* – *not knowing what was going to happen.*

Fear 2: *Being Out of Control* – *not being able to control what was about to happen.*

Fear 3: *Being Overwhelmed* – *fear of the intensity of her feelings once she jumped.*

And underlying these three fears was her ego's major fear: annihilation. *It feared* **complete destruction or obliteration.** *As she stood on the edge of the mountain, Annette's ego feared that its sense of 'I' would completely disappear. Annette's ego was telling her SHE would cease to exist.*

It wasn't at all true, but in that moment, it was 150% real to her ego self.

Can you can resonate with any of Annette's egoic fears in your own moments of challenge, whatever they might be?

Eventually Annette's ego ran out of arguments. Her helpers then took this as assent and pushed her and her ego over the edge… sometimes a little push can help!

As she left the edge, her ego <u>was</u> totally annihilated by the intensity of her fear, but this lasted only for a moment. Then she was flying on the wind, screaming with adrenaline charged fear that transformed into excitement. The longer she flew, the more she loved it and the happier she felt. At some moments, she felt like a part of the landscape itself.

> *Back on the ground, Annette could see that her ego's games were just that – they were trying to keep her safe with seemingly-real-yet-unrealistic stories that limited her potential. Since then, she's found it easier to challenge her ego's games on the ground and step into more moments of her unlimited self.*
>
> *Annette's story is an extreme example that helps to clearly identify the ego's games that occur on everyone's internal mountain edge in moments of challenge. Her story will help you to see these games for what they are. You'll learn more about how this process happens below.*

Your Mind Determines Your Experience of Yourself

To get a little more understanding of your ego and what lies beyond it you need to look more closely at how your mind and the brain that underpins it works.

Your mind experiences itself (and you experience yourself) as your brain interprets it: both your primal and limbic brains at the centre, and your cerebral cortex with its left and right halves on top. The left half of your cerebral cortex largely relates to intellectual and egoic function, and the right half relates to your feeling/intuitive/body and soul mind. These two parts of your cerebral cortex communicate (amongst other ways) via a sexy little membrane called the Corpus Callosum: the neural pathway that gives you access to the benefits of both halves.

For an amazing insight into how these two sides function, watch the TEDx Talk My Stroke of Insight *by Jill Bolte Taylor.*

Of course, the two sides of your cerebral cortex aren't completely separate, and all four brain areas interact with each other (and with your body) in ways more complex than can be discussed here. We focus here on how you *experience* your mind's workings, rather than on your brain function.

Your 'Other G Spot'

Overseeing all four areas of your brain is something science is still discovering, which has been known in the East for millennia as your 'God Spot'. It's part of your mind that lives at your crown and is commonly found in meditation. It allows you to be aware of your 'self' or your 'I', to 'see' the thoughts you're thinking and know the actions you're taking. It acts a little like an internal God watching over you.

As well as your 'self' consciousness your God Spot also contains your observer-consciousness which holds both your self-consciousness and your awareness of what lies beyond your 'self' in the reality around you.

Beyond your self conscious and observer conscious minds lies the transpersonal or infinite consciousness, that which lies beyond your mind, and your God Spot acts as the gatekeeper in between.

Your God Spot's job is– simply letting you know that you're here, that you're safe (without needing to be in control in an ego-based way), and that you're never truly alone because you're connected to something larger than yourself. It does this by observing and noticing what's going on for you without judgement.

Your God Spot allows you to safely access the magic, or the 'more' that you're seeking that lies beyond your ego. From this wholeness you no longer need to control, manipulate or otherwise harass your partner, vastly improving your potential for a loving relationship. It allows you to see more of the many aspects of yourself (see Illustration 6.2) and to see that your whole self is even greater than the sum of its many parts. This is what you develop greater access to through your ABC practice.

Nb. We have avoided labelling these aspects as masculine or feminine for Graeme and I believe it is easier to access more of them for ourselves if we're not struggling with gender labels we might be resistant to.

6: Stuckness and State Change

Corpus Callosum - the communication pathway between the two realities

Trans Persona - Witness/God consciousness, gateway beyond the mask where four value logic: I AM, I AM not, I AM both, I AM neither exists

L Brain

Self Consciousness

Ego Personality- I think, two value logic: I am/am not

Ordinary everyday reality

Logical, rational & analytical abilities

Linear thinking- exists in future, past and believes in polarity/2 value logic

Expresses through thoughts, words, ideas, judgements, actions

Believes it is separate, individual Needs to be dominant, unique, exclusive

Concerned with focus, purpose, goals, details, problem solving

Is Objective, relies on Facts, Story

Seeks to survive, to know, to be safe

Based in Will

Is hard, rigid, solid, reliable, protective, penetrating, provides

Seeks attention, diversity, ownership, connection/attachment

Seeks love, approval and things

All satisfaction is momentary

Creates masks to get approval

Fears the unknown, loss of control, overwhelm, annihilation/Ego death

R Brain

Soul/Infinite Consciousness

Soul Identity- No Self or Selflessness

Extraordinary reality

Intuition, meditation, dreams

Multidimensional, timeless/in the here and now, sees beyond polarity/has 4 value logic

Expresses through the body, feelings, senses, images, sounds

Knows it is whole, part of everything, is surrendered, is inclusive of everything

Sees bigger picture, is creative through intention, lateral thinking

Is Subjective, Descriptive, Poetic

Manifests, Seeks nothing, is free

Based in Passion

Is soft, flexible, flowing, wild, changing, receptive, nurtures

No need to be seen, connect or attach as it is in relationship

Is Desire, is Love

Has no need for satisfaction

No need for masks or protection

Is everything/ fears nothing, is timeless

Diagram 6.2 The Whole Self as it exists at an experiential level

Learning to Trust Yourself

When you're standing on the edge of your own internal mountain, not knowing what lies ahead, you have a choice. You can stay behind your ego's walls of protection. Or you can go within, using your ABC, and trust in the powerful mystery that lives inside you.

Each time you make this choice to surrender your ego, you'll experience a moment of vulnerability, an inner nothingness as Annette did in the story earlier. This is simply a letting of your outward defences, because you now *know* they're just your ego's game. This then allows you to fall into the essence of your authentic self.

> *"This is love: to fly toward a secret sky*
> *To cause a hundred veils to fall each moment*
> *First to let go of life,*
> *Finally, to take a step with no feet."*
>
> The Love Poems of Rumi, Rumi

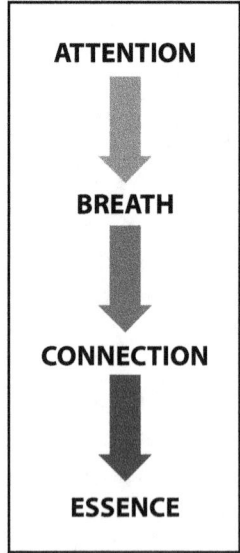

This step into your mystery always feels illogical and difficult. Yet ultimately, it offers much more than your ego alone can ever know. It allows your state to change, and your perspective – and even your world – to shift.

You'll feel your vulnerability and your humility, you'll find your humanity, your love, and surprisingly your power. You'll see objectively what you've been protecting and make friends with it. Your body will soften and you'll be more emotionally available to your partner. Your inner tension from your ego's right/wrong logic will recede, and all four areas of your brain will work together in the service of your heart/body-mind. Your sexuality won't be far behind, for your life force responds when you come into alignment with yourself.

You'll find a choice of infinite, no longer paradoxical possibilities from your heart's four-value logic. These possibilities include:

- Security/Support/Comfort/Belonging
- Familiarity/Identity/Fidelity/Longevity
- Fun/Pleasure/Adventure/Excitement
- Intimacy/Connectedness/Freedom/Autonomy
- Love/Sex/Mystery/Meaning/Happiness.

From here, you'll find taking the first step towards your partner and risking intimacy will be easier. You'll be able to see your that partner's comments about – for example – your lack of bookkeeping ability may be true, but they don't need to destroy you. You'll see that your partner's rejection of your kiss is about them having had a hard day, rather than your lack of desirability.

You'll also be slower to anger and quicker to feel compassion. Your responses to criticism will be more constructive. You'll find expressing your truth easier and more rewarding. You'll see beauty in your partner (and yourself) where previously you saw only imperfection. You'll no longer need to perform in sex – instead you'll open to the moment and to your sexual curiosity (this is another reason that we suggest the ABC practice as a precursor to lovemaking). And most important of all, with your walls down you'll allow yourself to be deeply loved, and love your partner in the same way. This surrender of your ego offers unlimited opportunities to grow your relationship and opens your heart to love.

> *"The way you become divine is to become wholly human".*
> Bishop Shelby Spong, The Star, Apr 21, 2007

Depending on the strength and fragility of your ego and your connection to your heart/body-mind, letting go into this moment of nothingness can vary from a slight feeling of unease to one of deepest terror. But it's only for a moment (or for as long as you choose to stay in your defensive 'rational' story or your 10% truth/90% bullshit).

The more willing you are to trust yourself and the process, the quicker the shift happens. One delicious way to think of it is being like letting go into the freedom and no-mind of an orgasm! And the more time you spend in connection with your body and your feelings the more comfortable (though never easy) the shift from ego into your whole self becomes.

If there's no moment of challenge involved, you're probably stepping into a new way of seeing your false self that your ego mind creates in the guise of surrender. This is especially true if this new self has you feeling more important, and even omnipotent than before, for the authentic self doesn't need to aggrandise itself. Your new ego self may work for you for a while, but ultimately, your whole self will keep pushing for recognition by challenging it.

This is a negative side effect of much of the self-help movement and individual counselling today, and is why these strategies often don't work for relationships. They're designed to build your ego self up more strongly through loving yourself and becoming more self-expressed. At the same time, you put it in greater fear of surrender and loss of control. You want your partner to do it instead. This means you create pain and suffering for yourself as a result. Remember: you need a certain amount of ego to exist, but too much gets in the way.

This is the challenge of intimacy: it will trigger you into this process of egoic surrender into your wholeness. This surrender is particularly challenging in the complex power dynamics that exist between men and women. Not understanding that this struggle is less about their partners and more about their own ego is why many people walk away from their relationships.

Yet if you drop your story of suffering about what your partner is or isn't doing, and surrender to your whole self, you'll never be quite sure (like Forrest Gump's box of chocolates), exactly what you'll get. But you can trust that it will be worth it!

Regularly practising your ABC, developing awareness of your God Spot, exploring your relationship triggers, and using the *Expansive Lovemaking* you'll discover in Chapter 8 will make this pathway into your authentic self (and the love that lies within you) easier to trust.

> *"Love is available unconditionally from the Soul and worthiness is irrelevant"*
>
> A Method for Tantra Bliss, Bodhi Avinasha

The more you develop the pathway between the two mind/body realities with the observer mind to keep you safe, the more authentic and powerful you can be.

Sexeptance

7.1 Acknowledging What Lies at Our Core

Most people think of sex as just something they do between the sheets at night with an intimate partner, but it's so much more than that. Treating it as such will change your relationship with it and with each other.

Sexual energy is the primal and creative energy of the universe. Everything that's alive was created by it: animals, plants, humans, and even the universe itself by the first big bang. We ourselves were all created by an orgasm, even though most of us cringe at the idea of our parents having sex. In fact, sex reminds us all of our humanity – almost everyone has succumbed to the urge to get vulnerable and naked and we're linked through the ages by those moments of total, sweaty abandon.

Yet sexual energy is so much more than just biology. It's your animating life force energy, the creative part of you that brings new life within yourself as well as bringing your offspring.

Sexual energy is present in a relationship as attraction, arousal, passion and pleasure. It's equally present in your enthusiasm for interesting projects in work or hobbies. It's the energy you use to run around the back yard with your children and grandchildren. It lies in your inspiration for new ideas and creativity, and it's the energy you feel when you've had a shift in your level of self-awareness.

You've probably noticed that after really satisfying sex, you find yourself with increased enthusiasm and vitality for living. When you say YES to your sexual self, you connect to a very deep part of yourself – even deeper than the love and pleasure you share with your lover. That place within you has nothing to do with actually having sex, it's your power centre.

Sex is power. This is why it's used to sell everything in the world from cars to ice cream; and it's also why the church, culture, society, parents and now pharmaceutical companies want to control it.

Being connected with sex in a healthy way makes you powerful within yourself. It makes you available to deep vulnerability, compassion and healing. It's worth cultivating your sexual energy for these reasons alone. And the more aware of, connected with, and authentic in your sexual self you are, the more your sexual pleasure flows.

It's a win-win situation!

It's a natural human desire to want to feel good

It's common to seek experiences of altered or uplifted states of consciousness. They can be as simple as having a glass of wine, watching a sunset, taking a moment in prayer – or as complex as taking mind-altering drugs or doing a BDSM ritual.

This is part of our longing to break free from the burden of our ordinary minds, and to connect with something larger than ourselves to make sense of the world. Almost every community on earth has some kind of ritual or spiritual practice to access something they call God or Spirit.

Suppressing and corrupting this energy is life-taking and unhealthy and denies our true nature. Suppression comes from our fear of and conditioning around its power. Sexual problems generally relate to unconsciously acting out the repression or the unhealthy expression of this energy rather than by its healthy expression.

> *"Modern men and women are obsessed with the sexual; it is the only realm of primordial adventure still left to most of us. Human lives otherwise are pretty well caged in by the walls, bars, chains and locked gates of our industrial culture."*
>
> Sex At Dawn, Edward Abbey

Sexual Energy is Natural, Powerful and Beautiful

Sexual energy is catalytic: you can't see it or measure it, but you can notice its effects and it leaves you feeling different afterwards. Sexual energy is not just physical. It's emotional, psychic and subtle, and it impacts your soul-body. When you're having sex you're connecting a lot more than just your bodies. It fosters your capacity for wonder, your absolute confidence and your openness to the world and to your heart. If you can experience this simultaneously with another human being in a loving, sexual context, it's absolutely magical.

It's the only way most people feel absolute freedom – in that moment of orgasm where they're free of their everyday, ordinary, limited minds. This experience is known as the surrender or 'little death' of the ego.

Almost all of us have been there at some time in our lives, and we want to go back as often as possible. We promote our sexual energy by saying YES to it through how we live, as much as what we do in the bedroom.

You say YES to your sexual energy and potential for ecstasy by:

- Eating plenty of fresh foods
- Living in an aware and embodied way (see your ABC tool)

- Developing a 'felt' sense of your body so you know its real signals, including hunger, thirst, tiredness, sexual desire etc
- Minimising your addictions
- Getting regular exercise, including some that challenges your body
- Getting adequate rest
- Taking a few minutes each day to stre-e-e-e-tch your body
- Taking regular breaks from your electronic devices
- Finding gratitude
- Appreciating beauty
- Doing something just for the joy of it
- Doing something purely for sensual pleasure daily
- Making life-affirming choices rather than life-defeating ones
- Being honest and in your integrity
- Doing something for others
- Doing something you love
- Keeping your mind active by learning new things
- Being willing to take healthy risks
- Finding a way to express your inner wild man or woman (the primal part of your nature) to balance the time you spend being civilised
- Developing some kind of spiritual practice, whatever this means for you
- Having life-affirming sex, rather than the energy-draining kind
- Keeping an open mind to the connection between sex and your spirituality.

It's equally important to explore the relationship you have with your own sexual energy so you can talk about it more clearly with your partner. How do you view it? How do you manage it?

7: Sexeptance

> **What does sex mean to you? Write down and explore your own thoughts**
>
> What are your own beliefs about sex?
> - Where have they come from?
> - How did you first learn about sex? Who from?
> - What were the messages you received about sex?
> - How well do they serve you today?
> - How would you feel about challenging some of your limiting beliefs about sex?
> - How do you feel reading this interpretation of sex?
> - How do you cultivate your own sexual energy? Where do you suppress it?
> - Do you own it, or give it away to others or to your conditioning?
> - What positive messages could you give to yourself about sex?

It's not important how often a couple has sex together. There's no magical numerical formula. Instead, it's the quality of the experience that counts, how satisfied it leaves you and what it brings to each of you and to your relationship. What's also important is that a couple thinks about, talks about, and makes conscious decisions about this powerful part of their relationship.

7.2 Sex - What's in it For Me as a Woman? (by Annette)

My work gives me permission to talk about sex for real. In it, I hear women of all ages and backgrounds expressing their desire for the delights of great sex. What I believe they're really hungry for though, is access to the part of themselves that's radiant, desirable, alive, powerful, loving, and even wild and free – a place that speaks to their very souls.

This place inside a woman is about more than just what she does in the bedroom. I believe a woman's sexuality IS part of her soul. It's not just about having sex, but about the unique connection her sexuality gives her to herself- helping her to be in her body, to feel her aliveness and her capacity for pleasure, along with access to her intuitive and other subtle senses as well as to her personal power. This has been reflected over and over in the women I've worked with, and I'm sure it's true for you too.

Yet many women with this desire still struggle to express it fully. They find themselves with low – or no – libido, or they're all revved up with no place to go. But then, given the right environment, they often find their desire shows up with bells on. In my own journey with sex, I've felt it all: huge, all-consuming desire, low desire, all the way down to no desire at all – not even a flicker of response, no matter how hard I tried.

I've also had chronic vaginal pain, anxiety, emotional neediness and low self-worth, all of which complicated my sexual desire (and vice versa). Yet my sexuality also has given me experiences beyond my wildest dreams and has taught me so much about myself. I've learned that where I'm at in my sexuality is often a reflection of where I'm at with myself. Believe me, sex doesn't have to be just another chore on your list. Instead, it can be a truly fascinating journey with learning, healing and rewards around every corner with the power to make life work for you.

It Hasn't Been Easy

Women have long had a confusing relationship with their sexuality – a history that impacts how they experience it, even today. This is partly explained because a woman's body and her sexuality have always been linked with her power.

7: Sexeptance

"For about two thousand years of Western history female sexuality was denied. When it could not be denied it was condemned as evil"

The Great Cosmic Mother, Rediscovering the Religion of the Earth, Monica Sjoo & Barbara Mor.

Women's sexuality has been feared, denied, rejected and invalidated. It's been stolen from them through centuries of abuse. They've been burned at the stake as witches for it and thrown out of their homes and communities – even stoned – for indulging in it. Their sexuality has been treated as medical 'hysteria' and viewed as a temporary insanity or something to be merely 'tolerated' for the ensuing benefits of motherhood. Women have been blamed for men's misuse of sexuality, and despite the advantages of modern science, the existence of their 'GSpots' – their sexual power centres – is still in hot debate.

A woman's most asexual roles – those of the mother and the safe, subordinate wife – are the ones given the most kudos. Meanwhile, the ones most vilified are those with a sexual aspect: the slut and the whore, which are wrongly seen as the lowest a woman can be.

It took radical feminism to give women the right to their own bodies inside marriage. The pill sexually liberated women in the 60s, and *Sex and the City's* Samantha gave them permission to be sexual aggressors. Yet a large percentage of women, especially those in long-term relationships, still don't experience the sexual fulfilment they were born for. Big Pharma has called this Female Sexual Arousal Disorder and defined it themselves with categories so broad that any average woman could fit into them, leaving women longing for a pill to give them a simple answer. However, the answer to a woman's pleasure is not simple but it is wondrous.

Impacted by their history, women are still looking for ways to give themselves permission to own and love this part of themselves. The good news is that women's sexuality has been feared, denied and controlled precisely *because* it is so powerful. That means we women all have the ability to reclaim some of that power for ourselves.

> *"Men's biggest sexual complaint about women is that women often cannot let go during lovemaking, and there is something to this. It simply has not been OK for women to let go and be themselves sexually."*
>
> Female Ejaculation & The G Spot, Deborah Sundahl

How we Deny Ourselves

Let's explore the many reasons that a woman, apart from her history, often doesn't fully own her sexual self. This isn't intended to blame women (they've had more than enough of that!), but rather seeks to understand her situation.

A woman's libido is different

A woman's *desire* for sex is different to her *capacity* for sex. Her libido commonly (but not always) *follows* rather than leads – it comes *after* arousal rather than before, and needs a context rather than just a place. She usually desires sex for reasons other than pleasure, making sex about being loved or desired, perhaps because it unconsciously feels safer. This is why a bad boy can make such an impression – he sets her body alight and helps her feel this denied part of her.

Women's main reasons for desiring sex:

- To feel loved, desired and desirable
- Seeking connection and intimacy
- Getting a man's attention
- Making babies
- Creating peace and quiet in the relationship (or even getting a new kitchen!)
- Seeking pleasure

- Exploring her spiritual dimension, which she intuitively knows is related to her sexuality.

Most of these desires can be fulfilled in a relationship, but the last two require more than just the safety and familiarity that relationship sex provides. And rather than rely on a bad boy, you can learn how to set this part of yourself alight on your own and then lead as well as follow if you desire.

How a Woman's Environment Denies Her Sexuality

Work disconnects her

Spending her days in a high-achieving, intellectual, high-stress work environment leaves a woman coming to sex worn out and out of touch with her adrenalin fatigued body. Caring for her family sees her coming to sex (or avoiding it) with an empty energy tank. Yet somewhere in the back of her mind, she carries high expectations about the possibilities of her sexual pleasure, and then sadly blames herself or her lover for not getting her there.

Fashion and beauty industries shame her

Women spend an inordinate amount of time finding the right 'look' to make themselves acceptable or beautiful enough to be desired. They try products that range from push-up bras to imperfection fixing makeup, all the way to breast implants and labiaplasty (labia reconstruction). Yet women's belief in their own innate, natural beauty is a vital part of their sexual attractiveness, and denying it significantly reduces their pleasure.

Porn and patriarchy keep her in fear

Patriarchy has taught women to unconsciously see other women as competition rather than a means of support, which keeps them afraid and striving to be sexy enough to keep their men. They fear their lovers will desire the perfect women they see in porn. This means they see other women as competition and miss out on the incredible support network that women can share.

Our society believes sex has an age limit

Society has few role models for sexual older women, and the few we do have are looking 'younger' than ever. Menopause is seen as a time to leave sex behind. I, on the other hand, see menopause as a time when women let go of libido. Rather than relying on our sex drive, we choose to explore and celebrate this beautiful and powerful part of ourselves in a whole new way. It's no less intense, but it's more heart-connected, full-bodied and multi-dimensional. Many of the suggestions in this book will help you move through your menopausal challenges and for more information see:

- http://www.oztantra.com/menopause-suffering-alchemy/
- http://www.oztantra.com/relationship-survival-strategy-men-living-woman-menopause/

Medications decrease her libido

Many over the counter medications will affect sexual desire such as antihypertensives, antihistamines antidepressants and antipsychotics. If you're on these check with your Dr to see if you're on the ones with the least impact.

Devaluing femininity and receptivity

As a society, we devalue feminine qualities, which leaves women resisting their feminine essence. Believing that the feminine qualities of softness, nurturing, playfulness, vitality and vulnerability are weak, irrelevant or scary causes women to intellectually armour themselves against these qualities and miss their power. Graeme and I have witnessed women many times in their soft, open, vulnerability in our client sessions. And every time, that vulnerability shows not as weakness, but rather as the incredible beauty and power of their hearts cracking open, which raises the soul of everyone in the room to the heavens.

When a woman surrenders into her heart, connecting to her own receptive nature and true feminine self, she feels paradoxically stronger in speaking up for herself and calling her man on his games. And her man, feeling her receptivity, is energetically drawn to her from his own heart rather than his ego.

Sex and spirit

Lastly, a woman's innate connection to her spiritual aspect has often been confused by religion, which tells her that being spiritual and being sexual are different – and even mutually exclusive. This shames sex and leaves her with only its mechanics, rather than its vibrant whole.

Personal experience

All of this conditioning lies on top of whatever a woman's own personal sexual history brings her. No wonder being a sexual woman is confusing, and she feels wrong about herself!

> *"Libido for women lives in the complex web of our lives and is influenced by our past experiences, our general health, our current relationships, and our hormonal balance."*
>
> Bodywise, Dr Rachel Carlton Abrams

I share the blocks below with you to show that you're not alone in your experience of less-than-perfect sex. Whether these reasons affect you a little or a lot, I hear you and I see you.

Women's Internal Environments Create Blocks to Fulfilling Sexual Pleasure

Can you relate to any of the following blocks?

- Not feeling good enough in yourself

- Thinking that sex is only for you to 'give' to men
- Being disconnected from your body and contracted in your pelvis
- Not understanding fully how your body works
- Believing your body is unattractive, ugly, dirty or smells bad
- Fearing that you won't get wet enough
- Endlessly comparing yourself negatively to other women
- Not believing you deserved to be cared about in sex
- Believing that you shouldn't want sex, and labelling yourself as a slut if you do
- Losing your voice in sex or suppressing your 'no'
- Fearing or resenting that you won't access the pleasure you long for
- Allowing yourself to be penetrated before you're ready
- Trying to have orgasm-focused sex and limiting your whole-body arousal
- Being able to 'endure' unsatisfactory sex
- Fearing that once it's unleashed, your sexuality will be 'too much'
- Not feeling safe to open yourself to vulnerability
- Disassociating from your body due to sexual trauma.

Over time, each of these blocks will short circuit a woman's sexual desire. If any of them are true for you, use the techniques in the *Identifying Your Beliefs* section of Chapter 4 to begin working with them. There will be other ways in the sexual healing and awakening tips to follow.

Your Journey is in Moving Beyond Your Conditioning

A woman's sexuality is an 'opening into the whole of herself' experience. I believe that, as women, we're yet to fully experience and own the power of our sexual selves. As our society becomes more driven by ego, and sex becomes more about performance, we're losing our access to the beauty of our sexuality.

A woman in expanded sexual pleasure is open, radiant, clear, full of love, joy, tenderness and abandon; and the lucky man she's loving knows no greater gift. This experience begins from her YES to her sexuality, and from her self-love, self-trust, and trust in her partner's ability to 'see' her for who she is.

And if you're thinking that as a woman, you've got a raw deal with the number of sexual challenges you face, I assure you that your man has his own share of conditioning and misunderstandings to deal with. The good news is that it's a healing journey you can share together.

Giving yourself permission to be in your sexuality is like reclaiming a part of yourself

What do I mean by being 'in' your sexuality? It means being fully in your body, using your ABC, and feeling all of your feelings – including your sexual ones – from a place of self-awareness and love.

It means seeing your sexuality as one powerful package, containing your secret inner power, your vitality, your passion for life, your inner radiance beauty routine, and your energy for chasing your kids or grandkids round the back yard or running a marathon, as well as a pathway to your inner wisdom. The specifics will look different for each individual woman, and this is before you even get near the bedroom.

In the bedroom, you reclaim your sexuality by connecting deeply to yourself, to where you're relaxed *and* energised, rather than hyped up and needing release. It's a state of being open, surrendered to yourself, and safely connected to your inner power. You can flow into raw heat and passion, giving, receiving, and feeling playful, creative, flowing, ecstatic, surrendered, dominant, blissful, orgasmic and even magical. Beyond merely seeking satisfaction, you come fully into the moment of being *whoever* and *however* you are, unattached to any outcome other than this. And you invite your man to meet you there.

Following your ABC practice and the many steps in this book will get you one step closer every time.

Get Started by Connecting to Your Sexual Self

There's much you can do to make a difference in connecting to your sexual self, both by yourself and with your partner's support.

Start by giving yourself permission to think differently *and to take action...* Think of each action, no matter how small, as not another chore and not even anything to do with sex, but instead as an act of self-love. Taking charge in this way helps you to feel good in yourself and builds your sexual – and general – self-confidence, reducing your stresses, insecurities and reliance on your partner to get you there. (Though of course you'll be very willing to accept the support he gives you!)

> **Connecting With Your Sexual Self**
>
> **Starting outside the bedroom:**
>
> 1. **Get in touch with the power of the sexual openness that lies inside your vulnerability.** See the value in it for yourself and learn to feel safe and empowered in it. Women everywhere are getting in touch with their external power and making big inroads into becoming their own women – yet without vulnerability and surrender into their hearts, that power doesn't translate into the more satisfying intimacy and pleasurable sex we all long for.
> 2. **Get in touch with your body more often.** See it as your sacred temple, and the holder of your pleasure and divinity. Stop, pause, breathe and feel. Stroke yourself with love. Listen to what your body needs and give it to yourself, eg water, good food, elimination, rest, relaxation or space. Even attending to these basic needs makes a difference. It's amazing how easy it is for us

to continually give priority to others and neglect our own body temples, but it doesn't serve us.
3. **Enjoy moving your hips.** Open up your hips and free up your sexual energy with a regular pelvic rock, circle, wiggle, jiggle or make small thrusts. Breathe. Smile.
4. **Make the choice to be in your body.** Sit your shoulders down and back, put your head up and your chest out and roll your hips when you walk. You'll feel fabulous!
5. **Be positive when you talk about yourself and sex.** Notice what you're putting out there, choose not to indulge in negativity, and share about sex in a genuine, heartfelt way. Applaud yourself and others who are doing the same thing. Create a network of sex-positive friends.
6. **Find an honouring name to call your genitals, as words carry energy**. I use 'Yoni', which encompasses all of my genitals and means 'sacred space' but find what works for you.
7. **See your man's approach to sex as part of his social conditioning.** Realise that he's just as much a victim of the patriarchal worldview as you are, and believe that underneath he wants the same things that you do: loving, pleasurable and fulfilling lovemaking *with you*! This can help you feel more connected to him, safer in expressing yourself in the bedroom, and more willing to take a team approach to getting what you both deserve.

 Connect with your sexual power directly through your body

This sounds like an unusual and downright weird thing to do, but your womb, ovaries and Yoni have their own intuitive intelligence just like your brain, your heart and your gut. This intelligence can reliably guide you into a strong and healthy relationship with your sexual self.

To access it, sit or lie comfortably, placing your hands low down over your belly in a downward facing triangle with your thumbs and fingertips connecting. Bring your attention to this area, breathe into it for a few minutes, then ask it questions, eg, "What do you need right now?"

Let your sexual body speak to you through feelings, images or intuition. Trust what it has to say. The more it knows you're listening, the more it will speak. (And this works even if the physical parts you're speaking to have been removed).

 In the bedroom:

Take time with yourself, by yourself, to get connected with your body.

The more you value this connection in yourself, the more it will be reflected around you in your happiness, femininity, truth, sexual aliveness and confidence.

Make it a regular practice to:

- ***Massage your breasts with a loving, rather than stimulating, touch.*** Start with your full hand, slowly ending at the nipples. Breathe into the area as you do so, kickstarting a cocktail of chemicals that brings a beautiful safety, openness and aliveness in you.

    https://www.oztantra.com/15-minutes-to-unlimited-female-sexual-pleasure/

    Let go of any negative messages about your breasts as you do this. Do it regularly as an act of self-nurturing – even just one minute will make a difference over time. You can even do this during lovemaking as it helps to open your heart and your pleasure. You don't need to wait for your lover to do it for you: doing it for yourself at times can be truly beautiful.

- ***Nurture your genitals.*** Moisturise them with coconut oil, sweet almond oil or even just your hands. Massage your butt, inner thighs, lower belly across the top of your pubic bone, outer labia and perineum. These areas hold – and withhold – much

sexual tension, so you'll be amazed at how freeing them up by massaging firmly with messages of love can open up your sexual pleasure.
- **Massage the inside of your Yoni.** Get to know it outside of the sex act. Touch simply to connect with it as a vital part of your sexual self. Breathe into it. Learn how it feels, where it feels pleasurable, and stretch and release any tension or even emotions it might be holding.

Being with your lover

- Listen to yourself. Listen to your body. Take your time – you're worth it. Give up performing.

- Connect with your heart, and what you're feeling in your body. Feel and release anything that keeps you from feeling safe and open. Pay a little compassionate attention to this part of yourself simply by breathing into your heart and allowing any accompanying feelings to release.

This will allow you to feel safe and connected enough for your arousal and desire to arise. Speaking your fears or concerns is not required, but doing so can help them to shift. It's important to ensure you make them about yourself and not your lover.

The more comfortable you are with these practices, the easier it will be for your lover to trust you and your process, knowing they are a pathway to your passion.

Value yourself

If you believe your lover isn't willing to take time with you, ask yourself whether this is real, or whether it's your fear, shame or lack of self-love? Ask your partner if he's willing to support you in taking time to fully open, because you really want to go there – and that ultimately, both of you will benefit. It's helpful to be aware that there may be a male/female language or communication difference in this space as well, so check the *Men and Women Are Different* section in Chapter 5.

When you're genuine in your desire, most men will be very interested in supporting you, especially if you let them know it will make sex with them much more satisfying!

Let his appreciation in

Men love to look at a woman's body, especially when it's willingly revealed for their gaze. Use your ABC practice to empower yourself in enjoying your body enough to reveal it to your partner, and allow his appreciation to soften the edges of your self-judgement.

> *"When a woman undresses in front of a man, she feels insecure, he feels only gratitude."*
>
> A diarist in Bettina Arndts' What Men Want In Bed

Get to Know your Genitals

Have a look at your genitals in the mirror every now and again. Look with love and curiosity rather than judgment, and take as long as you need to really see them with love. Let the shame and judgement drop away.

7: Sexeptance

Exploring your points of sexual awakening

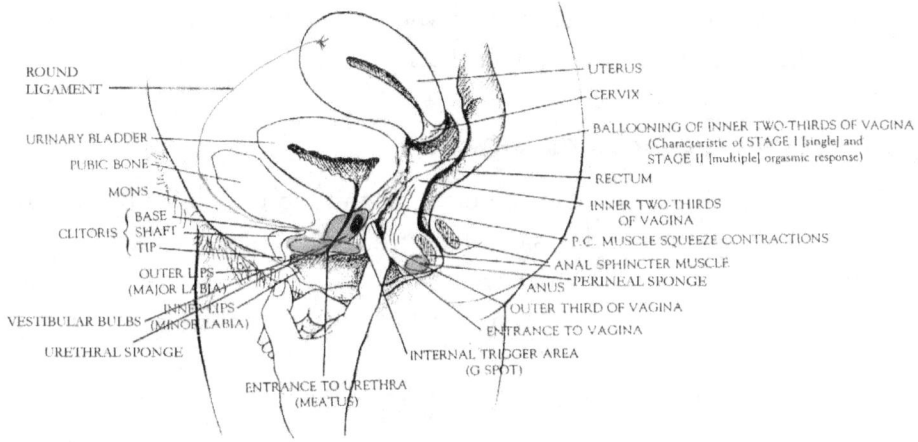

Diagram 7.1 Female Genitalia

The external appearance of a woman's genitals comes in as many shapes and sizes as women do themselves. Just like their ears, noses and feet genitalia are all unique and have their own innate beauty (unlike the airbrushed ones seen in porn). To see some of their great variety and normalise (even love) your own, Google search images from Jamie McCartney's 2008 exhibition of plaster casts of vaginas, or Yvonne Lumsden's book Heart of the Flower.

Get to know your external arousal tissues

The first stage of a woman's genital arousal starts outside her vagina, in the delicious tissues of the vulva.

Get to know this area in yourself: underneath your outer labia lie your clitoral legs, vestibular bulbs, and then way down behind your vagina is your perineal sponge. All of these areas are capable of arousal given the right attention, eg a full and relaxed hand 'melting' onto the area (without movement), circular massage, then gliding strokes, forming the gateway to your deeper levels of arousal.

You can tell these tissues are aroused when they puff and swell. This is the key to being ready for more direct clitoral touch.

Understand your clitoral network

Your clitoris is not just a little button at the top of your vulva. It has legs extending down either side of your urethral opening. Each clitoris responds to different stimulation – some want direct touch and some want very indirect (ie to hardly be touched, focussing more on the labia).

If you haven't already, experiment and find what your own style is.

The GSpot (AKA the 'Goddess' Spot)

The GSpot is also known as a the 'Goddess' Spot, or the 'Sacred Spot' – the latter term created by Charles Muir, a man who's awakened more GSpots than any other man living. This is an energy point, and is your connection to what can be defined as your energetic centre or your sexual soul.

Your GSpot has a physical location that's not actually inside your vagina. Instead, it's located *within* your urethral sponge (AKA your prostate gland – yes, you have one too), which lies inside the upper wall of your vagina, behind your pubic bone and below your cervix.

This spot can be aroused through massage, and it's common for neither you nor your partner to feel your GSpot until it IS aroused, which is why many women believe they don't have one. When arousal happens, your GSpot feels like an area of raised ridges like an almond, and can sometimes even feel like a small pearl. If either you or your partner can't feel anything at first, this is normal, most GSpots require 'awakening'.

Awakening this spot takes your sexual experience to a whole new level of full-body pleasure, including ongoing waves of orgasmic pleasure, unlimited multiple orgasms, emotion and even what can be described as spiritual experiences.

Fully experiencing her GSpot brings a woman to a place of self-love that never truly leaves her. Her pleasure from this area is very different to her pleasure from her clitoris.

Her GSpot may also hold the residue of any sexual suffering, hurt or abuse, which may feel like the blocked energy of anger, guilt, fear, shame or disappointment. This can cause her GSpot to feel numb or painful to touch and is why a GSpot needs *awakening* rather than just stimulating.

> "Deep inside, protected as the clitoris is not, it [The GSpot] is a place that can produce the most profound pleasure, both physically and on a psychic level."
>
> The Art of Conscious Loving, Charles and Caroline Muir

How is a GSpot different from a clitoris?

Both of these areas are part of the same genital landscape, with one external and the other inside the vagina. The clitoris is supplied by the pudendal nerve. It has a 'peak' orgasmic response and can generally only experience a limited number of orgasms.

Meanwhile, pleasure from the GSpot is supplied by the larger pelvic and parasympathetic nerves, and generally comes through relaxation in unending waves, rather than piercing peaks.

GSpot sensation can be very intense!

For many women, the GSpot still remains an unknown experience, and takes a greater level of self-awareness and even self-acceptance to awaken.

It's part of a woman's emotional body, and one of the major energy centres in her body. Experiencing it can bring a pleasure or emotional intensity that's unexpected or even frightening. But with knowledge and practice, a woman (either by herself or with a trusted lover) will find that awakening this centre allows her to access new levels of satisfaction that go a long way toward fulfilling the intense emotional longings and frustrations that she usually hopes her partner can fulfil for her.

How to awaken a GSpot

Keep your attention firmly on this part of your body. Breathe deeply, relax and feel without expectations. Just honour whatever comes up.

Insert one or two fingers facing upwards into your Yoni, with plenty of lubrication (or alternatively, ask your partner to do this, or use a GSpot vibe or a crystal wand). Move your fingers in past your pubic bone, rest your finger against the vaginal wall and see if you can "feel" a connection with your GSpot. Then pull them backwards in a 'come hither' movement until you feel a response. If you feel like you need to pee, you've found it! This is because the urethral sponge the GSpot lies within actually surrounds the urethra. Just breathe and relax until it starts to feel pleasurable.

Then tap or vibrate your internal finger gently, make more 'come hither' movements, or move your finger side to side like a window washer. Start slowly in the beginning, as your sensations may come and go. Alternate active touch with holding in stillness, or you'll scare it away. Squeezing your PC muscles (the muscles between your legs that you feel when you try to stop the flow of urine) will help to move the spot onto your fingers.

As you do this, get to know your GSpot's size, shape and moods: it can generally take much more pressure than your clitoris. Once it's warmed up, you can try my personal favourite: with your lover's finger on your GSpot, have him rest the palm of his hand on your clitoris. Then, with a *relaxed* arm, have him vibrate his arm, hand and finger rapidly side to side, sending delicious energy through both these areas at the same time – it's a winner!

Once your GSpot is awakened, you'll feel it more pleasurably in lovemaking too, especially with shallow penetration, being on top, with a pillow under your butt or in rear entry position.

Some of the reasons your GSpot can still be missing in action:

- You can miss your GSpot completely when it's not aroused, because it feels almost flat. If you can't feel it, know you definitely have one – just believe in it, visualise it, relax and keep touching. It takes time. Your lover can place the fingers of his other hand just above your pubic bone (on the outside), then press down with his fingers to help him anchor the spot between his fingers inside and out.
- GSpot arousal can be short circuited by focussing entirely on clitoral orgasm. It's best to build stimulation in your clitoris but stop short of orgasm, then begin to focus on the different sensations and possibilities in the GSpot.
- Whole-body tension is another short circuit. Often a woman will tense her body to create a clitoral orgasm, which is the opposite of what the GSpot requires. So, when you feel arousal happening, remember to relax, let your muscles go and deepen your breathing.
- Doing too much too soon can also short circuit your GSpot. It needs awakening, not just stimulating. It needs you to listen to it and hear its voice, rather than overriding it with a mental need for orgasm. Allow yourself a good **20 minutes** for your GSpot to come out to play.
- Finally, weak and/or tense PC muscles around the GSpot can short circuit it. These muscles can suffer from either lack of use or over-strain. Squeezing/releasing relaxed but toned PC muscles will stimulate your GSpot.

Your Pelvic Floor: Your Gateway to Greater Pleasure

You probably associate your pelvic floor with exercises to improve your bladder control post baby, or to increase your partner's pleasure. But your pelvic floor is also a strong barometer of your feminine well-being, and a pleasure pump for YOU! These muscles are the ones that contract in orgasm, and women commonly hold their fear, tension and sexual resistance in them. Getting to know them helps you to release their tension, increase tone and sexual lubrication, all whilst maximising *your* pleasure.

> ***Toning Your Pelvic Floor***
>
> 1. Imagine letting your pelvic floor relax like chocolate melting in the sun. Do this often, especially if your pelvic floor is tense. If this is the case, practice relaxing these muscles for a few weeks before you start any contractions.
> 2. Gently squeeze and release the outer ring of muscle at the entrance ten times
> 3. Repeat the squeeze, but this time include deeper layers by imagining you're using the muscles up inside you to 'sip' as you'd sip a thickshake up a straw. Sip, sip, sip. Hold in as long as you can, then relax fully, melting your muscles as did before. Start doing three repetitions, and build up till you can hold for 30 seconds.
> 4. Add your breath, inhaling and exhaling through your mouth, in time with moving your muscles.

Your GSpot's emotional life

- Sometimes a GSpot feels totally numb, so you might think it doesn't work and give up. Instead, what's really happening is that it's probably emotionally numb. With attention and love it can be fully activated, so keep practising and trust the process will work.

- Overusing a vibrator can either short circuit sensation by being too much too soon, or toughen and numb the spot, reducing its sensitivity. You can resolve this with sensitive massage as above.

- Sometimes your GSpot may be painful when touched, and it's easier to avoid it. This pain will be old, stored, unexpressed emotion from unhelpful sexual beliefs and experiences from the past. With loving attention, deep breathing, and making sounds, these past hurts can be released.

  As your GSpot is an emotional energy centre the feelings it arouses can be unfamiliar and intense. Understand that these emotions are an important part of who you are, and an energy that will become pleasurable when you accept it. Allow yourself to just feel or express any emotions that arise. Breathe into your heart and bring love into your GSpot. To fully experience your GSpot, you need to trust your body, and surrender into your sensations, letting go into them with every exhalation.

- Your GSpot may have a minimal nerve supply, in which case it needs to be trained to be responsive. All the same techniques above apply.

The fear of ejaculation

Ejaculate is the fluid that can be expelled from your urethral sponge or prostate gland when your GSpot is aroused.

Because little is known about female ejaculation, both women and their partners can view it with fear and shame as urine. However, it has a different chemical composition, smell and taste from urine. It's believed to help lubricate the urethra from the acidity of urine, reducing infections and sweetening the acidic environment of the Yoni to enhance sperm survival.

A woman often holds back in fear of 'wetting herself', but it's very difficult for her to pee when she's highly aroused, just as it is for a man when he has an erection. Her arousal tissues swell around her vagina and urethra, cutting off access to her bladder higher up and opening the para-urethral tubules that lie inside her urethral sponge just near the entrance of her urethra.

Ejaculation can happen with, or separately from orgasm. In Tantra, ejaculate is known as Amrita, the nectar of love, and is seen as a gift from God and letting go of Amrita leaves a woman and her partner feeling renewed.

The ASpot and the Cervix

Your GSpot is not the only area of interest inside your Yoni. Others include:

- *Your PSpot (urethral sponge or prostate gland),* which is linked to your clitoris but is that spongy area inside your vagina, just before your pubic bone. This is often confused with your Gspot, which is the energy point that lies within it. It can be aroused like your clitoris, though often with a firmer touch.
- *Your ASpot*, which is located the front wall of your vagina, right at the very end next to your cervix. You approach it the same way as your GSpot, just further in.
- *Your cervix itself,* which you can gently massage too, either with your fingers, a dildo or your lover's Lingam (the Sanskrit word for penis). Massage with slow, rhythmic movements over a long time, up to **40-45 mins.**

  The cervix is energetically connected to your heart, and if you have a deep level of trust in yourself and your partner, profoundly heart-opening experiences can come from here as well.

You can find each of these spots through gentle finger massage, or through slow, deep penetration.

Like with the GSpot, putting your mind's attention on each spot and feeling into it will help. These spots are better found when you're highly aroused, once the round ligament has pulled your uterus (and therefore your cervix) out of the way so that any vigorous penetration won't bang on the cervix itself (ouch!) but instead on a receptive bundle of nerves that was just *made* for the purpose. Massaging above your pubic area as part of your love-play not only feels good, but it also encourages this ligament to tighten.

Where You Start is Not Where You Finish

There are a multitude of 'spots' in a woman's body to explore. Your whole body can be an arousal zone. The more you take the time to explore, the more you'll awaken to new areas of pleasure. You can even build new neural and energy networks to experience pleasure in ways and places you've never have before, eg expanding from your clit to your GSpot or vice versa.

Just because you've always done things a certain way doesn't mean you can't build new areas of pleasure. And if at first you find no response, keep trying with the understanding that it takes time to build new connections. Play between the old and the new. Your interest in your own arousal will spur on your lover to join you in the search. And remember that from little things, big things grow. Appreciating every little moment of pleasure along the way will help more arise. Trust that it is there. Validate and appreciate yourself, and your fulfilment will match.

Being Empowered

The bedroom is not the place for a woman to play quiet. I'm not saying you have to show up in black leather with a whip (unless this is your bent) or do all the work for your lover. But you can do much for yourself that isn't about pushing yourself, performing or giving and that comes from a place of self-love.

Remember that you're a beautiful, powerful woman who's much stronger and more capable than you've ever dreamed. If you think this feels like hard work, ask yourself how much do you really value your pleasure? How much do you value yourself?

Taking charge in this way is stepping from the role of Princess to Goddess. Studies have shown that the closer a woman comes to orgasm, the more her capacity to regulate her behaviour deactivates, her judgement suspends, and her inner 'wild woman' is released. (Not wild, as in 'out of control', but rather fully alive and powerfully authentic). Along with this comes freedom from pain and access to altered states of consciousness.

That's well worth the effort of getting there, don't you think? And inviting your man along for the journey will create a connection between you that's second to none.

If you're feeling stuck

Taking risks is a direct route to opening up something new. Think about what risks you could take to get sexually energised and interested again. Remember: when you want to be desired, desire yourself first.

So, when you want to feel more connected with your lover, connect *with yourself first* via your ABC, which will automatically enhance your connection with your lover. When you want to be touched, touch yourself and feel your lusciousness. When you want to be kissed, sensually imagine the desire arising in your mouth and spreading through your body. Kiss your lover from this place or simply surrender to enjoying it in yourself. If you want to be touched a certain way, start it yourself and your lover will be inspired to follow.

The old saying goes 'If you want the same results, keep doing the same things!' If you *don't* want the same results, perhaps the risk you take might be:

- buying and using a vibrator
- wearing a skirt without knickers
- telling your lover one of your desires
- ask your heart, where are you resisting letting your man in to you?
- self-pleasuring by yourself or in front of your lover

- flirting with your lover (or the guy at work)
- reading some erotic literature (or having your lover read it to you)
- practising with a Jade Egg
- having a full body massage
- asking your lover to explore your GSpot
- surrendering more deeply into yourself and what lies within you; imagining the feminine power inside you; feeling and expressing it through your body – it might be water, flow, fire, mystery or darkness
- going to a Tantric workshop.

Can you give yourself permission to go there? Provided you do any of these things from a place of self-respect, good things will come from it.

What Does All This Mean if You're a Man?

Supporting your woman in exploring her sexuality is one of the most loving and highly sexual things you can do for her. Your reward is likely to be what you most desire in her: a woman with incredible beauty and an awesome sexuality. But bear in mind that a GSpot orgasm is not another goal for a woman to reach, just as ejaculation is not a 'party trick' to perform on demand. Both are a gift from her feminine soul.

Supporting your woman is about connecting with yourself and being fully present with both her and yourself. Your masculine energy on her 'spots' is extra powerful in the awakening process. Aim to be of service rather than to know it all, following her instructions (and my suggestions).

Read this chapter thoroughly and hear where she's going to be coming from. *Be willing to take your time with her*, as this is *incredibly* healing for her. Occasionally just want to hold her. Get grounded and in your heart through your ABC process so you can stay present in the face of whatever may come – fear, anger, shame, grief or multiple orgasms – and know that they're all part of opening her up to greater pleasure, self-love, and openness to you.

The art of being the ultimate lover lies firstly in being grounded and connected in yourself and then believing in her power and supporting her in discovering it for herself.

The Benefits of your Sexual Discovery

Your exploration of your sexuality will be unique to you. What I've learned is that my Yoni teaches me to care for and nurture myself. It's taught me to open where I was closed, and let go where there was hurt. It's taught me that in opening my heart to my lover with abandon and trust, I could be safe – not always without hurt, but OK.

I've learned that I can experience unlimited pleasure and unlimited love that feels like an expansion and freedom inside me, and flows effortlessly through me to and from my lover. I'm not playing out a role, I am whatever arises naturally from within me at the time: surrendered, loving, gentle, playful, emotional, wild, lustful, naughty, wanton, filled with passion or experiencing extraordinary spiritual realities. I honour each and invite you to do the same for your own.

There's no longer any paradox for me in my sexual self. I can be good and bad (sometimes at the same time!) without shame or limitation. I can now love deeply, letting Graeme in without losing myself, and this is still growing. This flows into the 'me' I am in my relationship, benefitting all areas of my life, where I'm more whole, open, empowered and loving.

I believe this is the ultimate gift that sex has for a woman – that of finding herself without games.

Further reading:

- http://www.oztantra.com/gspot-oztantra/
- http://www.oztantra.com/painful-sex/
- http://www.isismedia.org/ with Deboah Sundahl for everything you need to know about your GSpot.

- http://laylamartin.com/for Jade egg info
- DVD: http://www.theartandscienceoffemalearousal.com/
- Book: Woman's Anatomy of Arousal by Sheri Winston
- Book: Wild Feminine by Tami Lynn Kent

7.3 Actually, Men DON'T Want Just Sex (by Graeme)

All men are capable of experiencing much greater sexual pleasure and satisfaction than they have ever imagined. Experiencing this pleasure requires accessing much more of what you, and also your partner, are seeking in sex. Accessing this will bring an end to your loneliness by creating a deep connection with yourself and your woman. As an added bonus, it will bring you freedom from the need to continually perform, plus relief from that old chestnut, cultural sexual shame, that men carry collectively.

All this is possible for you if you're willing to take a fresh look at what happens for you in the bedroom.

After coming to terms with my own sexual abuse and exploring sexuality both in my own life and then in my work with men through Oztantra, I believe that most men achieve only around 10% of their capacity for pleasure in sex.

Sex surveys show that the average length of time for sexual penetration (the standard measure of a man's sexual satisfaction) is around six to seven minutes. This is much, much less than what's possible. And most of these surveys don't even consider the amount of actual pleasure that man can experience. I believe we don't even have a language yet for fully understanding the male sexual experience.

> *"Understanding how men think and why they do what they do is not as simple as popular 'wisdom' suggests. Men are neither all the same, nor do they want all the same things. As an escort, I learned to empty my mind of assumptions and focus on the man in front of me, taking him as a unique individual."*
>
> Sex Secrets of Escorts, Veronica Monet

This disparity can also be applied to women and their sexuality; but in many ways, women have made more significant moves forward. And whilst they still have a long way to go, it's time for men to start their own sexual revolution. Having both sexes moving forward will not only remove this gap, but it will also resolve the ongoing frustrations in both male/female sexual experiences.

Misdirected Sex Education

Much male sex education has been about becoming a better lover for your partner by focusing on pleasing her and holding back, thus numbing or otherwise diminishing your pleasure. There's very little, if any, focus on increasing your own capacity for pleasure and achieving deeper satisfaction during sex, which is why sex education for men hasn't worked.

So, at some level, even though you know how much you love to give and see your woman experiencing pleasure, you feel left out. Your benchmark of success is measured by her pleasure. I regularly find that when a man gives himself permission to fully experience his own pleasure, he's pleasantly surprised and in awe of its potential. This significantly reduces the pressure he feels to perform and focus on end results. He no longer needs to 'disappear' in his pleasure, but can show up and share it fully with his partner, bringing them closer together in a way that was unimaginable before. In this space, his heart is open beyond anything either of them thought was previously possible.

You've probably been 'doing it in a hurry' for most of your sex life

- Historically, sex had to be quick in case a wild animal, or neighbouring tribe, came along to disturb your procreation of the species
- As a boy, your masturbation needed to be quick and furtive to avoid the shame of getting caught (and because getting to the end felt so good)
- The same was true with your sexual exploration in adolescence
- During the brief time of honeymoon sex, you might have played with lasting longer
- The next stage was having sex quickly before the kids woke up, your partner changed her mind, or you fell asleep after a hard day's work
- And, as you get older you hurry before losing your erection!

So, in all these cases, you've been left not knowing what is possible.

Managing to ride the bucking bronco

You've also probably, like most men, felt a degree of confusion over the intensity and power of your sexual energy, and how to manage this potent pressure coursing through your body. This goes all the way back to those unpredictable moments with embarrassing 'woodies' in your speedos, or having an erection on the school bus from seeing that attractive girl walking past you on the street. This confusion is why a man will often emotionally disconnect from himself, bypass his heart and disappear into sexual gratification. It moves him out of his intense feelings and back into the safety of his more familiar emptiness.

And if you're a man who *doesn't* have intense sexual energy that's continually ready to go, you probably carry shame about NOT being like this. It's hard to admit that you're just as happy with a kiss and a cuddle as a with sexual marathon.

There IS another way...

Remember your best orgasm ever, then multiply this pleasurable feeling of intensity by up to 10 times, and imagine holding this feeling for as long as you want... And this can be before you start making love, or even having an erection! Ask yourself too, what it would be like to get to your point of 'no return', and instead of automatically ejaculating, choosing to have your deeply pleasurable orgasm as many times as you desired. You could ejaculate later on, if you chose, but you didn't need to.

This is not an urban myth: it's what all men are capable of.

This is what men can achieve. If you're trigger-sensitive, feel numb or have erectile issues, you're still capable of feeling this much pleasure. Even after prostate surgery, much is still possible for you...

What are the benefits of improving your sex life?

Besides the obvious pleasure, the benefits of creating a more satisfying sex life exist not only in the bedroom, but also range from the clubroom to the boardroom and everywhere in between. You'll find yourself with greater self-confidence, increased self-worth and decreased stress levels – with all the related health benefits. Not to mention, you'll also have a happier, more exciting relationship.

Do men want just sex?

OK, I agree that the majority of men – including me – have earned this judgment of just wanting sex, and we've been unfeeling fuckers for generations.

7: Sexeptance

*Women need romance, foreplay and heart connection.
Men only need a time and a place.*

There are reasons for this, but there are really no excuses. For years we've lived from our patriarchal conditioning: being a man's man, earning a living and providing for our families, and having sex when we can get it. Only when we come home to find a note on the table from our recently departed spouse saying 'I just don't love you anymore' do we get the chance to ask questions about ourselves.

Luckily, this conditioning is changing – but most men are still controlled by it to some degree.

Sensitive men

Of course, not all men fit the macho image mentioned above. If you don't, understand that even if this stereotype feels totally foreign, you still have much to gain from using the sexual practices I suggest in this section. They'll help you to define your masculine identity from within, rather than according to any external stereotype.

Men DO Want Heart-Connected Sex

If I give a man a safe space to talk about sex, I've found the common perception that he 'only wants sex' is mistaken. Most men do seek intimacy and heart connection as well. They might seek it through sex, but they're still seeking it. What a man wants most is a space where sex (and he himself) is valued enough to talk about.

If not now, then later

In his early years, a man's sexual desire is driven more by his hormonal urges. As he gets older his drive diminishes, he feels less excitement, and his erections become less reliable. This is the 'mid life crisis stage' that most men experience to some degree. If he's smart he'll start looking for more understanding than he's had before about sex. If he's *not* smart, he'll keep trying to recreate the past by looking outside of himself for the answer. This is the stereotypical guy with a forever-new younger woman, lots of porn, a new sports car, Harley Davidson or anything else to replace what's lacking inside him.

Relationship Sex is the Best Sex

Despite the fantasy of a hot mistress or casual hook-up, a man's intensely pleasurable sexual potential is best achieved and maintained in a committed, healthy, long-term relationship. This is because for a man to tap into his full sexual potential, he requires more than just a few new tricks. Instead, he'll find his answers deep inside himself.

This takes time, emotional awareness, heart connection and courage, yet the benefits are huge.

Learning something different

My approach to male sexuality within a relationship is about showing you how to take control of, deepen and significantly increase your access to the other 90% of your sexual pleasure. In doing so, you'll learn to last longer, feel more, and find yourself more focused on relaxing and feeling. You'll surf the waves of unimaginable sexual pleasure, and discover that real pleasure comes from having *more* sensitivity rather than less during lovemaking. You'll also understand that men who are trigger-sensitive (having premature ejaculation) actually have a gift, as they're very close to achieving those amazing levels of pleasure.

Your relationship with sex will change as you become more connected to your heart, to yourself, and to a love that's indescribably powerful, nurturing and rejuvenating. Sexual connection will no longer be just putting your body inside your partner's. It will be a place of rawness, softness (that isn't weakness) and depth that's impossible to put into words. Through feeling sexually connected and fulfilled (rather than just spent), your heart will open and become vulnerable, yet powerful and readily accessible to those around you.

Boys, feeling and intimacy

The way men are conditioned to make love starts early. Boys are generally touched and hugged less than girls, and almost all touch stops at an earlier age. They're conditioned then taught the right way to be 'manly' from a very early age: how to be tough, unfeeling and not show any emotion. This will massacre any man's capacity for pleasure.

They soon learn to view 'coming' as a fast way to relieve the pressure of their unfelt feelings, both sexual and emotional. They then carry this method of 'stress release' into adulthood. Their unfamiliarity with intimacy, emotions and being vulnerable interferes with their capacity for leisurely, pleasurable and fully satisfying lovemaking.

> *"There are many times when a man wants nothing more than to be held or comforted. But he can't get it. He can't admit his feelings and he can't ask to be held. And that is very sad."*
>
> The New Male Sexuality, Bernie Zilbergeld

Men are also conditioned to cut off from their bodies and not trust their feelings, living more in the safety of their heads. The only socially acceptable way for a man to feel powerful is through actions such as aggression, achievement, success or power over someone or something. Men are especially not taught to express anger in a healthy way, so they suppress it – and then it most often seeps out as aggression and violence.

Men and Shame

> *"Shame (for men) is being wrong. Not doing it wrong, but being wrong."*
>
> Daring Greatly, Brene Brown

The way a man is expected to feel *is* through his sexuality. Yet he's caught in a bind: to feel sexual is to feel 'wrong', because sex itself is seen as wrong. Every time a man proposes sex, he steps into a place of shadow and shame to do so, which is why being rejected sexually is doubly powerful for him.

Additionally, the way he feels sexual in his relationship is conditioned to look a certain way, where he must be focussed on his woman or he's being selfish leaving little space for his raw, primal lust. Even in this day and age, men carry a lot of shame and guilt around their masculine identity and sexuality.

Many men also carry subconscious guilt and shame about the rape and violence committed by other men throughout the history of mankind. Their use of porn increases this emotional bind because of the shame energy it carries. It's a big part of the reason a man will visit a sex worker, even though he may have a loving wife at home – the sex worker often validates this shamed part of themselves.

Men's sexual shadow

Much of men's shadow behaviour in sex emerges from being unaware of their buried emotional hurts. They unconsciously project their hurt outwards into the behaviours that push their women away. These behaviours range from being emotionally unavailable, shaming, overriding her needs, disappearing in sex or just disappearing, all the way up to physical or sexual abuse. Or, a man might manipulate his woman into giving him what he thinks he wants, or focus on being a good lover for her, all while denying the deeper connection with himself.

"I couldn't feel so I tried to touch."

Hallelujah, Leonard Cohen

Men's Inner Warrior

What helps a man to find the courage to go into the vulnerable, feeling part of himself where truly great sex lives is what I call his Inner Warrior. This is an essential part of every man's heart and his sexuality, yet it's one that's intensely shamed in our modern culture.

As society has become more civilised, the term 'warrior' has received a bad rap. I see the masculine Inner Warrior as being of pure heart, as evidenced in times past when men defended their homes and families in up-close-and-personal battles. In those times, each man relied on what he could access within himself – his deeply personal feeling or soul connection – to both defend and survive. This is depicted beautifully in Tom Cruise's movie *The Last Samurai*. And in my work with Annette, we validate this aspect of a man in every sense of the word.

A man's Warrior in shadow is without heart. It's war-mongering, mindless destruction, competition and selfishness – as seen in news media stories about the abuse of power, money and sex. But equally, shutting down his Inner Warrior results in him losing direction, empowerment, passion and compassion.

Not the Marlboro Man

A man who's connected with his Inner Warrior will stand up and protect his heart, himself, his family, his community and his place in this world. In this age of political correctness, it takes real courage to be your own man, whatever this looks like for you, rather than be a cardboard copy of The Marlboro Man. It requires you to challenge your own – and often your partner's – beliefs, along with societal norms about how you should be.

When this part of you is activated, you'll begin to feel your true power. It's not about having to run through the forest with a spear, but recognising and owning both your heart intensity and your sexual power. It's similar to a martial arts expert who carries his power within him without needing to use it, though all around him can feel and respect it. Making love from this place is like nothing else: you're fully in your power, feeling it surging through your body, or simply being in quietness and stillness.

A well-known Warrior

A well-known, healthy masculine Warrior was Nelson Mandela, who endured years of persecution and incarceration, never wavering from his beliefs, but keeping his heart open to end the ugliness of apartheid. And by all accounts, his sexuality was alive and well up to the end of his life.

Becoming Your Own Inner Warrior

Our world desperately needs more heart-connected men. Breaking the destructive cycle of masculine disconnection happens through supporting men in their journey of self-discovery by:

- *Validating their masculine heart, emotionality and heart-connected sexuality*. Annette and I see men melt into this place over and over again when they're simply given permission.

- *Connecting with other men in a healthy masculine space*. It takes a healthy masculine community to create a healthy masculine man. It's up to men to take responsibility for their actions and create change – either with other men, or on their own until they find them. Even if it's just taking the time to ask the men you meet "How are you going?" and really listen for the answer, you'll be surprised at the response.

- *Regularly grounding and connecting to yourself through the ABC practice*.

- *Making the shift from tension-release sex to more pleasurable, expansive lovemaking*.

Surfing the Edge in Expansive Lovemaking

Pleasure from ejaculation feels pretty damn good, but it's actually a separate experience from your orgasmic pleasure. Did you know that ejaculation and orgasm are two separate functions? Just because both usually happen at the same time doesn't mean they're the same thing.

Men who ejaculate a lot *only* experience their ejaculation, not orgasm. They may also feel limited amount of orgasmic pleasure, but it's still only a very small percentage (perhaps 10%) of their orgasmic pleasure potential.

Ejaculation is the primal rush and release of semen, while orgasm is the pleasurable heat and peak of tingling sensation that accompanies it. After ejaculating, you're generally finished – unless you're young enough, or inspired enough to ejaculate more than once. But through learning to 'surf your edge' by identifying and expanding your orgasmic potential, you'll be able to have as many orgasms as you want, whilst meeting your partner in her passion and expansion fully.

And you can do this without the 'down' after ejaculation: it's that good, satisfying and complete. Or if you choose to ejaculate afterwards, it won't leave you with the same level of 'down' – instead, your full-body pleasure will leave you 'high' for days.

In the beginning, it can be a struggle to achieve pleasure separate from ejaculation. It can feel like you're giving up your ultimate moment in sex – but this is actually an illusion that comes from your primal and cultural conditioning.

How to have your cake and eat it too

This section will show you how to identify the sexual energy (your sexual pleasure) that exists in your body and that you were born with. Then it will show you how you can *go further into* and expand your pleasure *while you last*, rather than giving it up.

Imagine your ejaculation pleasure – the pleasure that feels like an intense heat and a primal desire to fuck – as the fire under your pot of boiling water. Your orgasmic pleasure is the tingling, expanding feeling that bubbles up like the water inside that pot.

You can learn to get your fire going (ejaculation energy), and then enjoy endlessly bubbling water – either bubbling higher or simmering – by managing the amount of wood you put on your fire. Each time you increase the heat (orgasmic energy), you can reduce the amount of wood on the fire and still retain the heat in the room (your body). Your potential beyond this point is not only limitless pleasure, but a life-changing experience of connection that's well worth the effort of exploration.

Men's Ultimate Challenge

Imagine making love like this, with your Lingam (the Sanskrit word for your penis or cock – it literally means 'Wand of Light', so yes guys – you have a lightsabre between your legs!), energised and feeling. Imagine your Lingam joining together with your partner in penetration, rather than *simply taking* from her. Imagine being able to really feel inside your lover and bring more energy to *all* the pleasure spots, bringing both of you alive with love and connection.

Sex like this lives inside of you, rather than in the hottest babe or the best technique - and it gets better with age, rather than worse.

BUT there is a condition attached to this type of sex, and it's non-negotiable. To move away from performance and go into your deeper, full bodied pleasure, you *must* open to and connect with your heart. Feeling and connecting with your heart creates fuel for sexual intensity and unlimited pleasure in lovemaking.

You'll find this heart connection in staying present with the intensity of vulnerability and feeling that arises just prior to ejaculation. Most men miss it because they escape into coming.

This is not about giving your heart away to your lover and losing yourself. It's about experiencing your heart opening in a way that allows you more loving sexual power, centred within yourself. It's about becoming softer inside and harder where it counts, rather than the other way around.

What Can Men Do for Themselves?

So what do you do if you don't totally focus on your lover, try to hold off from coming, or really go for your last few seconds of pleasure? The following outline will dramatically increase your capacity for pleasure in sex and help to open your heart. You can take a few or all of these steps towards greater sexual understanding and fulfilment. How far you choose is up to you, though each step will bring you something worthwhile.

Being selfish in sex

You can start by being more selfish in sex – and I bet you've never been told that before! Equally, I can assure you that it's not easy for many men to do. Being selfish doesn't mean taking what you want and disappearing. Instead, it means being centred in yourself, focused on experiencing your own body, your sensations and your heart, and moving towards your lover from there.

The more you feel yourself, the more your partner will feel you, and the more the sexual energy will flow between you without needing to be hooked into any performance or agenda. Bringing this into your lovemaking practice will support your woman in surrendering to herself, probably in a way that neither of you have experienced before. And it's a way that makes her infinitely desirable to you as well.

Being selfish includes finding the clarity and focus to manage this energy into full-bodied pleasure. Seeing your ejaculation as giving all of yourself

– all of your heart and the force within you, which has the awesome power to create new life. It also includes holding yourself in this place of vulnerability to wholly meet your partner in lovemaking. You can most unreservedly satisfy your lover, not by relying on the right 'techniques', but by becoming most fully yourself. Annette and I call this 'man's final frontier'. Again, the more you're aware of and can feel yourself in sexual space, the more your partner can feel you. If *you* can't feel you, neither can she, and this is what I mean by being selfish.

Getting down to the how

1. Choose to believe you're worthy as a person, even without having any external goals to achieve.

2. Know your pleasure is just as vital to lovemaking as your lover's, and that you can feel pleasure the whole way through, not just at the end.

3. Trust that the more of yourself you feel, the more your partner will feel of you, and that this is what she wants. If she doesn't, know that it's about her, and is most likely her own fear of vulnerability and opening her heart. Don't let it stop you from leading the way and using this as a new beginning in connection.

4. Make your goal one of getting present and connected with yourself and understanding your pleasure. Start with understanding what your genitals look like.

7: Sexeptance

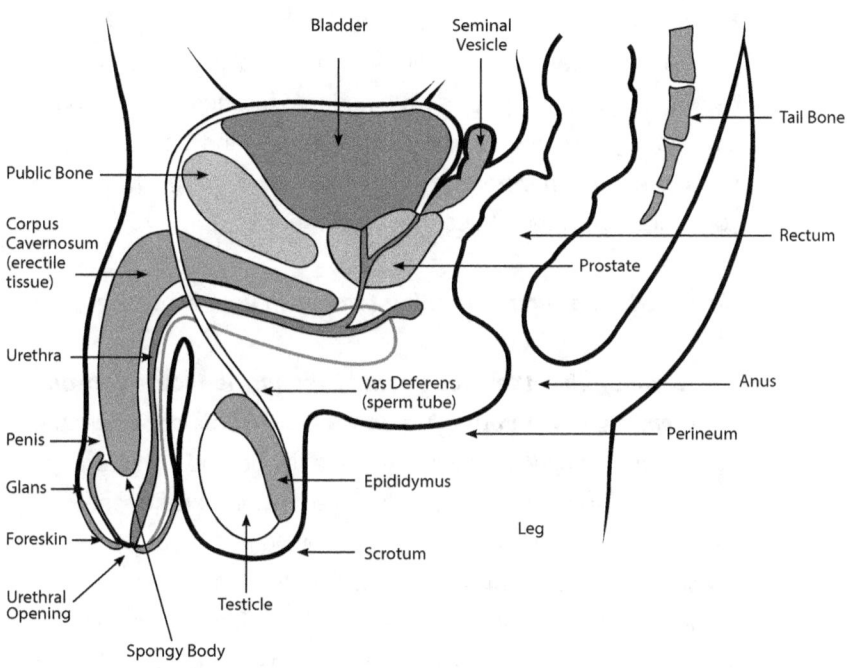

Diagram 7.3 Male Genitalia

Sexual Energy Mastery Level 1

Learn what you're actually feeling in sex

1. ***The next few times you're being sexual, enjoy the visuals and the touching; but also take note of what you're actually feeling within you.*** What are you feeling, and where in your body are you feeling it? There can be physical sensations, eg heat or tingling, but also more emotional feelings. This is about discovering your own unique internal sexual landscape.

2. ***Notice what's happening with your breathing.*** Where do you hold your breath? See if you can deepen it in those places instead.

3. ***Notice whether you're holding tension in your body.*** If so, use your breath to relax it.

4. ***If you recognise that your sexual feeling is located in one spot, simply close your eyes and feel into this spot***. Breathe deeply, and notice the feeling expand. Notice how this energy then moves in your body. You can also expand and direct your sexual energy by focusing on it and moving it around.

5. ***Practise being present in your own body***. Focus your attention *inside of yourself* until you become aware of first your own body, and then your lover's. Self-pleasuring (masturbating) with your 'other' hand on your heart is great to help you learn this.

6. ***Touch your own Lingam at times to connect with yourself and your own feelings.*** You don't have to wait for your lover to do this. Touching yourself during sexual intimacy with another person helps you to stay connected within yourself. Mix up touching your own body with touching theirs until you really get this. With practice, it will become effortless.

7. ***BREATHE more deeply and slowly.*** Mouth breathe (especially when you exhale).

8. ***Slow down.*** Be more in the moment, and feel yourself both sexually and emotionally.

9. **Practice your ABC.** This will help you to get comfortable with feeling your emotional realms.

Once you've managed this, you'll have the skill to actually be in your body, in the moment, when you're being sexual. You'll also establish a level of understanding about how your body usually works, which is essential before taking it to the next level.

 Sexual Energy Mastery Level 2

Separating ejaculation and orgasm

This is a *beginning practice* that helps to practise ejaculation delay, separate your ejaculation from your orgasmic energy, and increase full-body, heart-connected pleasure. You can invite your partner to share this with you later, but it's important to practise it through self-pleasuring on your own first. Use a long-lasting lube or coconut oil.

1. **Centre into your body with your ABC and some deep belly breaths, exhaling out through your mouth.** Feel your body relaxing and drop inside it. Let go of any external fantasies or thoughts, and just be here now. Continue this through your session. Make occasional eye contact if you're with your partner.

    It's not a good idea to use porn here, as your focus will be on the image. This will take you outside of yourself: the opposite of what we're going for.

2. **Start stroking your Lingam slowly at first.** Then use a basic gripping touch to stroke firmer and faster as your energy builds.

3. **Notice where you are on an arousal scale of 1-10, where 1 is just starting to get an erection and 10 is about to go over the edge into orgasm.** When you're at 6, pause and take three or four strong, deep belly breaths, breathing out from the back of your throat. Remember to let your body relax as you exhale. This will spread your sexual energy (the expansive heat and tingling)

through your body, which will reduce your need to come, and will open your heart. In turn, this will begin to separate your pleasure from the need to come. If you're still feeling this need, focus on breathing and spreading your energy.

4. **If you do this correctly, you'll notice a shift in your arousal away from your Lingam.** Your arousal will go back to at most a 4, and you'll feel your erection soften slightly. When this happens, start building your arousal up again. Keep repeating – each time you pause and breathe, you're moving towards full-bodied pleasure as your subtle orgasmic energy becomes more obvious.

If the shift in your arousal doesn't happen, take a couple more breaths. Imagine a channel between your genitals and your heart. Feel/see the heat of your arousal moving up that channel to your heart, and spreading out to the rest of your body. You can use your other hand to stroke up your body from your Lingam to your heart to help activate this shift and move the energy up.

5. **Repeat as desired.** To help build your arousal more quickly, you can stroke more firmly or add short sharp breaths and/or quick pelvic floor squeezes. Rocking your hips will also help to build and spread your energy. Play with your own combination as you go up and down your arousal scale.

Your Pelvic Floor: Your Gateway to Greater Pleasure

Your pelvic floor is the sling of muscles between the front and rear of your pelvis. Lying directly between your legs, these muscles help you to choke off a fart, and stop the flow of your urine.

You've probably heard that pelvic floor exercises can improve the strength of your erections. They can also increase your pleasure, as they surround your prostate – the seat of your sexual pleasure. Contracting and then relaxing these muscles at different times will enhance and spread your pleasure.

Practice: Toning your pelvic floor

1. **First identify the muscles correctly.** Stand up and point your toes inward so they meet each other (this stops you from involving your buttock muscles). Gently squeeze and release your pelvic floor muscles ten times.
2. **Slowly build up until you can hold the squeeze for 30 seconds.**
3. **Add your breath.** Inhale as you contract your pelvic floor muscles, hold your breath as you hold the contraction, and then exhale through your mouth as you relax them.
4. **Totally relax.** To know what this feels like, stand out on the back lawn one night with your hands behind your head. Exhale whilst fully relaxing your pelvic floor muscles and letting all your urine drain out until your bladder is empty. The aim here is to identify and practise your relaxing skill without squeezing.

Now you've had a taste of moving your sexual energy through your body and learning to enhance it with your pelvic floor. You may also have had some experiences of orgasm that are separate to ejaculation, or at least some feelings that are totally out of the ordinary and good enough that you want more – despite the fact that you're not heading straight for the goal line.

This will stand you in good stead for the multiple orgasm practices that come next (if you'll pardon the pun!)

 ### Sexual Energy Mastery Level 3

Building your orgasmic pleasure

1. **With practice, you can surf closer to your edge – 8, 9, 9.5, 9.75 and even 10 – and still maintain choice over ejaculating.** As you get closer to 10, drop your energy back by **totally relaxing** your pelvic floor muscles. The more intense your pleasure is (especially if you're trigger-sensitive), the more this momentary relaxation will take you back from your edge.

This is about keeping your intensity, and instead of ejaculating, moving your energy away from your Lingam and bringing it up into your body, especially around your heart. Your awesome multi-orgasmic potential kicks in at your 10 if you can avoid ejaculating.

2. **Then you can concentrate on building your orgasmic energy.** By this time, it should have moved to 10 or beyond on your arousal scale. Alternately squeezing then relaxing your pelvic floor will build your energy, and deep breathing and rocking your hips will focus your orgasmic energy into orgasms. This is very subtle at first, but with awareness and practice, it can become your new normal. You may find your orgasms blending into one long, continuous orgasm.

3. **You will notice your orgasmic heat and tingling moving up along your spine.** If you become aware of your physical response as you alternate PC squeezing with relaxing (especially focusing on the relaxing) you'll notice how this moves your intensity away from your genitals and into full-body pleasure.

    The intensity may also move around your ribs to your heart, up along the back of your neck, and even over the crown of your head and back down the front of your body. If your energy is really running, rotate your ankles or lift up your toes every now and again to keep yourself grounded. Moving your hips and being seen in your sexual vulnerability like this really increases your heart connection.

4. **In the beginning, you'll notice more pressure to ejaculate.** Over time, this intensity will steady, especially as you focus your awareness on the shift in energy flow between squeezing and releasing. Most men are conditioned to ejaculate, so don't give up if you're feeling challenged in learning these new skills. You'll have more orgasmic energy in your whole body: the squeezes will increase your energy and relaxing will spread it though your whole body. You'll feel relaxed and aroused at the same time.

7: Sexeptance

> Once your ejaculation energy feels under control, you can mentally decide to bring it up into your orgasmic energy as you breathe to intensify its heat, like putting more wood on the fire. Then you'll be able to mentally put it aside until you desire it again. In this way, you can control the amount of pleasure you experience.
>
> You'll find yourself going through different phases in your practice: intensity, relaxation, shaking, stillness, expansion, love, a primal 'I want to fuck you' feeling, and more.
>
> Enjoy it all.

"A man who exercises this kind of sexual control often seems to give the woman freedom to finally lose control of herself. Her orgasmic potential increases with this discipline, and it's a wonderful thing for a man to feel he can influence the depth of a woman's orgasm; it does wonders for his feelings of self-worth."

The Art of Conscious Loving, Charles Muir

When your erection (or your libido) doesn't want to play

Not having an erection or sexual desire does NOT make you less of man. Given acceptance, it actually makes you a more resourceful and creative man. Erections have minds of their own, as you might have noticed. They're nothing like the artificially manufactured ones in porn, which are assisted by Viagra, editing cuts, and 'fluffers' whose job it is to encourage them back again.

In normal sex, erections come and go for a variety of reasons. It might just be tiredness or over-indulgence in alcohol. Or it might be a natural shift in the energy of your lovemaking. Your erection is definitely susceptible to an uninterested, judgemental or closed-hearted partner, though this is separate from her physical attractiveness. More serious erection complications can also be due to some medications, eg antihypertensives, antihistamines and antidepressants; illness, eg prostate problems or diabetes or decreased testosterone levels that can come with age. Viagra and its derivatives give an erection back to about half the men who try it (it's not been the huge success it was initially thought to be) but it doesn't impact their full body arousal and intimate connection so it's only a part solution.

Your erections also, believe it or not, have their own innate intelligence; and they'll sometimes refuse to play if you're pushing it, being out of integrity, or avoiding something you need to look at within yourself. Manage your erection loss by:

- *Not making it wrong*: just relax, change the focus and come back later.

- *Getting healthier*: get more sleep and decrease your stress.

- *Sharing honestly with your partner*: let her know it's not about her and that you know how to work together to move through it. She will love you for your vulnerability here as it lets her in closer to your heart.

- *Checking with your GP about your medications and testosterone levels*: see whether there are alternatives.

- *Exploring feeling without an erection*: the two aren't mutually inclusive, once you let go of the mindset of needing to have an erection. Try to stroke yourself, breathe, play with your pelvic floor muscles, massage your prostate through your perineum, touch your whole body, and play with energy practices (in Chapter 8) with your partner. You might surprise yourself.

- *Doing the Lingam Massage practice in the resources below regularly*: use it to heal over time any sexual shame and closed heartedness that impacts your erections, and to explore your prostate pleasure.

What Does All This Mean if You're a Woman?

Ask a woman what she desires to feel from her man, and most often she'll respond with, "I want to feel his heart opening to me…" Feeling your man accessing his Inner Warrior during lovemaking will allow you to feel met, held and safe, enabling you to open more fully to yourself into a place of heart-connected surrender with him.

Feeling himself and being at ease in his own pleasure allows a man to enjoy that place in himself that he just *loves* to give from. And all the giving comes direct from his heart, which is truly yummy for you! It takes away the subtle (and not so subtle) manipulations that can occur when he tries to make his pleasure happen outside of himself *through* you. This allows more intimacy and authenticity, which means even more pleasure you for both.

Also, when he's connected with himself, he'll be increasingly aware of the subtleties of his experience and where you're at. You can support him in this by believing in the 'heart on' that is happening inside his 'hard on' and responding to him from there.

Supporting man to move beyond his sexual shadows

You can help heal your man's conditioning-generated wounding. Start by not being merely charmed by what he can do for you, but instead calling him into his heart from yours. Hold space for his vulnerability and give the man in him – rather than the boy – a chance to show up. Support him in working through his ability to access greater pleasure through the suggestions here, knowing that you'll gain from it in the long run.

Stepping into greatness takes men and women acknowledging that fears, vulnerabilities and wounds exist on both sides, and that it's time for the games to stop. The intimacy of a relationship is the perfect place for this to happen.

This is What's Possible

Once you start down this pathway, not only is there no turning back, but it also becomes a limitless, timeless and never-ending journey. When you actively introduce heart connected masculine empowerment into yourself and your relationship, it creates a depth of heart-opening sexual loving that will keep growing and deepening.

You can then journey as far and as deep as you have the courage to go into yourself, connecting your heart and sexuality. This power grows stronger and deeper with age, and is the place in a man that a woman craves to feel safe, nurtured and – most of all – met.

Only when you're truly empowered in yourself can you make love (and life) from this place.

Resources:

- http://www.oztantra.com/lingam-massage/
- http://www.oztantra.com/anal-play-exploring-your-hidden-depths/
- http://www.oztantra.com/tantric-lover-oz-tantra/
- http://www.androlygyaustralia.org/your-health/

Sexploration

8.1 When Two Become One

Ah, the ever-so-desirable notion of sexual union: two people joining together for pleasure, passion, even ecstasy, and putting an end to feelings of separation and aloneness, at least for a little while...

The simple act of sex promises so much – especially relationship sex that not only includes the physical act, but is also the stage for love. How your sexuality looks is of course totally up to you. Here Graeme and I offer you some understandings and tools that provide both safety and newness in your erotic desires and take you closer to the sex life of your dreams, whatever they may look like.

Having Real Sex = Making Love

Your relationship is the one place that offers you the opportunity to actually make love rather than just have sex. To have real sex rather than just perform for each other. To fully go to the edge in sex means going beyond your ego's performance into the unknown of the present moment, in real-time vulnerability. This is the place of full-on sex. It's where masks get dropped, roles and agendas are released, pleasure is enhanced, and people meet each other for real. It's the freedom of 'being' in sex, rather than 'doing' it, and the difference is mind-blowing.

It's more than romantic love and physical sex. It's the scary-but-ultimately-safe place where lovers can fully express their open-hearted sexual selves. From here, truly satisfying connection happens, where even simple things can be profoundly satisfying. Healing happens where you show little parts of yourself that you've held in contraction, fear and shame. Sex becomes making love with extraordinary pleasure, where two *do* become one, and even become love itself.

This expanded sex is incredibly simple, yet it takes time, practice and trust. This means the best place for powerful sexual love is the strong container of a committed relationship.

Sexual love also takes a significant amount of self-respect. It takes owning that you're a sexual being who desires to feel and share sexual pleasure. It takes believing you're worthy of receiving that love and being willing to ask for and give it. Few of us start out this comfortable in our sexual and emotional selves, yet the rewards of cultivating it are huge.

No, it's not easy to go to this depth, but it *is* the way to make relationship sex totally fulfilling and desirable. This kind of 'real sex' can lift you out of your everyday reality and into something extraordinary, where you feel powerfully free and connected at the same time. Magically, it becomes a living creation – loving, playful, passionate, erotic, naughty, raw, healing or blissful, but never boring and for years to come.

It all depends on how present and heart-open you are with yourself and your lover, for the limitlessness in sex comes from *inside* you.

And no, sex doesn't have to lift the roof every time, but it will happen more often. Experiencing lovemaking at this level is one of the payoffs for sticking out the tough bits together and doing your own work. In the intimacy and ecstasy unveiled through what Graeme and I call Expansive

Lovemaking, we see people regain their sense of innate innocence and capacity for wonder.

When you can look at your life partner and know that the places you go with each other plumb the depths and heights of meaning in life, it's hard to look past them to another person, or to stay mad at how they leave their socks on the floor or their hairs in the bathroom sink.

Moving from Friction Sex to Energetic Sex

Expansive lovemaking includes friction sex combined with energy sex, and sometimes energy sex alone.

Friction sex is about two physical surfaces rubbing against each other over and over with a build-up of body tension until a peak is reached and the tension is released. This mechanical approach alone is pleasurable and stress-relieving but ultimately limited. There are only so many times you can do it without boredom setting in.

This kind of sex also keeps you in your ego brain, focused on performance and attached to predictable outcomes. You'll get much more pleasure if you can relax at the *beginning* of sex rather than just at the *end*, and we'll show you how to do this in this chapter. This relaxation also opens you to experiences of energy flow in your sex.

Energy sex is where there's less – or even no – friction. Instead, surfaces exchange energy between them. Energy sex is focussed on relaxation, breath and creating pleasure through energy movement rather than relying on friction alone. It creates a pathway to the more expansive lovemaking and its benefits described above. We'll explore more aspects of energy sex shortly, but here's a way to get an idea of it.

Awakening Your Energy:

1. Try this by experimenting with your own bodies. Move one hand lightly over your arm, finding a pace and depth of touch that allows you to feel a slight buzz or tingling between the surfaces of your arm and hand. This is the energy exchange happening.

    Continue to do this, and begin taking some deeper breaths into your belly, exhaling out of your mouth. This allows your body to relax and your energy to activate, which will send tingles through you. Energy flows better through relaxed muscles. You can see this by shaking one hand hard and quickly for a few moments. How different does it feel to the other?

    Then go back to a light, relaxed touch. Move your hand up over your shoulder, through your hair and around your face, down over your chest, belly and legs. Feel your body awakening to the touch.

    In lovemaking, the same thing can happen to your whole body, brain and beyond. This opens up the spontaneous, pleasure-feeling part of your brain that is creative without an agenda.

2. Share this with your partner. Lie together and both of you breathe deeply. Focus your mind on imagining you're breathing in light from your toes to your crown, and exhaling it down again.

    As you do this, begin to kiss and stroke each other in long, light strokes, without focusing on your genitals. Rock your hips gently. Make sounds. Enjoy the moment without trying to get anywhere. You'll be amazed at how much energy is created by this basic activity, just like when you were teenagers!

If you're wondering whether this means the end of other types of sexual experiences, from bread and butter sex to a quickie in the broom closet, playing with vibrators, watching porn or experimenting with a full array of naughty sexual possibilities, then of course the answer is 'Not at all!' It simply means that if you bring these empowering, heart-opening and energy-moving tools into other types of play, they'll be even better.

So to get your love life back on track, or to take it to the next level, bring in some of the tools of Expansive Lovemaking and watch the sparks fly!

Principles of Expansive Lovemaking

Expansive Lovemaking is a combination of structure and flow, of active doing followed by moments of allowing. Choose one or several of the principles below to play with, then introduce more as you feel inspired... If you need to start by yourself, do so. Your lover will be motivated to join you when they feel how good you feel.

Take responsibility – be a creator

Know that you and your lover are *equally responsible* for creating your experience. It's not up to your partner to give the experience to you, nor you to them. This keeps the point of power within yourself.

Don't just lie there thinking 'he's not doing it right' or 'she's just waiting till it's over'. Instead, ask yourself whether you're connected with your body, heart and genitals from the inside. If not, start getting connected with yourself through your ABC. And yes it's ok to do it here for you'll soon find the benefits are worth it.

Get present

Let go of your ideas of what sex 'should look like' and be present in the moment instead. The more you think about *how* to do it, the more you'll miss it. Instead, give your mind the job of doing your ABC, breathing, noticing what you're feeling, and experiencing *what's right here and now*: the sights, sounds, smells and feelings. From here, you'll find the next step will arise, then the next and the next.

If you feel disconnected from your partner, you're already disconnected from yourself, so reconnect with yourself before making it about them. If you find yourself checking out, don't hide it. Instead, name it, pause, re-centre through your ABC and move on. This is easier said than done, but every moment you're really there is worth a lifetime of going through the motions!

The ABC practice teaches you how to stay present with your more intense feelings – both pleasurable and uncomfortable – which will take you to greater levels of pleasure over time.

Don't wait until you're turned on

Trust that getting into your bodies via your ABC will allow the desire to flow. Expanded Lovemaking shifts you into a more open place, getting you out of the busy place you might've been in that day, and *giving* you the energy to make love, rather than draining it.

Start with being selfish

By being selfish, we mean being centred *inside yourself* through your ABC. The more you do this, the better you'll feel, and the more your lover will feel you. So what starts out as feeling selfish is actually a very loving thing to do. It's surrendering your head into your body and into your heart.

See your partner as your lover

When you're fully in the energy of sex you see your lover as someone different to their ordinary, everyday selves. They're more attractive, more alive, more powerful and desirable. So drop any thoughts about them being the one who irons your shirts, disciplines the kids, or earns the money, etc and see them purely as your lover because you'll find that you see them differently.

Treat them as your lover outside the bedroom. Send them sexy text messages, kiss them sensually, massage their neck, or stroke their shoulders, hips, butt with *appreciation* rather than an agenda to get anything (with women, this makes *all* the difference). Try complimenting them, letting them know you *see* them and yourself as sexual beings.

Regularly give them long (at least 30 seconds), delicious *full-body melting* hugs, with your chests and genitals touching, and your hearts and sex centres connected. This subtly reminds each other of your loving sexual connection, and the potential in it.

Let go of agendas

As paradoxical as it sounds, the more you let go of focussing on any particular goal or outcome, the more likely you are to achieve it. Let your body or your energy move you, rather than the other way around.

If you're willing to play in the moment, you'll not only feel a lot more, but you'll also have a much more willing partner who'll help you to drop any expectations, manipulations and disappointments. This will allow you to feel safe in your erotic explorations; and feeling safe – with your boundaries in place – invites spontaneity, creativity and love.

Breathe

This is our Number #1 tip for better lovemaking.

One of the main reasons people give for not making love is feeling too tired at the end of a hard day. Breathing more (part of your ABC), especially at the beginning, will transform your tired body into a more alive, energised one.

If you're like most people, you're probably not aware of your breathing until things become hot and heavy just before orgasm. At this point, your breath becomes short and fast, or stops altogether. This is way too late to focus on breathing for the more you breathe, the more pleasure you feel – not only in yourself, but also in your partner.

There are many varied and fancy ways to breathe, but the best way is to keep it simple so you'll DO it! Simply bring your attention to your breath in the beginning, and slowly allow it to deepen. Breathe more fully into your chest, your belly, or even – dare we say it – right down into your genitals. Then exhale first through your nose then when you get comfortable, through your mouth, letting your breath just fall out of you.

 Playing with your breath

- Become aware of your breath, and slowly allow it to deepen and take on a life of its own.
- To increase your pleasure, breathe shorter and faster. To spread your pleasure through your body breathe deep and slow. Holding your breath occasionally (being guided by your level of health and your skillset) then releasing it fully will intensify your feelings before spreading them though your body (but you need to have built your energy up first).
- Alternate nose breathing with mouth breathing, or breathe in one way and out the other. They each have a different effect.
- Take three deep breaths together with your partner, and notice your pleasure spread through your combined energetic egg (this is where your individual energies that circle through, and around your bodies combine into one large circuit. You might experience this as sensing your bodies merging with one another).
- Play with alternate breathing – breath in as your lover breathes out then vice versa. This helps your energies to activate each other and more fully connect.
- Breathing not only helps you to feel more, but it also prevents your body from becoming sexually numb.

Feel

Again, use your ABC here. Again, the more connected you feel to yourself the more you'll feel connected to your lover, it's like magic.

Note: if you feel nothing, keep breathing and relaxing, and make it OK! This is especially important if your lover IS feeling something.

If you stay with your nothing and go through it without making it wrong, you'll notice it shift into something else. But if you try to fake it and perform instead, you'll miss the real thing that's waiting for you.

Be you!

Sometimes when you start being sexual, you feel anything *but* turned on and ready. You might feel shy, embarrassed, scared, resistant, resentful, blocked, emotional, etc. If so, this is a *good* sign: it simply means you're opening more deeply to what is real.

All feelings and emotions are welcome in Expansive Lovemaking, for it's all energy – just like sexual pleasure

This is true whether you're a man *or* a woman. It isn't unmanly or over-the-top to feel emotional in sex. And if you can hold space for the one who's feeling emotion without taking it personally, or needing to fix or get rid of it, you'll be the lover they keep coming back for.

This is where your emotional skills training from Chapter 2 comes into very good use. If you simply let your feelings be there, accepting and breathing through them, they'll likely pass into something deeper and freer. It might help to briefly talk about what's happening in order to let it go, but most times you can just feel it.

Occasionally, you might end up connecting with an old hurt or negative belief. If you do, see it as an opportunity to learn more about yourself (or about your partner if it's their feeling – just remember *their feeling is about them, not you,* and don't get in the way by taking it personally!)

This can be scary, but don't hide anything. This is why learning to hold yourself in vulnerability is also a sexual skill. Trust what shows up and share it, as this is the juice of real lovemaking and why it can be healing if you allow yourself to be really seen. It also allows your lover the chance to show up with surprising tenderness, empathy and love.

Remember how to kiss

Being heart connected through your ABC will take your kissing to a whole new place. Give kissing your total attention, rather than using it as a lead-in to what's next. It can be a lead-in of course, but not if your head is somewhere else.

Start tender and slow, slow. Vary the moves and the rhythm. Nibble top or bottom lips. Breathe. Imagine the tingling of your genitals up in your mouth. Stroke your lover's lips, teeth and tongue with your tongue. Leave full on deep throat with your tongue until the moment the passion's rising and you're both really getting in to it – too much too soon is a put-off.

In the meantime, tease and taste it all.

Touch

Touch your lover with presence, starting slow and playing with different levels of intensity. Listen to their feedback.

Long, slower strokes will help them to feel relaxed and encompassed by your touch, especially if you use your open hand, for your hands are the messengers of your heart. Shorter strokes and fingertips help to focus on one area. Massaging moves the muscles underneath the surface bringing a deeper opening. Play with a variety of touches, and vary the location, speed, depth, intensity (all the way from feather-like to a scratch or slap, but always ask first!). Use the whole of your body to touch with - your lips, tongue, hair, nails and teeth (start gently!) Include moments of simply holding your lover in stillness.

Let your partner know if you're going to build the intensity of your touch, so they can say yes or no to it.

The Differences Between Men's and Women's Bodies

You've probably noticed that men's and women's bodies are different: different on the outside, on the inside and in how they work.

A Woman's Body

A woman's sexuality is built of many layers, and – like a crockpot – it's at its best over many hours. *In her body, sexuality works from the outside in, from her extremities to her centre, her yoni.* Her multi-dimensional sexuality isn't separate from intimacy, emotion and spirituality, although she can enjoy sex at any level. She's capable of a high level of energetic intensity and touching her from the outside in really pays off. If you don't, her body will not only not awaken fully, it can turn right off.

When you touch a woman, to keep it simple, no matter where you're touching her, start from the outside and work slowly towards the centre. With her body start at the top of her head and the tips of her fingers and toes, and work your way to her centre. Imagine that she has a bikini on and the parts covered by the bikini are touched last. If you touch her breast, start at the outside and slowly make your way to its apex, the nipple. If you touch her sexual centre, her Yoni (genitals) start outside with her belly, inner thighs and pubic area. When you move to her Yoni itself, start at the outer lips, then the inner lips, the clitoris, and then move inside. And when you touch the inside, begin at the entrance and then move to the GSpot then the cervix area.

Given time and proper awakening, a woman is capable of high states of bliss, where relaxation, pleasure and love merge into one. When fully awakened, she's capable of orgasms in many different places, many times over – even in her heart, mind and soul. She's also capable of ejaculation, which we talked about in Chapter 7.

A woman's sexual energy is magnetic, attracting, and negative in polarity.

Lovemaking transforms this negative energy into positive, which is why a woman often has an excess of energy after sex and wants to talk. When her energy is fully transformed, she feels whole in herself, and open to her lover but not needy of him. This awakening can take anywhere from a few hours up to a lifetime.

A Man's Body

A man's sexuality has traditionally been thought of as straightforward like a microwave: give him two or three minutes and beep, beep, beep, he's done. His ejaculatory orgasm is generally seen as the apex of his experience, with sex and love being completely separate. As we discussed in the previous chapter, this is of course a gross misunderstanding. It's merely the outcome of his conditioning, rather than his ultimate sexual reality.

As mentioned, given time, a man is capable of matching a woman's sexual intensity, including her capacity for multiple orgasms (both with and without ejaculation). Given time he can meet her in her multi-dimensional sexuality too, that includes intimacy, *emotion* his spirituality – a sense of something greater than himself. *His sexuality works from the inside out, from his genitals to the rest of his body.*

When you touch a man's body, start at his sexual centre, his Lingam. Start here, then invite him to spread his sexual pleasure through the rest of his body, rather than remaining and being released from here. Help him by keeping one hand on his Lingam and use the other and the rest of your body to stroke his pleasure outwards to his extremities. Beginning at his centre, he can relax and expand, seeing that he doesn't need to wait until those few moments right at the end for his pleasure. The one exception to this is beginning at his PSpot (his prostate gland) – he needs to warm up to this one! Do remember that his breasts and nipples are pathways to pleasure and heart opening just like a woman's so don't be afraid to give these some attention along the way.

This is where his practising *his* ABC really pays off, leaving him more familiar with feeling himself in a relaxed way and connected to his heart.

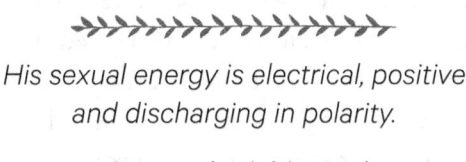

His sexual energy is electrical, positive and discharging in polarity.

Lovemaking transforms his positive energy into negative, which is why it can be draining for him to constantly discharge his energy from his body. This is where Tantric-style lovemaking, where he moves his energy up and through his body first, is a more restorative pathway. It allows him to charge his body with positive energy and retain more of it when he ejaculates.

As with women, this awakening can take anywhere from a few hours up to a lifetime.

Connecting together

Though you might start in different places one way to connect both of you to your bodies at the same time is that while the man is pleasuring the woman, she can hold his Lingam, either in stillness or lightly stroking it. Using lubrication will help him to relax into her touch.

Because this connects him with his sexual centre, he'll be happy to touch and stroke her, taking all the time she desires. It's also a great motivation for him to practise his energy spreading practices so he can enjoy this for a long time.

Eye contact

You've probably heard it before, but eye contact is so powerful that it's worth bringing up again. It's one of the simplest and deepest ways to share intimacy – to literally see and be seen, for the eyes truly are the windows of the soul! (That's why we like to hide them.)

Gaze with soft eyes into your lover's eyes and feel what it brings. If this is too full-on to sustain, try just a moment or two here and there, and slowly build up. If it becomes uncomfortable, breathe, relax and see if you can stay a moment longer before you leave. You might be surprised how this opens the connection you've been missing. If your lover is somewhere else just enjoy gazing at them from the depths of your own soul.

Come back often, occasionally all the way through orgasm.

Sound

Give yourself permission to make sounds: your vibrating vocal chords help to create vibrations throughout your body. This is not about trying to sound like a porn star – in fact, it's the exact opposite. Instead, just let out any sound that's authentic for you. Even small sounds can be a powerful pleasure activator. They can be a great shame-buster as well, particularly if the sound comes from deep in your belly, or even your soul.

If you're worried about the kids or the neighbours, make any loud sounds into a pillow (placed over your mouth only). You can make quite a lot of sound this way without it travelling very far.

Let it flow

Real sex is variable. It has more than one speed and one flavour. Real arousal and real erections (unlike the medicated ones in porn) come and go. They can involve glorious fucking or sublime stillness. Have an open mind and see what happens.

Being in the moment and going with the flow will drop you into a place where your pleasure becomes your lover's and vice versa – a phenomenon known as entrainment. Plus, the more you focus on feeling and being in the moment inside of yourself, what comes next will take care of itself.

Variation is the key

As mentioned above, include your partner's whole body in your touch, and vary the speed, pressure and type of touch: this helps your mind to let go. One variation to this rule – if your woman is rising to a peak of orgasm, don't go faster unless she asks you to. Instead, maintain your pace (as it's obviously working!) and let the orgasm happen, otherwise you can override her sensations.

Active giving

Surprisingly the best kind of giving is in moments of surrender. It's where you are totally in service to your lover, responding to their desires and cues with no thought of yourself. Your ABC will help you drop into this and will invite moments of entrainment, where you're giving without effort, it's just happening.

Active receiving

This isn't passively laying there – instead it's giving your lover the gift of being actively present to their touch, with your mind engaged in the moment, and allowing yourself to fully let in what they're offering. Active receiving is firstly a mindset: one of opening your mind, letting go of control, and allowing whatever happens to be just as it is.

It involves breathing, feeling the sensations fully, letting go of any inner resistance you might have, and totally surrendering to yourself through the touch. It's the essence of the ABC practice. Although your surrender is to yourself and not to your lover, you'll automatically feel more connected to them as a result (and they to you).

Note: this might *look* like surrendering to your lover, but the internal reality is very different: you remain connected to and safely in charge of yourself, trusting that you'll be OK whatever happens. This doesn't mean tolerating something that feels uncomfortable for you, but instead asking yourself:

- Are you letting the feeling in?
- Is there any resistance you can drop?
- Is there any emotion you can acknowledge?

This practice can help you go underneath yourself and into something unforeseen yet wonderful. If it still doesn't feel good, ask for it to change.

Active receiving is one of the most precious gifts you can give to both yourself and your lover. It opens not only your heart through the gratitude it brings, and your spirit through the acceptance it takes, but also the doorway to greater pleasure through the expansion it offers.

Holding on to yourself

There will be times in all of this amazingness when your lover might be in a different place to you or have a different desire to yours. It's important in these situations to hold on to yourself, breathing through any feelings and being OK with wherever they – and you – are at.

Be open to sharing what's opening up for you and hearing what's opening for them – and see what newness comes out of it. You may need to pause to get grounded and come back to yourself before discussing what is happening.

Internal Energisers

We commonly get energised (or turned on) by external factors such as a time, privacy, naked bodies, loving or sexy words, clothing and images, sensual touch, and giving and receiving. These are all wonderful things. There are also many things you can do from *inside* yourself to activate the pleasure from within, which create as much as energy as, or even more than, your external environment (and they never wear out!)

Here are some for you to try.

Attention

Give your mind a job – to notice the feelings in your body via your ABC without judging them or thinking about what to do next. This will help your thinking mind to turn off and keep your energy within you.

Then bring your attention to your genitals, breathe into them, and allow their energy to awaken. Open to the tingling pleasure that lives inside of you as well as feeling it from the touch on the outside. Breathe into your heart as well, allowing it to open. As you centre yourself in your open heart, love will expand from within you, for both you and your lover to enjoy.

Breath

We can't overstate that your breath is the key to awakening your body from within. Continue to breathe consciously as often as you can throughout lovemaking. Breathe slow, fast and in between, with a closed or open mouth. Eventually, you'll become present to your breath the whole time. Occasionally, after you've built up your energy, try breathing all the way out and holding your breath out as long as you can, then a little bit longer, then inhaling strongly. This will drive pleasure through your whole body (but don't do this if you have a tendency to high blood pressure!)

Rock rather than thrust

After your breath your hips and pelvis are the most powerful generators of sexual energy in your body, whether you're in sexual union or not. So rock your hips backward and forward by arching and flattening your lower back, rather than thrusting your hips as thrusting contracts your butt and thigh muscles, limiting the flow of energy.

Try moving your hips around in circles as well, and letting them shake freely. As much as possible let your body move you, rather than you moving your body. If you usually prefer to hold your body in tense stillness in order to come, practice bringing in some movement with breath: it might be distracting at first but it will open up much more feeling with practice.

Muscle contractions

Contract your pelvic floor muscles to build energy and pleasure – and, for women, lubrication. Imagine that you have a bladder of energy in your pelvic bowl, and as you tighten your muscles gently in and up, you release energy from the bowl. Relax the muscles fully in between each tightening.

Women actually have three rings of muscle inside their Yoni: an outer, middle and inner ring. With practice, these rings can be contracted separately or together. Men will find that they can contract their anus, perineum, base and tip of their lingam. Building up pelvic muscle strength over time not only helps with erection strength for men, but it's also a pleasure builder for both. In fact, you can both lie still after penetration and each just squeeze to be in orgasmic heaven.

NB. It's important to relax your muscles fully as you exhale so you don't build unnecessary tension in this part of you.

Oral Sex

To get the most out of oral loving, remember that it's less about your technique and more about your degree of presence and enjoyment. Start from the outside in for a woman and vice versa for the man (unless they desire otherwise), explore the whole genital area, not just the obvious. Breathe through any resistance you might have to giving or receiving and find a place of enjoyment in it for yourself. Your enjoyment will spark more pleasure for both of you. Be in the moment and relax. Do pelvic muscle contractions to enhance your own energy and imagine breathing it into your lovers' genitals for some extra zing.

Orgasms, Orgasms and More Orgasms

As humans, we're capable of many different types of orgasms. We're more or less orgasmic at different times in our lives. Each of us tends to be more comfortable with one particular style, but with practice many more can open up in Expanded Lovemaking. These can include:

- Whole-body orgasms
- Multiple orgasms
- Rolling like a wave, flowing with/without muscle contractions
- Spine-tingling, erupting, shuddering, imploding (erupting within us) orgasms
- Ejaculating and non-ejaculating orgasms (for both men and women)
- Heartgasms (orgasms in the heart)
- Valley orgasms (in stillness)
- Breathgasms (orgasms through breath)
- Melting waves of pulsations
- 'Orgasms' at the third eye (sixth chakra)
- Visual orgasms (images that evoke physical state shifts)

- Orgasms that allow us to experience a sense of the 'Divine' – of something larger than you can understand (whatever this may mean to you)

Expanded Lovemaking orgasms can be short and intense, or last for hours. Not everybody will have orgasms, nor do they need to. All we're saying is that they're a learnable skill.

The main skills are having an open mind, being present in your body and letting go of trying to 'get there' or tensing up and short circuiting your pleasure.

Instead of tensing and striving, relax and open into yourself. Rather than letting yourself go over the edge of your first orgasm as your pleasure intensity begins to build, pause, breathe deeply and allow your pleasure to spread through your body, then begin again.

Once your pleasure has peaked, rest for a few moments, then breathe, and open further to discover new heights. Over time, your pleasure will awaken between your orgasms, taking you into a state of erotic ecstasy that's well worth the wait!

If your orgasms are more subtle, or you're not sure *if* you're orgasming or not, again relax and open into what IS there, you'll be surprised at what you find.

And despite the playful title of this book we suggest you don't become overly focussed on coming at the same time as it puts you in your head and this is not where you want to be. Orgasms are great *whenever* they happen. Plus it limits you to the idea of one orgasm in total, and we hope you get the idea this doesn't need to be the case.

Plus play with the moves we've talked about in the Men's and Women's sections on being orgasmic earlier in this chapter.

Stillness

Contrary to popular belief, there's great value in stillness because you can often feel *more* in it. Drop into complete stillness at times and just breathe, as this allows the energy you've created to spread, allowing you to enjoy it twice over. Let your energy move you, rather than vice versa.

Also, remember that love requires space to show up in, so ensure you give it some, to turn your sex into lovemaking.

Sex Positions

You can have fun hanging off the chandelier, upside down over the edge of the bed or on the laundry sink. However, Graeme and I find that there are five basic positions which, with minor variations, provide for great connection and energy flow:

1. **Missionary position – man on top.** This allows for strong penetration by the man and ease of surrender in the woman underneath. This doesn't mean that the woman needs to be passive here: she can also move her hips whilst her man slows or pauses at times as this can even help her surrender and open more deeply.

    The feel of this position can change depending on how high or low the woman places her legs, whether her legs are wrapped around her lover's calves, thighs, back or shoulders. The man can have his legs straight, one knee out to the side or be up on his knees. The woman can also use pillows under her butt to help change the angle of penetration.

2. **Woman on top.** This position can allow a woman to feel powerfully feminine *or* masculine. It also allows her to find the right position to connect with her Gspot. It allows the man to gaze upon his woman and relax in his energy play.

3. **Spoons position with lovers front to back.** This position allows little eye contact, but it's relaxing. Although it can get hot too, on occasion!

4. **Rear entry position.** The woman faces downwards, either on her knees or flat on her stomach. This creates a strong primal response in both lovers, and is great for G/PSpot activation.

5. **Scissors position.** The man lies on his side, and the woman on her back with both of her legs over the man's hips, and their genitals connecting. She can stay here or slide her uppermost leg between the man's so that their legs are entwined. Either partner can support themselves with pillows if desired, and connect a hand to their lover's heart to connect their upper bodies, completing the energy circuit.

6. **Yab-Yum.** The position is an iconic one that you might have seen in Tantra or even Kama Sutra images. The woman sits in the man's lap so that they're facing each other. This can either be on the bed with cushions, on the edge of the bed, or on a chair. This creates a position of equality that allows energy to flow freely from base to crown energy centres.

Deep Lovemaking Strokes

Amongst your usual variety of penetrative strokes, play with these. They're not in any particular order but it's great to start with the first one.

- Enter *slowly*, going deeper only as you feel your woman's Yoni fully opening to you. Be really present and look into each others eyes here.

- Move in and out just two or three inches deep. This helps to stimulate the woman's GSpot.

- When you're all the way in, remain deep, moving in and out just an inch or two, which helps to stimulate her cervical spots for deep, heart-opening pleasure. Be really present with this one and give it the time it deserves. (All the more reason to practice gentlemen).

8: Sexploration

- If it's feeling really good for both of you, stay in deep and slowly circle your hips, first one way several times, then the other. This can drive a *fully receptive* woman wild!

Each of these strokes can be intensified with moments of eye contact, as this takes the level of presence, vulnerability and trust right up for both.

When you're in deep, stop moving, and then both squeeze and release your pelvic floor muscles (which you've been practising, right?) This stimulates her GSpot and his PSpot, sending pleasure through both of your bodies.

Personal Lubricant

Take the pressure and the guesswork out of sex, use lubricant as a normal part of your love-play. A woman's body isn't necessarily moist even when she's hot, so having lube handy takes the shame and guesswork away. This doesn't mean overriding her need for arousal, but it does help to take away any 'performance pressure' she might put on herself.

Or, if you're pleasuring a man, lube will give him a more sensitive experience and decrease numbing from an over-hard hand grip. Look for lighter water-based lubes or use coconut/almond or other natural oils.

NB: be aware that oil-based lubricants, including natural oils, degrade latex condoms – so avoid these if you're using them for anal play or with latex/rubber sex toys.

Sex Toys

If you enjoy (or would like to try) using sex toys in your love play, Graeme and I encourage you to bring the skills we've mentioned here into your play with them. That way, you become the driver of your sexual pleasure rather than leaving it to the toy to do it for you.

And this way, you'll have the benefits of the toys without numbing your response over time.

Focusing On One Thing

Rather than pushing yourselves to do everything from start to finish each time, try exploring one thing thoroughly for a change. Try just:

- Kissing
- Oral loving
- Different types of touch
- Breasts, butt or clitoris only
- GSpot or PSpot loving, etc.

Another fabulous practice is to have **'one person receiving'** sessions. This is as simple as it sounds – the focus is totally on one lover receiving, with the other lover in service to them. Separating the focus out like this means you can learn an awful lot about each other that would usually get lost in the mutual experience.

Go Both With, and Underneath Your Gender

While gender-fluid and transgender identities are becoming more acknowledged and accepted now, most of us are born with an innate sense of our gender as male or female. There's immense power in exploring the qualities of your gender and its opposite in lovemaking.

Give yourselves permission to play with being the more active or dominant lover – the one taking charge or being more active, which is often seen as the masculine aspect. This gives the other person a chance to enjoy actively receiving. At other times, give permission to be soft, open, receptive and surrendered – which is often seen as feminine. And guys, not being dominant at times doesn't mean that you're less of a 'real man' – you're just a more adventurous one in a delicious new way. Plus you get to enjoy the freedom and play in not having to be in charge occasionally. And ladies it's fun to step into the dominant role, all the way down to imagining you have a Lingam and balls of your own and experiencing what that feels like!

Even deeper than this, try dropping gender altogether and just let what arises outside of that be. Let the sexual energy or Spirit move through you and create something more than your gender conditioning limits you to.

Have Adventure Sessions

These are lovemaking sessions where you give yourselves, and each other, permission to simply explore new ways, touches, tastes, sensations, positions, etc without any expectations of a particular result. Removing your expectations decreases any fear, resistance or shame.

Don't limit yourself to just the obvious things: include feathers, furs, oil/no oil, cornflour (yes, cornflour), toys, fantasies, foods, lighting, music, positions, faster/harder/slower/lighter strokes and breath, making sounds, giving/receiving, speaking up, self-pleasuring and sexual healing.

If at first you feel resistance or even nothing when you try something new, breathe more and stay open. Remember that some things take time to awaken. You can also explore parts of your body that feel shut down or unfamiliar: parts of your sexuality that feel taboo, role plays, power plays with agreed boundaries, and more. Opening into these areas will bring not only greater ease and wholeness in yourself, but they'll also create greater glue in your relationship.

Begin with talking about what you'd like to try, and express your fears and concerns. Even just talking about them can be amazing. Some of the things you try you may bring into your lovemaking on a regular basis, some occasionally and some never.

At the very least, you'll be fostering an openness to play and trust in the bedroom.

Anal Play

Anal play isn't something you *have to* do, no matter what anyone says. But if you do go there, you need to take your time to make the most of it.

For it to feel truly amazing, you need to be emotionally open as well as physically – and if you can do this, it's worth the effort!

See http://www.oztantra.com/anal-play-exploring-your-hidden-depths/

Energy Sex

To take your lovemaking to another level still, play with some of the suggestions below about sexual or life force energy – that tingling, expansive feeling we experience as sexual pleasure. These suggestions are based on the idea that we're all energy beings with channels of energy running through our bodies, which has been taught in the East for thousands of years.

If you're a New Age sceptic (in which case, good for you!) you don't have to believe in these ideas. Just try them with an open mind and see what happens.

The more you play with energy, the more you'll experience it.

- *Believe it or not, you have an energy channel that runs like a central pipe from between your legs to the top of your head.* When one of you feels your pleasure building up, both pause, take three deep breaths and pc squeezes together, and imagine breathing the energy up through this channel to your hearts. Then exhale out though your mouths, 'sighing out' your breaths as you allow the energy to spread through your whole bodies, feeling the pleasure expand throughout both of you. Enjoy the moment then building the energy again.

- *Imagine this life force energy as light, love or water flowing through your central channel and filling you up.* Breathe it from your toes up to your crown at the top of your head and back down again. Imagine it being like ocean waves rolling through you, helping the pleasure to spread through your body. Play with it. Imagine light flowing from your heart out through your hands and into your lover. For where the mind goes the energy follows.

- *Place the tip of your tongue on the roof of your mouth to create an energy circuit within your body.* Do this whenever you are being sexual. Or try connecting the tips of both your tongues and breathing together moving the energy circle within both of you.

- *Place the palms of your hands on your lover's butt.* Get primal, then breathe the delicious extra energy up your spines and forward to your hearts.

- *Place the palms of your hands on different chakra points (yours or your lover's) to activate them.* If you know the colours associated with a centre, imagine them as you do so – if not, you can find this information at www.oztantra.com/chakras-and-your-relationship

- *Together, each inhale and pc squeeze your energy from your genitals up to your third eye, then each exhale it out into your lover's third eye and down to their genitals.* Create a circuit, repeating it two to five times, then both rest in stillness. This will make your lovemaking a more meditative experience – subtle yet powerful.

- *Include some of the self-pleasuring practices we talk about later in the chapter in your lovemaking.* Even a few rounds of *Fire-breathing* will build your energy instantly.

Once you start playing with energy, it will start playing back with you. Have an open mind and see what happens. Remember to ground yourselves after playing at this level.

How to Begin with Sex

One of the most difficult parts of sex is the beginning. This is the point where your hopes, fears and vulnerabilities are all highest. Foreplay is a strategy that's supposed to overcome this, but it's generally fraught with anxiety, agenda, frustration and even manipulation. To bypass this place of mind games, there's a simple solution. Start by simply relaxing and getting into your bodies. This will turn off your thinking brain and turn on your feeling one.

 Beginning With Relaxation

1. Lie side by side with your eyes closed and your arms around each other, **without movement.** Lying naked is best, but it's not essential.

    Being held by her man helps a woman feel safe and nurtured, giving her as much time as she needs to fully arrive. She can also gently hold her man's Lingam to allow him to relax and connect with himself, and know he isn't being left till last.

2. Both belly breathe and allow your minds to become quiet. Take as much time as you need to go inside *yourselves*. Practice your ABCs here.

3. If your mind is busy, take your attention off it to focus on your breath, the sensations in your body, or the feel of your body lying against your lover's instead.

4. Bring your attention to your heart and to your genitals and allow whatever's there to just be there.

5. Keep breathing deeply and stay present inside yourself. This will feel like a dropping into nothingness, which is the opposite of the 'doing' that you might normally look for.

    Inside this nothingness, lies your sexual energy and your connection with the freedom in your authentic self. Give it the time it needs to show up. The more you can trust finding this,

> the easier and more satisfying the rest of your lovemaking will become.
> 6. Once you feel this connection, begin to stroke your lover lightly and gently rock your hips, allowing your sexual energy to arise.
> 7. If one person is connected first, they can enjoy being in the moment until both are ready to move into a more active space.
>
> From here, move into whatever lovemaking practices you desire.

How To Finish Making Love

Traditionally this is a no brainer: sex finishes when the man comes! In Expanded Lovemaking, it's less clearly defined. So like everything else, the ending becomes a choice. It's one of the freedoms that not being attached to a genital orgasm brings.

If you can feel the energy flow, you'll know when it feels complete. A genital orgasm and ejaculation may feel just right for both of you. Or perhaps you come to the end of the time you have (despite what you've heard about Tantra, you don't always have to last for hours or days, though you can if you want). Finish by acknowledging each other, lie in the bliss, go to sleep or get up for a cuppa – whatever feels desirable. It can be different each time. Having spread your sexual energy through your heart and body without draining it, you get to stay in it for as long as it remains, uplifted and heart open, carrying it with you into your day.

In Conclusion

As you can see there's much to play with, even with this gentle beginning.

Lovemaking becomes a combination of doing, non-doing, building, flowing, spreading, opening and surrender. There are times of giving and of receiving, at others it seems like neither of you are doing, it's just happening. At others it can feel like you're lifted into another dimension and something larger than you is doing you.

The incredible thing about these practices is that they build sexual energy between you over time rather than drain it. This keeps the spark in your lovemaking happening with less and less effort over time, rather than the other way around.

And what you're creating in your lovemaking positively impacts how you approach your relationship, and even your world through encouraging you to be more open, loving, trusting, creative and empowered.

So it's worth a little effort, don't you think?

8.2 Mmmm... Turn Your Volkswagen Into A Ferrari!

Be warned, you're about to enter forbidden territory here. We're going to talk about that thing that almost *everyone* does behind closed doors – perhaps under the sheets or in the shower – but that few will admit to. That thing, of course, is masturbation – or what Graeme and I call self pleasure – the one thing in your sex life you likely have the most resistance to, or shame about.

So why do we include this topic in a book about relationships? Isn't masturbating merely a second-best choice for when your partner isn't available? No!

*Self-pleasuring is not a lesser choice: it is
a time-honoured Tantric practice.*

A person who can gain fulfilment in their own self pleasure is much more likely to find it with a lover. There's so much you can learn and enjoy in touching yourself, we promise, without having to go blind (or even wear glasses!)

After all, how can you:

- Expect someone to desire you if you cannot desire yourself?
- Teach your lover to how touch you if you don't know yourself?
- Learn to create expanded pleasure that lasts for longer if you don't practise?

Self pleasure can help you to:

- Be free of socially conditioned sexual shame
- Avoid having to rely on your partner to 'give' you pleasure
- Love, energise, revitalise, nurture and awaken yourself – which is always time well spent.

The Art of Self Pleasure

How do you make the shift from mere masturbation to glorious self pleasure?

First, decide that ***you have the right*** to experience feeling totally ecstatic and blissful by yourself through being proactive in your own sexuality. Schedule self-pleasuring into your life, for 20 to an occasional 60 minutes.

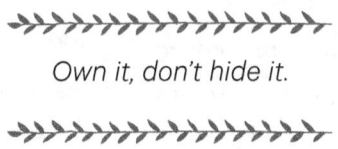

Own it, don't hide it.

De-shame your sexuality in a big way by affirming it rather than being covert about it. If your partner is home, let them know what you're doing. If you come across your partner self-pleasuring, see it as them connecting with themselves rather than them rejecting you and affirm them for it. This can be challenging the first time, but it's a huge relief afterwards.

This kind of self-pleasuring is about self-love rather than tension release. There is no goal except for self-connection. Slowly build the time and intensity with which you can self-pleasure. Begin with your ABC, then do your own thing. Or try different combinations of the following ideas – there are no shoulds here, and no particular way for it to be except for shame free.

An extra gift of self pleasure in the loving, embodied way described here is that it gives you a sense of your own mind, body and energy connection, plus your own wholeness, worthiness and beauty.

"I now proclaim that masturbation has come of age"

Sex For One, Betty Dodson

Tips include:

- **Self-pleasuring works extra well after some vigorous physical activity.** So, the next time you've been for a walk or run, been to the gym or danced around the living room to your favourite songs (highly recommended) and you're feeling all tingly and alive, take a little extra time to do yourself a delicious favour and expand that into some juicy sexual energy.
- **Keep your attention inside your body.** Scan your body and notice what you're feeling, rather than focussing on fantasy or porn, which take you away from yourself. This can be hard at first but it's a step you need to take to get the most out of your practice.
- **If your mind is all over the place, imagine that it's filled with the colour white.** White is soothing and healing, so the more thoughts that come, the whiter you imagine your mind until your mind gives up.
- **Place one hand over your heart and the other over your genitals.** Take a few minutes to breathe into both areas, feeling them connect and awaken, rather than starting with mechanical stimulation. If any

part feels blocked, just keep breathing gently into it, allowing it to open in its own time. There's no rush here.

- ***Notice your breath and gently increase its depth.*** Keep following it into your practice and play with it as in Expansive Lovemaking.

- ***Break any habits of going straight for your genitals.*** Instead, expand your repertoire of self-touch. Touch your body all over with open hands, brush/pull your hair, lick your lips, suck on your fingers, caress your breasts (guys too) and squeeze your pelvic floor muscles to help awaken your pleasure from inside you. Though for guys you might like to start at your genitals and then include the rest of you (this is an OK option for women as well of course).

- ***Try a range of body touches.*** Go from very light and very slow to occasionally harder and faster, and from taps and tickles to slaps and stillness holds where your hands melt onto your body, and everything in between. Love yourself!

- ***When you're ready to move to your genitals (if you're not there already), aim to explore rather than simply 'get off' with an orgasm.*** Keep one hand on your heart and the other on your genitals to build a more full-bodied experience.

- ***Have plenty of oil or lubricant handy, so that when you're ready for genital touch you can glide rather than rub.***

- ***Breathe your pleasure up through your body.*** Imagine you have an energy channel up the centre of your body (as in fact, you do) that your pleasure can move up through. As you inhale, move your hand along the front of your body to help your imagination lift the energy up. Then relax as you exhale. Trust the images of the energy that your mind might come up with, whether they're sparkles, colours, water, light, etc.

- ***You can also move your pleasure up to your heart or third eye as you inhale.*** Place the tip of your tongue on the roof of your mouth to create a conduit. Or move the pleasure up along your spine, over your crown to your upper lip as you inhale, then down to your belly as you exhale. This may initially seem to make your pleasure disappear, but if you keep going it will return even stronger.

- ***Try some of the tips from the Men and Women's sections and the Expanded Lovemaking earlier in this chapter just with yourself.***
- ***Practise making sounds whilst there's nobody to hear you.*** Try as many different sounds as you can, small or large: purr, sigh, moan, groan, grunt, scream, shout! Breath in, sound out.
- ***Your goal is self-connection, rather than orgasm.*** If you happen to go into orgasm, take several short, sharp breaths as you do to expand your pleasure. The longer you can inhale, the longer your orgasm (a great reason to practice your breathing). Making sound helps too of course – and yes, you have permission!

Leave yourself literally filled with love, expansion and energy.

Do remember not to rely on the one form of stimulation – variety is key here to train your mind and body to respond to a number of approaches to prevent genital numbness and broaden your response to the different touches your lover brings. Your body is like any instrument: if you only play it one way, you'll only get the one sound.

For women include your breasts, lower belly, inner thighs, outer lips, perineum, vaginal entrance, Gspot, cervix and anus in your touch along with your clitoris (start with your clitoris as well as the other spots, then the other spots alone).

These different areas may take longer to respond initially, but freeing up your sexual response will make your efforts worthwhile. Keeping one hand on the outside to keep your familiar pleasure going, use the finger(s) on your other (or a dildo, especially a crystal one) to explore touch inside your vagina. Playing with your pelvic floor muscles too (especially with a

Jade Egg inside) helps to build your inner sexual connection, increasing your likelihood of pleasure here during penetrative sex.

Having one only masturbation technique is often true for men too, so along with your favourite, try some variations – plus stroke your nipples, balls, perineum, anus, etc as well for the same reason.

It's fine to use a vibrator (or other toys) if you wish – just remember what we said earlier about not allowing yourself to get numb as you do so.

 Opening Up Your Sexual Energy

Hip/Breath Combos to build your energy circuit. Do 2-10 minutes of each:

Rock your hips, and breathe in time with them.

1. Receptive breath: fill yourself with energy by inhaling through your mouth as you rock your hips forward and exhale through your nose as you rock them back. Feel yourself fill with energy.
2. Discharging breath: breathe in through your nose as you rock your hips back, then breathe out as you rock them forward, and feel yourself powerfully discharging energy.
3. Breathe slowly and fully through your open mouth whilst rocking your hips quickly, letting your hips shudder and shake if they want to. Play with the speed of your breath here too.

 Fire-breathe to build up your energy

Do as many as you desire.

Breathe in through your nose as you arch your back, pull your hips back and relax your pelvic floor muscles. Then breathe out with pursed lips as if through a straw, as you rock your hips forward, flattening your back and contracting your pelvic floor.

> **Fire-breathe to heaven**
>
> **Allow 15mins.**
>
> Once you're comfortable with fire-breathing, imagine that with each inhalation, you breathe the energy up through one or all of your chakras, one at a time. For example, inhale energy from your first chakra up to the second and exhale it back down to the base. Repeat this for each chakra one to three times.
>
> When you reach the crown chakra, you can either allow the energy to move out through your crown and shower down around you, you can send the energy to any chakra you sense needs it, or you can send it to your belly (a great energy storehouse). Enjoy the feelings that arise as a result, whether they're pleasure, emotions or Core Heart Feelings.

In your self pleasure you may experience feelings other than pleasure – like fear, shame, irritation, boredom, frustration, numbness or sadness. If this happens, just accept them as they are and keep breathing, staying present with them until they dissolve. (Or, if they don't, see *Identifying Your Unique Blocks to Pleasure* in the following section and find the gifts that live within the most uncomfortable feelings.)

Finally, acknowledge yourself for going there. If you don't experience much at first, try again – many people can become numb to feeling without realising it and it takes time to undo this. The more you get present, breathe, relax and say YES, the more your body and your psyche will open. Moving sexual pleasure up through your body heals shame and opens your heart, making self pleasure a healing experience too.

Share the gift of self-pleasuring with your partner now and again too. You can either self- pleasure in front of your partner (extremely shame-busting – although if it's too confronting, you can wear a blindfold, which is kind of sexy too) and vice versa, or both of you can self-pleasure together. This is also a great chance to learn the ways you each like to be touched from each other.

8.3 Identifying Your Unique Blocks to Pleasure

There are many reasons that, even though you may long to experience satisfying sexual pleasure and connection, you can't access it and instead find frustration, shame, insecurity and an inability to feel. Because your ego is attached to getting only what it wants it's normal to make this situation wrong. It's then common to project this lack of fulfilment onto your lover: to find things wrong with them and make them responsible for your lack of desire. Or you might project it onto yourself, believing you're unsexy, undesirable and even unlovable.

But if you can step out of this blame game and get curious enough to look closer, you'll see that what's happening is that you're coming up against the individual blocks to pleasure that lie hidden deep within you. Some are social, cultural, or gender-reflected, and some are the result of your personal experiences; all began as protective mechanisms. This section explores how to identify and move through them.

You may find it reassuring to know that Graeme and I have – in amongst our sexual heights of multi-orgasmic pleasure, ecstasy, bliss and deep heart connection – experienced *all* of the blocks below. And yes, that includes sexual shame, painful sex, no sex, premature ejaculation, no libido, no erection and no connection. You name it, we've experienced it!

It takes a lot of courage to stop playing the pretend game in bed but it's worth it.

It takes self-connection not to blame your partner for what isn't happening for you and take responsibility for it yourself. Equally, it takes self-connection to not make your partner's lack of desire about you, but doing so IS the way through to the pleasure you deserve. Your ABC practice will help to you stay grounded and open as you look at what isn't working, seeing everything you discover as clues for how to turn your pleasure back on.

Closed Hearts

In our work, Graeme and I find that *the main reason* for lack of sexual desire between partners is the closing down of their hearts due to the unresolved hurts and sufferings in their everyday relationship.

Sexual desire is more complicated than just your body's physical sexual arousal. Desire is more about the heart, about wanting to connect emotionally, and it's much harder to feel when your heart is closed from hurt. When you don't acknowledge these hurts, your heart becomes armoured and you're less inclined to want to be vulnerable in the face of possible sexual rejection, or of lack of sexual fulfilment.

But when you speak, feel and validate this hurt, your heart is very forgiving. An open heart is very, very sexy, so use the many tips in this book, especially *Speaking The Unspoken* to get your heart(s) back on track.

Beneath this, there's likely to be a fear of deep intimacy. You might not even know you have this fear, but everyone does (refer to Chapter 6). It often manifests as criticism, doubt, inadequacy, resistance and denial. If you see any of these arising in the bedroom use your ABC to feel through whatever it is into what lies beneath it, as this is the way through into intimacy beyond your imagining.

Differing Levels of Desire

It's very common for one partner to desire more sex than their partner. Traditionally, the man has had the higher level of desire, but nowadays more women find themselves having their sexual advances rejected.

Regardless of your gender, being repeatedly rejected sexually by the person who's supposed to love and desire you hurts like f..k and results in a lowered sense of self-esteem and even self-worth. Meanwhile, being the one who's pursued and made wrong for saying no – all while feeling guilty and fearing any physical contact in case it leads to sex – is no fun either. And nothing dampens desire like obligation.

This difference in desire can lead to a cycle of pursuing and avoiding that skews desires on both sides till neither person knows what's real for them.

Graeme and I find that honest, vulnerable communication helps enormously here. So does approaching sex from the many understandings and practices in this book that help people to get into both their bodies and their hearts. When this happens, desire is a natural outcome and lovemaking becomes incredibly satisfying, with frequency becoming less important so lovers on both sides of the fence are happy.

For more on this topic, see http://www.oztantra.com/desire-mismatch-pursueravoider-cycle/.

Ebbs and Flows are Normal

It's normal for a couple to have reduced desire at times – in fact, it's difficult to sustain unfailing desire in the face of demands from work, children, outside interests, personal healing, hormonal changes, health concerns and even ageing parents.

It's also normal for there to be ebbs and flows in your own sexual arousal, because as a human being, you have ever-changing needs, desires and interests. And sometimes sex is like giving a presentation, preparing a meal or playing golf – no matter what you do, it won't come together (this includes erections)! These times have nothing to do with your underlying love for your partner or your/their level of desirability. Even though personalising it can feel like a natural response, doing so makes it into an unnecessary problem. Instead, choose to let it go and return to the ease inside yourself through your ABC practice.

Lack of Physical Touch Outside the Bedroom

Unconditional nurturing touch helps you to get into your body and feel more connected to your lover. It helps you to relax, trust and open your heart, and is an important part of any intimate relationship – even for men, who often don't understand it or can give themselves permission to receive it.

You can offer neck, shoulder, back or foot massages, but it doesn't need to be this complex. Instead, it can be as simple as a relaxed hug, lying together on the couch or snuggling in bed.

This does NOT work if the only time you offer it is as a prelude to sex - the only thing this leads to is your partner feeling used.

Waiting for Your Partner to Go First

Surely sex is God's cosmic joke on the human race: we need to move through so many layers of difference and vulnerability to get there. It can seem so much easier to wait for your partner to make the first move so they can help you 'get in the mood' and minimise your risk of rejection. Don't let these power games control your sex life: take heart and step up first, dealing with any rejection by falling on your sword and coming safely out the other side.

> *"It's the act of choosing, the freedom involved in choosing, that keeps a relationship alive."*
>
> Esther Perel, Mating In Captivity

Giving Yourself Permission

Sex is not an easy thing to do – at least apart from when the hormones are raging and it just happens, or when you're in a new relationship and you only have to *look* at each other to become aroused. Outside of these times, it takes quite a lot of chutzpah to own yourself as a sexual being, to make sex a high priority, and to ask your partner to join you and believe that they'll want to (and not just because they 'should').

The risk of humiliation makes it seem easier to turn on the TV instead. Don't DO it!

Having a go at offering sex is VERY affirming if you're willing to take the risk. First, find where you are in *your* YES. Then, even if you get a 'no' from your partner, see it as being about them rather than your delicious, desirable self. You can then choose to take care of your own pleasure, or use the energy of your desire in some other creative, or productive way.

Regardless, it's all a great boost to your sense of self-worth.

Owning Your Responsibility

Remember that your pleasure and the feelings of love and fulfilment you desire are YOUR responsibility, not your lover's. Even the best lover in the world can't overcome your resistance if you're not willing to show up too. You're also not responsible for your lover's experience – *continually caretaking for your partner in sex is the death knell of your own desire in the long term.*

Pleasure and intimacy is co-created and you get back what you put in. You're responsible for being fully present in your mind, body and heart, and sharing from this place and that is it. Sharing *with* your lover from your own desire rather than doing it *for* them is the match to the flame.

> "The core of healthy sexuality is full presence in your body and your connection with another person."
>
> Wild Feminine, Tami Lynn Kent

Saying Yes when You mean No

Don't say 'yes' when you really mean no. Saying 'yes' when, if you were being emotionally honest, you'd rather not – or when your partner's every move towards you makes you cringe inside – won't bring you anything in the way of connection or pleasure.

You're much more likely to check out, fake enjoyment to hurry things up, or simply count the minutes until it's over. You'll completely override your body and abandon yourself and shut your sexuality down. It's no fun for your lover either. And in the long run, you'll ruin the chances of creating authentic, loving connection between you and your partner.

It's totally OK to say NO sometimes because the clearer you are in your 'no', the clearer you'll be in your 'Hell yes!' If you have a continual 'no' look at some of the other blocks to lovemaking and see if they can help you find your 'yes'.

Believing Great Sex has to be Spontaneous

Sex definitely doesn't need to be spontaneous to be great. We would bet your golf game (or speech making or cooking) – even if you're a natural – gets better with practice. Remember how hot your longing for weekend dates with your teenage boyfriend or girlfriend used to make you? And they were anything but spontaneous.

Let go of this much-quoted – but quite untrue – myth about sex. Instead, fill yourself with desire by trusting in your ability to create something delicious when the alloted time arises.

Leaving Sex Until the Last Minute

Of course, sometimes leaving things till the last minute is unavoidable, but it's not a habit you want to encourage. Benefits come from making sex part of your everyday connection. This keeps your engines ticking over, so that when it's time for the main event, you're already on the starting line.

Think about the preliminaries for sex that happen automatically during the romantic days of a relationship – things like:

- Regular contact, eg sending loving, thoughtful or HOT text messages
- Spending time together
- Sharing about your day
- Giving compliments and surprises
- Making eye contact when talking
- Non-genital touch such as relaxing hugs, or stroking the back of your lover's neck or shoulders
- Lingerie (if you're into it)
- Even showering, cleaning teeth and kissing.

These often go out the door once a relationship is secure. But these actions aren't simply niceties: they're actually *part of* creating intimate and sexual desire. Things like giving your partner space to decompress or doing the dishes and putting the kids to bed can be real desire burners too. So, check in with your partner about which ones really work for them, and get back into the habit of keeping your erotic tanks filled up!

Not Making Sex a Priority

It's easy to let everything else come first, for it's only selfish pleasure, isn't it? https://www.oztantra.com/sex-just-how-good-is-it-for-you/

Beautiful lovemaking can be, as one of our clients described it, the well-oiled hub of your relationship wheel, making everything else turn smoothly. So, put bedroom play in your diary for at least once per week or fortnight (you can have more of course: this is just a starting place). Then ensure you make it happen, like you do other appointments for the dentist, the accountant or your child's school teacher.

And if you're worried about not being 'in the mood' on the day, use your ABC to get into your bodies, acknowledge and breathe through any resistance and trust what shows up, whether it's simple or earth shattering.

Being in Thinking Mode

Do you find ever yourself planning the next day's activities or reviewing this morning's meeting instead of succumbing to pleasure when you're being sexual? This is particularly common for women, who can generally multi-focus. Meanwhile, men worry more often about how they'll perform. We humans go into thinking mode in sex for the same reason we do in the rest of our emotional lives – to avoid feeling.

 How to Get Out of your Head During Sex

- *Firstly, don't make yourself wrong for being here.*
- *Secondly, rather than focus on the stories in your head, ask yourself what is it that you're avoiding feeling.* Is it fear, anxiety, vulnerability, anger, lack of trust, or even desire, lust and passion? Go into the feeling, accept it and if needed, express it with breath, movement or sound – you'll usually find your sensitivity and pleasure come flooding back in again.
- *Thirdly, if there's no feeling, don't try to analyse the situation.* Instead, to move away from mind distractions, turn your mental attention to your breath and fully experience what you're *feeling* in your body or genitals instead.

If this doesn't work, imagine your mind filling with the colour white, or with cotton wool. Imagine that every thought you have makes the white or the cotton wool more intense. Eventually, your mind will give up and turn off.

Having an Agenda

This is having a fixed idea of what sex has to look like, based on:

- Sex you've had in the past
- What you've seen in porn or movies
- Your fantasies or dreams
- What your friends, parents, religion or ideas on the internet have told you.

Having an idea of how sex *can* be is good as a starting place. But trying to act out that idea and making anything that doesn't fit into it wrong is a limitation. Being present in the moment, in your body, expressing what's up for you and being open to what happens works much better.

If it's been a long time since you've had sex, just start wherever you are and keep it simple. The more you try to push it, the more you can push it away.

Performance Anxiety

Worrying about 'doing it right' can be a big issue for both men and women. Hopefully, by now you're getting a sense that 'performing' isn't necessary. Start with showing up and being authentically vulnerable. Whatever happens after that is a bonus.

> *"Whenever closeness (sexual or not) feels like a requirement – something owed rather than inherently gratifying – it inevitably switches from an aphrodisiac to an anti- aphrodisiac."*
>
> The Erotic Mind, Jack Morin

Negative Judgement

Whether you're judging yourself, your partner or sex itself, this can be a major block to pleasure. Sexual or life force energy arises in a climate of YES! Focussing on the negatives actively shuts off your access to pleasure, literally turning off your desire.

Thinking that your thighs are too fat, your is cock too small, that sex is dirty or that your lover is inadequate is shooting yourself in the foot when it comes to feeling good. So without judging yourself for judging, move your attention onto your breath and into your body instead.

Not Knowing What to Do

Most difficulties in lovemaking between partners come not from an unwillingness to give, but a lack of knowing what to do and how to talk about it.

Overcoming your fear or resistance to speak up for what you need becomes easier if you remember this quote. For some suggestions on talking about sex see pg172 -179. Having a 'sex lab' session every now and again, where you agree to simply experiment with what feels good, what works and what doesn't can help, as can self-pleasuring and learning about your own body's responses.

NB: If your partner is still unwilling to give you what you need once they know what it is, there are probably relationship issues that need to be addressed outside the bedroom.

Fantasising

Fantasy can be fun, but it benefits from the right container. The more strongly you're in a fantasy within your mind, the more disconnected you can be from what you're actually feeling in your body rather than what your mind is telling you you're feeling. And from how your lover might be enjoying, or not enjoying, being there alongside you.

If you really want to piss off your lover, consistently be mentally somewhere else: they're likely to feel abandoned, invalidated or both unless they're busy having a fantasy of their own. If you want to enjoy a mutual fantasy together, this works – but otherwise, save it for when you're alone.

Limiting the Ways You Self-Pleasure

When you self-pleasure the same way every time (perhaps the same way you've been doing since you were twelve), you teach your brain and body a habit – especially if you just focus on tension release. This limits you to responding in this one particular way, which then becomes tricky when you get with your partner. Your body needs to be in exactly the same position and touched in exactly the same way for you to respond and this isn't always possible.

Instead, try touching yourself all over your body, lie on your side or your stomach, and open or close your legs. Relax, stroke your *whole* genital area, rather than just the hot spots, and teach it all to come alive. Rock your hips, breathe and break yourself free.

Limiting Your Ability to Feel

Turning the lights off, getting under the covers, and then hiding behind the push for orgasm is easier than being emotionally open, vulnerable and appearing uncool. Yet your emotional feelings are just as much a part of your lovemaking picture as your sexual ones, for they're all energy, right?

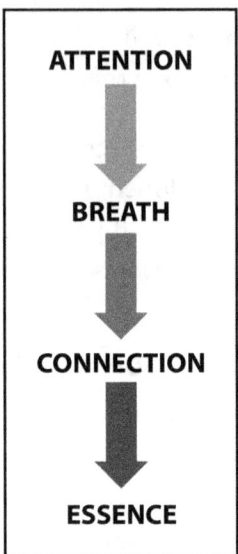

So practice your ABCs, get back into your body and get comfortable with feeling whatever's there, not giving a rat's ass about how you appear. Acknowledging these feelings will feel SO DAMN GOOD (after you've felt them), not to mention greatly increasing your sense of sexual intimacy.

Holding on to Tension

Tension is your worst enemy when it comes to ecstatic sex. Tension anywhere in your body limits the flow of energy through you and keeps your focus in your head. Wherever you identify muscle tension in your body, breathe into it and gently let it go.

Relying on Drugs in Sex

Humans have always used drugs in some form or other to enhance their sexual experience, especially alcohol. As with most things, it's not what you do but how you do it that counts, and using drugs is best as an occasional indulgence. Using any drug comes at a cost because, rather than giving your body energy the way it seems to, it actually draws on your body's own energy to create the high. Over time, this can be draining and unhealthy, so using your breath is much safer.

"Each drug high draws upon your store of Jing (life force), initiates premature ageing and moves you one step closer to death."

Higher & Higher, Jost Sauer

Making What You Feel Wrong

We all have moments in lovemaking where the pleasure, intensity, excitement or feelings of any kind seem to disappear, or even refuse to show up at all – especially if we're trying new things. Or we can feel an emotion surfacing and stuff it down, thinking that emotions aren't cool. And the most common thing to do here is to make what's happening WRONG, which is absolutely the worst thing we can do.

"Emotion plays an enormously important role in sexual desire, arousal and fulfilment. Feelings make sex matter."

The Erotic Mind, Jack Morin

The emotion isn't wrong, it just *is* – and there's no point arguing with reality. Remember that being with the truth of whatever is in the moment is the doorway to something greater. So hold on to yourself, take a few deep breaths, practice your ABC, come back to yourself and start again.

Be OK with the vulnerability that's here: and know that crossing a difficult place brings a surge of sexual energy (like surmounting any challenge) that raises you to greater heights in the bedroom.

Not Being Able to Orgasm

This can affect both men and women, although it's much more common in women, and much more common than most women know. Everyone is *capable* of having an orgasm, but we encourage you not to make yourself wrong if you can't at any given time. If you instead make your way through the pleasure suggestions here, loving yourself along the way, it will likely happen. You might also explore your unconscious beliefs through listening to your body via the healing sexual numbness practice what follows.

Limiting Beliefs About Partner Sex

What judgements and justifications do you carry about how sex should be that might be influencing your sexual behaviour? Explore them, own them, and be open to hearing those of your partner. You never know what you might learn.

To help you get started, here are some common beliefs about sex with another person:

- Relationship sex should only be in bed, at night, with the lights off
- Men should want sex all the time, and they're wrong if they don't
- Women shouldn't want sex at all, and they're wrong if they do
- Women only want connection, not sex and vice versa
- For a woman to be sexually desirable, her lover needs to have an erection
- If I'm in a relationship, my partner owes me sex
- A man needs to 'come' every time, while a woman doesn't
- If we've both had an orgasm, that was fulfilling sex
- Erotic or naughty sex needs to be kept outside my relationship, and my partner will reject me if I mention it
- Once I've passed menopause, there's nothing in sex for me

- I need to have sex at 55 the same way I had it at 25
- The man always needs to be in charge in sex
- If there's no libido, there's no sex.

To help you see how the power of how these beliefs might play out, read through the real-life scenarios below

> ### Women vs Men – Most Unhelpful Beliefs
>
> Jennifer wanted to enjoy sex more, but she couldn't help it: all she felt when Chris rolled over to her with his morning erection nudging her in the back was anger. She was angry that he hadn't connected with her at all for the past few days, and now he wanted sex!
>
> **Belief: All men really want is just sex.**
>
> What Jennifer didn't see was that Chris had also felt the distance between them and was looking to connect with her from his heart. And she didn't realise that allowing himself to have his erection felt, judged and possibly rejected involved a high level of vulnerability for him.
>
> Meanwhile, Carrie wanted to have an orgasm so badly, and got SO frustrated when Richard went straight for her genitals without kissing her or stroking her breasts. And to top it off, he couldn't find the right 'spot' on her clitoris.
>
> **Belief: it's the man's responsibility to give her an orgasm,** and it was Richard's fault she couldn't have one.
>
> Carrie didn't realise how closed off she was from herself, and that her judgement was closing off her pleasure and pushing Richard away. It wasn't totally his fault for going straight to the 'engine room' to get something happening for he was avoiding the hurt from her closed heart.

> ### 💬 Men vs Women – Most Unhelpful Beliefs
>
> *Hal wanted to be a good lover, so he searched the internet and read all the right blogs and books to improve his technique.*
>
> **Belief: a man who can give his partner a good orgasm is a great lover.**
>
> *What he didn't realise was that in perfecting his technique, he was keeping himself emotionally separate from his wife Thea, who didn't relish the idea of being merely tuned like one of Hal's prize Porsches. She hated having to have an orgasm for his satisfaction and was ultimately more interested in feeling his heart open to her.*
>
> *Meanwhile, Ian was angry that Robyn didn't want sex anymore, no matter how much he pleaded with her, bathed the kids and did the dishes. Ian thought Robyn owed it to him.*
>
> **Belief: as a husband, a man is entitled to sex.**
>
> *He didn't see that his sense of entitlement and heading straight for penetration left Robyn feeling obligated, unaroused and ignored. Nor did he see that his shame about his self-worth was causing him to get in and out of sex as quickly as possible to avoid really feeling, which just left Robyn further unsatisfied.*

Make it a practice to explore your own beliefs about partner sex. Then, when you see them limiting your experience, feel the feelings inside them. Share them with your partner. Let them go with your breath and choose new, more helpful ones. Over time, they'll give up.

Subconscious Needs

Your subconscious mind is very sneaky and persistent about getting its needs met, and it can sneak many needs in under the guise of sexual desire. Carrying these needs unseen inside you can leave you unconsciously manipulating either yourself or your partner to meet them. This not only detracts from the free flow of your life force energy, but it also leaves you more open to being hurt or triggered. When you identify and acknowledge these needs, however, they no longer act as blocks.

Ask yourself whether you're having sex to:

- Relieve stress
- Be needed
- Be validated
- Get love
- Act out or relieve shame
- Express anger covertly
- Be physically close but avoid intimacy
- Have power over something/someone
- Get high to avoid real life issues.

Just naming the truth of what's happening for you goes a long way to clearing it. Name it first to yourself, and then to your partner. See this sharing as a way to open yourself up for enhanced pleasure and connection. Then explore what's in sex for you outside of these needs. Plus, explore other ways in your life that you can seek to meet these needs and minimise the amount of baggage you bring in to the bedroom.

Unconscious Patterning

Your very first experience of sex with another person strongly colours your perceptions and future experiences of sex.

If your experience was a positive one, you'll continue to view sex in a positive way – and vice versa. The same is true with sexual values from your family, culture, religion and gender. Any negative experiences and beliefs can create frozen or blocked areas in your body and set up unconscious expectations, needs and desires.

> *"The human libido is not a hardwired, invariable biological urge but can be curiously fickle, altered by our psychology and the history of our sexual encounters."*
>
> The Brain That Changes Itself, Norman Doidge MD

However, Graeme and I see these not as problems, but as further riches to explore. For example:

- If your parents never spoke about sex or made pleasure wrong, you might feel guilt or shame *whenever* you feel sexual
- If your first experience of self pleasure was by yourself in the dark, it will automatically be easier for you to find sexual pleasure here
- If you were shamed about touching yourself, you might believe that sex and your body is dirty, causing it to freeze in shame
- If you were caught out in an innocent sexual act by someone else, you may have an a fear of, or attraction to, being seen in sex
- You can also become contracted in your sexual confidence by sexual shaming from current or previous partners.

You can uncover this patterning through doing your ABC, being more present and embodied in your lovemaking, and acknowledging with compassion then being willing to release any stuck, unfeeling, or shame-based places you might be limiting yourself. (Again refer to Identifying your beliefs in chapter 4.) This allows you to rescript your sexual experiences with healthy beliefs and desires.

Making Your Fantasies Wrong

Everybody probably everyone thinks their own fantasies verge on the bizarre – this is often part of their allure. But they're not likely to be as unique as you think amongst the world's population – or as shameful – as you fear.

See your sexual fantasies as a normal and healthy part of you, and explore what real-world need they fulfil, eg power, freedom, validation, naughtiness, comfort, shame, etc. If you feel able to, sharing them with your partner invites a deep level of intimacy. And you never know – they may be willing to explore them with you in creative ways. If not, however, remember their 'no' is about them, not you.

Sex after Childbirth

This deserves a special mention, as the time after a new babe arrives is the hardest period to schedule in intimate time. Mum is sleep-deprived and overwhelmed with the baby, especially in the first 6 weeks – 3 months, while Dad is a bit out in the cold and unsure.

It's crucial to find a place for your adult relationship as soon as is practical after childbirth. The longer this gap lasts, the harder it will be to fill. Yes, the child's needs are important, but having disconnected and resentful parents as they grow up is not what they need either.

For more on this important topic, see http://www.oztantra.com/and-baby-makes-3/.

Sex at 40, 50, 60 and onwards is not the same as at 20

Focusing on being sexual at 40 or 60 in the same way as you were when you were 25 happens because you misunderstand the true nature of your sexuality. Just like nature, it's always changing. You're not the same person you used to be then, so the way you have sex needs to change as well (and the great news is that it gets better!).

As we get older, most of us become more comfortable in ourselves, who we are, and what we want. Sex at this time is less about hormones, libido and goal-chasing, and instead becomes a choice we actively make to be sexual. It's less frenetic and more based in relaxation and heart open authenticity. Orgasms become more full-bodied, less of one big genital peak, and more heart opening.

If you want to keep your love life vibrant and alive, you need to shift into this different type of lovemaking. From here, your desire for sexual connection will continue long onto the future.

For more info on dealing with sex in menopause, see:

- http://www.oztantra.com/menopause-suffering-alchemy/
- http://www.oztantra.com/relationship-survival-strategy-men-living-woman-menopause/

Painful Sex

This is when sex creates feelings of anything from a burning, stinging irritation to extreme muscle tension and resistance. It's more common in women but it can also affect men.

The pain can be based in physical, mechanical or emotional causes – but regardless, it's a real concern and is *not* something to be tolerated. Women especially are very good at 'putting up' with things, but this is NOT a good idea. Instead, do something about it. Even if the pain has become chronic, there is much you can do about it.

For more on this, see www.oztantra.com/painful-sex/

Sexual Abuse

An incredible number of people have experienced sexual assault. An estimated 1.3 million Australian women and 360,000 men experienced an incident of sexual assault since the age of 15, according to results from the Personal Safety Survey 2005 (ABS, 2006a). This figure translates approximately to 1 in 6 women and 1 in 20 men. And most commonly, childhood sexual abuse figures worldwide average between 15-30% for females, and between 3-15% for males (Fergusson and Mullen 1999).

Even more devastating than the abuse itself are the self-beliefs that victims take on as a result, which impact their lives and relationships until examined and healed. Turning this negative experience into a positive one is definitely possible through sexual healing practices, which help victims to reclaim the dignity and sacredness of their sexuality.

However, the approach needs to be a multi-stranded one that includes working with the physical, mental, emotional and sexual impact of the abuse. Many of the practices Graeme and I offer impact directly on this delicate area. You can start many of these yourself, such as being present, feeling blocks and emotions, expressing feelings and sounds, using conscious breath, de-shaming sex, receiving sexually, and replacing unhelpful beliefs and painful memories with positive ones. However, you don't *have* to deal with this alone – see a good therapist if it feels too overwhelming to do it yourself. See the practice on healing sexual pain below.

For further info see www.oztantra.com/sexual-healing/.

Genital Numbness

Numbness happens when the sensitivity of your genital tissues becomes reduced (or even completely numbed) over time through repetitive mechanical, painful or closed-hearted sex.

Genital numbness means that it takes more effort to feel, and that pleasure and orgasms become delayed or non-existent. Erections are less potent, breasts less sensitive, and Yonis become deadened. This is especially true for people who've experienced obvious sexual trauma, but it can happen to most of us at some point in our sexual lives.

These changes are NOT, as commonly thought, merely age-related. They are, however, a normal part of our sexual complexity. We've been taught to manage this numbness by pushing harder and faster, which may work short-term, but it compounds the problem over the long run. Or we might shut down and pull away in shame, which is a real shame.

The solution is to avoid making this situation (or yourself or your partner) wrong. Instead see it instead as your bodies way of getting your attention and forcing you off automatic pilot to look deeper. It's time to re-sensitise your genitals, and free up the underlying emotional shutdown. The good news is that many of the tips in this book will begin this process; and making the following exercise a normal part of your lovemaking means you'll be keeping it alive for many years to come.

 Feeling Into Sexual Pain and Numbness

If Graeme and I could give you only one practice to enhance your sex life and resolve genital pain and numbness, this would be the one. There's so much to learn about yourselves and each other through it. Here's what to do:

- Any time you become aware of pain or numbness (or lack of arousal) in sex, feel into it, rather than override it.
- Stay with the feeling in your body (let your partner know what you are doing) to explore what's inside it, using your ABC. You may find memories arising, if you do simply observe them. As with any other feelings, doing this will make it pass into something more alive. Breathing and making sounds here can help. If you need further assistance see the Seeing Your Shadow activity in Chapter 9.
- If you're self-pleasuring, take the time to feel into those moments when you've pushed yourself, or over-ridden your boundaries, then release them on your breath.

The more in pain or numb you are, the longer this will take. But it will happen, and it's worth waiting for. Believe us – we've been there! Trust that the pleasure you long for is still there inside you, stronger than you ever imagined possible. For the more you trust it, the more it will trust you and show up.

If this does not resolve, get it checked out by your GP to ensure there's nothing going on that requires medical attention.

> To support your partner here just be encouraging and don't get in the way by making it about you.

Giving Up

Just because you don't have what you want right now doesn't mean that it's not going to happen. Even if you judge your partner as being a long way from the lover of your dreams, it doesn't mean that they don't want to – or can't – meet you in your desires.

Whatever your blocks are, don't sell yourself or your partner short by giving up. Each step forward you take is an incredible gift.

The Shadow and the Spy

9.1 Embracing The Shadow

What exactly are 'shadows', and why should we be interested in them? Your shadows are the dark or 'wrong' parts of your egoic personality that lie in your unconscious. They can be anything: feelings of inadequacy; problems dealing with anger; addictions; the inability to speak up for yourself, let someone in close or be sexually expressive. All the way to the covert, or even overt potential for violence we all carry.

Shadows can be generated by your past experiences, including past and childhood relationships. They can come from your cultural, religious, or societal background, your gender, your career and even your physical environment, eg cities, small towns or war zones.

Shadows are normal, and we all have them. They're part of what makes us unique. And they should interest you because they hold a lot of energy. Bringing them to light rather than making them wrong brings *juice* to your relationship.

"The term 'shadow' refers to the 'dark side' of our psyche – those aspects of ourselves that we have split off, rejected, denied, hidden from ourselves, projected onto others, or otherwise disowned."

Integral Life Practice, Ken Wilber

Shadows underlie the little and large irritations that trigger hurt in a relationship, leaving you believing that you've fallen out of love with your partner. The reality is more likely that your love still exists, but that a shadow lies in the way of it. Back in Chapter 3, we covered how to deal with shadows when they show up as emotional triggers. This chapter will show the process that underlies them more clearly, and help you see how to remove your triggers altogether in the long term.

> ### What Can a Shadow Look Like?
>
> *Julia had an authoritative and demanding mother who was always in the right, and as a result, she never developed much self-confidence. So when her husband John expresses a forthright opinion or raises his voice, Julia is triggered right back to standing in front of her mother, unable to find her own voice.*
>
> *Julia, who otherwise feels safe with John, then occasionally unleashes the torrent of anger at him that she'd been unable to express to her mother. John is left feeling hurt and confused, wondering what he's done wrong and who this completely unpredictable woman he's married to is.*

Your Shadows Fall for Each Other Too

We've talked about how the unconscious part of your brain actually chooses your partner for you. Your conscious brain might have thought you fell for their good looks, their cute smile that made your heart turn over, or your shared values – but underneath, darker doings were underway. Your unconscious brain contains incomplete material that needs to be completed for you to become whole, and it subtly influences you to choose a mate with just the right triggers to bring up whatever's unresolved in you, or to reveal your hidden talents.

In other words, you attracted a partner with shadows that perfectly mirror or complement your own so that you can see your own, because your psyche – just like your body – is built to heal.

Being messy isn't failing, but staying there is

Your conditioning tells you to see the messy parts of your relationship (your shadows) as failures. Graeme and I say that you can choose to see them as gold. Rather than shaming yourselves for your shadows, you can see them for what they are: part of your humanity that you can accept and learn from.

Even though they're deadly serious, at times you can even make them fun if you take the shame out of them by not taking yourself too seriously. They can be like the deliciousness in occasionally over-indulging in a chocolate dessert, flirting, saying the unmentionable at the dinner table, or being 'naughty' in sex.

Looking into the closet

Bringing a shadow out to the light, owning it and freeing the feelings attached to it totally disempowers it. It's like turning the light on in a dark room.

When your psychological shadows are shared and made OK, they form an incredibly strong matrix that holds your relationship together. True intimacy depends on you both being comfortable with (or at least willing to) reveal some of the shadows that lie behind your masks of social acceptability. Doing this brings you each the joy of being loved for who you really are, rather than for who you, or others think you 'should' be. You can easily love each other for what you admire, but sharing the vulnerability of your darkness takes you deeper, and is necessary for your relationship to thrive.

How Shadows Form

Our shadows form as we become 'civilised', sociable and acceptable human beings who can live together in society and follow rules to get along with each other. But our unacceptable, withheld parts don't disappear – they simply retreat and drive us from within.

Shadows are what show up in your life *today* as the parts that don't work for you or your relationship. They're the parts that leave you and your partner feeling misunderstood, hurt, angry and alone. The more you try to hide them, the more they leak out in unconscious ways. Think of the 'nice guy' who covertly takes his anger out on his partner by constantly 'tuning her out' in conversation.

Your shadow's negative effects are most strongly felt by those you're closest to, and they can slap you in the face when your partner is no longer willing to tolerate them. Think of the woman who disappears into being 'the perfect wife', and then can't believe that her husband has an affair with someone he can 'feel'.

There's safety in our shadows

Our shadows always have a positive in them for us, which makes them harder to both see, and to give up. Exposing them with compassion helps them to let go gently.

9: The Shadow and the Spy

> 💬 **Seeing the Positive and Its Shadow Underneath**
>
> Being a civic leader with no time for his relationship allows John to avoid his lack of sexual potency.
>
> Vivienne's drinking means she doesn't need to confront her fears about getting a job that will keep their mortgage payments up.

Converging Shadows

This happens when both partners project their shadows onto each other at the same time, and it's difficult for them each to see the wood from the trees.

> 💬 **Playing Three-Dimensional Chess Whilst Blindfolded**
>
> Stella niggles Ben emotionally with criticisms and subtly shaming comments that needle him until he strikes out violently. This allows her to shame him further by exclaiming, "See what an abusive man you are!"

Stella's projection that Ben is abusive is supported by the strongly held societal belief that men are always the domestic abusers in relationship, making Stella the victim. Of course, men can be abusers, but they're not automatically so, and refusing to look at her own actions prevents Stella from seeing the unhappiness that perpetuates her need to take Ben down a peg or two.

Stella's gold is in looking at her lack of self-worth and exploring ways to become more self-empowered and self-loving, so she can drop her need to infuriate Ben.

Meanwhile, Ben labours under his idea of himself as a 'good man' who protects his woman by tolerating her niggling, because he's *bigger and stronger and could really hurt her. This is until his own trigger point is reached, and he lashes out at Stella in ways he immediately regrets.*

His gold is to believe it's OK for him to walk away from Stella's insults, to open his heart to himself, let her know it's not OK for her to shame him, and trust it's not unmanly to let her know how much it kills him when she does so.

Don't Try to 'Fix' Your Relationship

Your shadows underlie most of the big problem areas in your relationship. And most of these problems aren't about the relationship at all: they're about you or your partner as individuals. So instead of pointing the finger, it's time to say 'I', rather than 'you'.

Your deepest shadows formed back during a time before you and your partner even met –in your childhood – where your strongest beliefs developed and where your most vulnerable feelings are found. These shadows carry extremely potent triggers from your past that you use to try to hook your partner into your suffering in the present.

So, when you're in a stuck place in your relationship, it's time to look within to where your shadows might be lurking in you, rather than trying to fix the relationship.

The general rule with your shadows is that if you don't own them, they will own you.

Once you own the shadow, your relationship 'problem' will fix itself. You may have to own a shadow more than once (sometimes many times), but each time it's seen and owned, it has less power over you. Graeme and I always advise troubled couples to address their shadows in their current relationship, rather than simply separate and take the shadow with them into their next one. By the time they've cleared their troubling shadow, most find their relationships have discovered new life.

Using your ABC to feel yourself fully and drop into your heart is the most direct way of 'seeing' your psychological shadows and owning them with compassion

Look for the 'I' rather than the 'You'

Here Are Some More Real Life Examples:

- *Andrea had indifferent parents, and is now is needy of Clinton's attention, but can't see that her constant demands put a wall between them that he can't penetrate. Her childhood invalidation leaves her emotionally closed and unavailable him. Her gift is to find emotional security in her connection with herself and come to Clinton from desire rather than need.*
- *Stan learned to manage his high anxiety by being the caretaker in his family of origin, as keeping everyone happy made him feel safe. Now he constantly avoids rocking the boat in his adult relationship with Beth. He'd be less anxious if he stood up for his own authentic needs and desires, which would make him more emotionally available, and sexually desirable, to his wife.*
- *Claudia unknowingly pushes Alistair away with her constant criticism, not realising how painful this is for him. She grew up with a critical Dad, so for her, criticism was just a normal part of 'love'. Seeing Alistair's pain and feeling her own is the gift she needs in order to change her behaviour in the relationship.*

- *Simon had an emotionally explosive past partner who constantly manipulated him, and now doesn't realise his need for emotional distance in his relationship with Laura is driving a wedge between them. His gold is to heal the past and learn to trust.*
- *Stavros, who has a Greek background, feels hurt that his English girlfriend Alma can't display the open affection he grew up with. His challenge is to let her know how important they are to him and offer her examples without pressuring her to return them, until she feels secure enough to do so.*
- *Shirley denies her partner sex after menopause because she believes this is what older women 'do'. This leaves her husband Clive mourning the loss of their closeness and turning to occasional internet porn. Shirley's challenge is to find new value in her sexuality for herself, which she can then share with him.*
- *Gerald is a man used to his own authority. Taught by society and his father's example that 'this is how men are', he doesn't see how his unwillingness to listen to his wife June's opinion and share the decision-making with her enhances her feelings of disempowerment. Then, he feels contemptuous of her. His gold is to loosen the reins and enjoy the support of being part of a team. This would leave him feeling freer and more loved, rather than less of a man.*
- *Donna is frustrated because Angus isn't showing up with her sexually and doesn't see that her angry sexual taunts create a trauma in him that feels like a physical assault. When she connects more fully with her own feelings instead of focusing on Angus' lack, Donna sees that she's projecting an early sexual abuser onto him, and then playing out her misplaced anger. Healing her wounding from her abuse allows Donna to relax in sex and gives Angus room to come closer.*
- *John is an angry man with a violent temper, and feels unloved by his wife Joan, not seeing that his abusive anger has driven a wedge between them. His task is to learn that the more vulnerable feelings that lie underneath his self-protective anger*

are about the loss of his childhood friend to suicide, rather than about Joan, and allow her in closer.
- *Angela feels totally overwhelmed and controlled in her relationship with Theo because of his narcissistic tendencies. She reads on the internet how painful it is living with a narcissist is and feels increasingly trapped. Her goal is to believe she has the right to set firm, clear boundaries and to leave the relationship if she can't be heard. These are the parts she needs support to find more of- the part that is less accommodating and that can stand up and say "no".*
- *Patrick, a man who feels shame and guilt about his sexuality, doesn't feel free in himself to fully make love with his wife. So he becomes righteous and shaming about her sexual behaviour, rather than allowing himself to be more sexually free, which is where his gold is.*
- *Sexually attractive Natalie complains about Blair's jealousy of other men without realising that she hasn't let him in close enough for him to feel secure with her. Natalie doesn't trust men enough to let them close because of her sexually inappropriate father. Her gold is to heal her past, see Blair for the trustworthy man he is, and let him in.*
- *Dylan doesn't trust himself enough to fully meet Claire in their relationship. He's tried hard to be successful in life, coming up through the army like his father, and successfully serving in Afghanistan. His military training makes it difficult for him to let down his tough exterior and show Claire the many beautiful layers of his inner world, which is where his gold is.*
- *Nicole was head over heels in love with her first boyfriend, but he overrode her non-existent sexual boundaries. She doesn't realise that her inability to feel anything sexually now comes, not from her current boyfriend Zack's technique, but from her closed heart. Her gift is to heal her pain from the past and show up in her vulnerable heart in the present.*

- *Chen was brought up to think he was the strong man in the family with no wants or needs of his own. He was there to provide not to receive. It was only when he started to connect with himself through his feeling realm that he was able to let himself be loved by his wife Jia. He felt his own preciousness as a result, leading him to make some healthier life choices.*
- *Paula and Stuart both grew up in sexually repressive households. Paula's family was Catholic and Stuart's was overly permissive, with their overt sexual expression and nakedness creating shame in him. Both Paula and Stuart found gold in moving through their sexual shame into an empowered and loving sexuality in their relationship.*

We're Built to Heal

Graeme and I feel grateful to our own shadows for the self-learning, intimacy and freedom they've created in our relationship. As a result, we don't seek to be perfect: just perfectly human. We know that having little to fear or hide in ourselves is a powerful and loving place to live from.

Annette Reveals Her Personal Shadow

As a shy child, I developed the persona of a 'good' girl, because I saw that being 'good' meant being accepted, included and cared for. At the same time, I covered up my insecurities and squashed my temper – a temper that came from not feeling able to speak up for my needs. And for much of my life, this good girl persona worked for me, allowing me to fit in with my caring-but-busy family of origin, my nursing career and the husband I wanted to be good enough for.

Over the years, however, it became evident that the nicer I appeared on the surface the more scared, covert, manipulative and resentful

I became underneath. This was particularly true in my marriage, where my deepest needs for love and intimacy lived.

Not owning the 'real, but imperfect' part of me kept my heart closed to both my husband and myself, denying me the love I craved as I projected my emotionally unavailable self onto my partner. There were even times that part of me enjoyed my shadow behaviour, feeling it was revenge on my ex for not being everything I 'needed' him to be.

In my current relationship with Graeme though, I've allowed myself to be seen warts and all, slowly making friends with and integrating the more colourful aspects of my persona. It was by no means easy, but with his unending love and understanding, it happened.

Graeme's challenge has been to believe in my innate wholeness, the part which had attracted him, and not get caught up in my persona's manipulations, which denied him the authentic intimacy he craved. And he needed to do it without stepping out of the relationship, which at times felt like his only answer.

Graeme's Thoughts on His Shadow

A difficult early life taught me that as a male, I was inferior, unlovable and sexually inadequate. I didn't realise that this self-defeating belief permeated every aspect of my life, personality, sport and business. As a result, I spent most of my life disconnected from myself, not really trusting my deeper self and creating a 'false floor' for my personality to live from.

This floor remained firmly in place until my early 40s, when I 'fell' through it and connected with the true self underneath. I know now that my ego had taken over, giving me the perceived safety of creating an external, material life that I believed I really wanted.

However, I felt empty at achieving it and wondered why I felt so devastated at 'having it all'. It didn't make sense.

Because I knew nothing about the concept of my shadow at the time, it took relationship breakdown, bankruptcy and total life change to come to terms with this aspect of myself.

My process has given me a different perspective on the power and control that shadows can have, and also the challenges facing those who seek to bring their shadows into the light. The most difficult instances of shadow to deal with are when people don't believe they have one and refuse to accept this aspect of their personality. The devastation in my own life is a testament to how much pain I had to endure before I admitted to and brought my own shadow out from under my home-built protection.

Annette's challenge was to see my whole person, and not play into my belief that I was unlovable. It was to see my gold within, believe in my process of finding it, and eventually see the gift of my mirroring her own lack of self-connection.

In my relationship with Annette, our shadows co-existed – her neediness and trying to manipulate getting love, and my not believing I deserved it. This lasted until each of us gradually realised that we wanted the more authentic, loving connection that bringing our individual shadows out into the open could bring.

Even then, the slippery little suckers took a while to let go. Shadow work takes time, skill and really good support – and each individual can only go into this area if they choose to. You can choose to ignore your own shadow, but in time it will come out in a way that won't be easy or comfortable.

The sooner you look and more open you are to seeing yourself, the easier, though never easy, the process is.

The Gold in the Shadow Itself

As we mentioned earlier, there's always gold in our shadows, and Graeme and I can personally appreciate this. My 'good' persona became a caring nurse/wife/facilitator, while Graeme's wounded child brought him a deep capacity for understanding and empathy in his work. And it's the same for other people: the obsessive/compulsive person who's very good at home maintenance; or the successful but unscrupulous businessman who can financially support his stepchildren.

The value in owning your shadows is that you can enjoy their positive aspects without allowing them to deny you the more well-rounded parts of yourself that live underneath.

Shadows can Also be Golden

Golden Shadows contain no negative behaviours. Instead, they hide your innate gifts and talents. It's only in hiding them that pain develops.

> **Kieran's Golden Shadow**
>
> *Kieran had a talent for painting but grew up in a business-oriented family that didn't value the arts. So he suppressed this part of himself, and instead went into the family business. However, this led to treatment-resistant depression that severely impacted his relationship with his wife and family.*
>
> *Giving himself permission to express his artistic talent greatly reduced Kieran's depression, and allowed him to become an active participant in his intimate and family life.*

Shadows Bring the Gift of Humility

Whether your shadows are large or small, the added bonus of confronting and honestly owning them is an authentic love and realness in your relationship that can't be matched. It's an intimate realness that draws your partner towards you despite your deepest fears of rejection, as you reveal the wholeness that lies within alongside your flawed humanity.

Doing shadow work reminds you that you're not the perfect image (or the totally flawed one!) that your ego likes to think you are. It will also let you see where you've hurt your partner. An important part of shadow work is to be honest with your partner, who's usually suffered as a result of your shadow, and to listen to their side of the experience with empathy and understanding.

Even though your partner is ultimately responsible for how much they choose to let your behaviours control them, your actions do of course impact on them. This listening requires feeling shame that is healthy and appropriate, but still uncomfortable. If you make it welcome, like all feelings, it will move through you. When this process is genuine, it invites understanding and forgiveness from your partner, so it's a powerful meeting in the heart, and great relationship glue.

Be aware that your shadow has hurt *you* too, so another step is to be gentle with yourself for not knowing what you can't see, rather than beating yourself up for it. And to forgive yourself for the suffering you've caused yourself.

Bringing Your Shadows to Light

The trick in acknowledging your shadows are not to make them wrong, for this will only push them deeper into shame and make them much harder to find and do something about. Instead, try to become a loving detective in your own life, and root out your shadows. In this way, you gain energy from them, building in relationship longevity and having some fun in the process.

9.2 Doing Jigsaws: How To See The Unseen

Shadows are seen more easily in an atmosphere of acceptance. Remember that being blemish-free DOESN'T mean being closer to perfection. It's much like the way the slightly speckled piece of fruit from your Grandma's old peach tree has more flavour and juice than a perfect-looking, cold-stored, genetically modified one.

So don't imagine yourself and your partner as flawed, imperfect beings that need to 'fixed'. For the more you think of yourselves as flawed, the more ashamed, fear-based and resistant to change you become. But don't think of yourself as someone who's 'above all that stuff' either as doing this leaves others to deal with the results of your unconscious behaviours. It means you not only push your partner away, but you also miss out on the freedom and resilience that shadow work brings.

> *"To change, a person must face the dragon of his appetites with another dragon, the life energy of the soul"*
>
> The Soul of Rumi: A New Collection of Ecstatic Poems, Rumi

Instead, think of yourself and your partner as jigsaws with many unique, individual pieces to be explored and enjoyed. The more pieces you identify and put together, the greater access to your whole selves you'll have – and the greater freedom, resilience, longevity and love you'll each have in your relationship.

So if you're ready and willing to look into your own darkness and find your way to increased energy, serious freedom and a healthier relationship in your life, how do you actually see the unseen? Start by imagining yourself putting on your Sherlock Holmes hat, and picking up your magnifying glass with an attitude of curiosity.

Coming Together

Your biggest laughs can come from seeing the reality behind your veil of projected illusion, and how far from reality your projections had become.

How to See Your Shadow Self

You can look at your shadow self through the gift of your mirrors, projections and triggers – your psyche's way of letting you see what's hidden within you. They're also found in your strongly defended 10% truth / 90% bullshit.

Different ways to recognise your shadows:

1. *Spend more time in your ABC process.* Drop into your heart, trusting its powers of insight and wisdom to show you where you have walls, resistance or contraction, and where you're not being in your authentic self.

2. *Notice the places where you become most self-righteous.* Look for places where you're 100% certain that your partner is at fault and you're not. These points are SO painful because they're deeply personal and lodged deep in your individual psyche.

   These places usually carry a feeling of unexplainable urgency to get sorted, or a need to urgently have met. Remember that this is your psyche urgently projecting your hurts outside of you, so that you can see them. It reminds you to look inside yourself for your solutions, rather than at your innocent (or even not so innocent) partner.

3. *Shadows live in the places where you get triggered into major emotions by relatively minor events.* So if this is happening for you, know that it's about something inside you: either an unhelpful belief or an unresolved experience from the past you're still carrying.

4. *Shadows also live in the places where you find it hard to move on after a fight.* You might feel the need to keep your distance, to hold onto your 10% and definitely not give in, in order to protect yourself. You may even feel that you should make your partner work hard to get your love again, because you blame them for your hurt, whilst you're left feeling unloved and wondering where all the magic went. Your desire to protect yourself, although understandable, keeps you from resolving your pain.

5. *Do you have a primary emotion that seems to be your particular default setting?* If so, then no matter what the situation is, this emotion is your first line of response. In this case, your default emotion is probably a secondary one that you've used to hide the primary one from yourself eg using anger to cover sadness, fear or shame. Use your ABC to go underneath your default secondary emotion to the primary feeling that lies underneath it. Feel this one and you'll free yourself.

6. *Notice what triggers you in your partner.* What pisses you off in others is what you hold in fear or contempt in yourself. For example, if you're scared or irritated by your partner's frequent anger, ask yourself whether there's unacknowledged anger in you. If you resent your partner's ability to speak up for their needs, can you identify where you deny your own need to speak up? If you see your partner making independent choices and make them wrong for it, are you denying your own independent self?

7. *Notice where you continually cross your partner's boundary. There will be a gift hiding there for you.*

8. *Sometimes, the merest hint of a shadow can flicker around the edges of your awareness.* It can give you just a subtle flash of what might be lying underneath your awareness. Trust these flashes and be open to more of them being revealed over time.

9. *Check in with your beliefs.* For example if you see you partner as untrustworthy even though they deny it, ask yourself whether you're projecting your own unacknowledged distrust of yourself onto them.

Or if you fear your partner is having an affair, and your allegations confuse and hurt them (because they have no desire for one), is it your own insecurity, your fear of having an affair or your denial of your sexual self you're projecting?

The more resistance you have to identifying what's happening for you, the more deeply your shadow will hold it. If you look at this part and say vehemently, "No way. That's not me!" it's probably in you somewhere.

This revealing is part of the mystery in relationship and in life, and it really *can* be like doing a jigsaw.

 Seeing Your Shadows

This is a good way to see where your own shadow might lie around your partner's behaviour. Unlike the ABC process, which we discussed for dealing an emotional trigger as it's happening, you can do this exercise any time you want to explore. Be open to magic here.

Part 1

1. Centre and ground yourself with your ABC, then think of something your partner does that pisses you off or hurts you. Take the time to really flesh out this experience in your mind – how your partner looks and what they say/do – and find the feelings in you that always come along in this situation.
2. Once you've got this clearly, detach from the image of your partner in your mind and focus on your own feelings as separate from them instead.
3. Identify where in your body your feeling is. Feel it fully, breathe into it, and stay with it even if it's painful.
4. Trust that this feeling has a message for you; and as you sit with it, notice whether there's a word, image or other deeper feeling that you can identify. Follow these signposts deeper into your psyche. (If you feel unsafe at any time, you can imagine someone you trust being there to support you.)

5. Ask yourself what this feeling/word/image is showing you. Keep feeling until you find your original pain point in the situation. You've got it when you start to see it's really nothing about your partner at all, but instead something unseen within you. This may be all you need to do. But if it feels like there are still layers hiding within you to be resolved do Part 2.

Part 2

Keeping in contact with the feeling, ask yourself the following:

- How old were you when whatever caused this pain point happened? Who was there with you? What was happening at the time? How were you responding? Allow the scene to fill out in your mind's eye. Notice if the story is coming from your body's intuition, or your egoic mind. If it's the latter, drop this story and go deeper into your body feeling.
- Ask yourself what's unresolved here. What didn't happen at the time that you needed to happen? Did you need to speak up, get angry, say no, say yes, say sorry, be heard, be understood, be protected, or to forgive or be forgiven?
- Imagine it happening *now*. You can resolve the past in the present because your imaginative mind doesn't know the difference between the two. You *cannot undo what has been done*, but you can resolve it. Imagine yourself saying or doing whatever you didn't then. Choose new beliefs to replace the unhelpful one.
- Ask the other people in the story with you what was happening for *them* at this time. Then imagine stepping inside them and seeing the situation from their perspective and trust what comes. This doesn't *excuse* any wrong behaviour, but it does bring understanding and reaffirms your belief in the safety of mutually imperfect humanity. This is often where the biggest shifts are.
- Ask yourself what positive benefits you received from this shadow, eg protection, safety, anonymity, power, etc.
- Ask yourself what negative beliefs you took on as a result of this experience.

- How do those beliefs impact you today? How willing are you to let go of them? Are there any new beliefs you can take on, or behaviours you can choose as a result of what you've learned?
- Keep exploring possibilities until you feel yourself dropping into your heart, and feel your hurt shifting.

6. Imagine yourself observing this annoying behaviour in your partner in the future and notice yourself feeling neutral instead of triggered, and choosing to respond differently, creating a better outcome.
7. Take some conscious breaths into your body, feel your feet on the floor, stretch and open your eyes.

Welcome Back!

NB. This process doesn't mean you always let your partner's behaviour go unchallenged to focus on your own reactions. Sometimes you need to set boundaries for yourself and not put up with behaviour that is abusive. Using this process allows you to do so more clearly.

To be led through this process, see www.oztantra.com/tantric-meditations.

How do You Know When You've Fully Seen and Owned a Shadow?

- The first step is being able to see it as something separate from your essential self, like when the picture in a jigsaw becomes clear.
- The second is seeing how it controls you in unhelpful ways.
- The next step is being able to see it as something separate from you with more detachment and less emotion.
- When it's fully shifted, you might experience an inner feeling of letting go. Sometimes you can 'see' an imaginary veil clearing before your eyes as you move out of the illusion and into greater clarity.

- At this point, your heart will feel open and your partner again becomes that wonderful being you fell in love with and feel mysteriously connected to (even if you'd felt like murdering them before this process!)
- You can also sit in ease in situations that would have triggered intense emotion in the past, and have a really good laugh at yourself.
- You can even try playing out any sexual shadow – eg the bad boy/bad girl, the naïve innocent, the powerful dominant, the slut, etc – with the consent of your partner (once the shadow has been cleared, unless you have support to clear it in the sexual play).

NB. Our deepest shadows often hold more than one layer, so they might require more than one visit before they're fully cleared. You'll find different aspects each time you visit.

Seeing Your Partner's Shadows

Whilst it's vital to see and own your own shadows, you can also play an important role in helping your partner to see theirs. Offering your partner a reflection of their behaviour by showing them how it impacts you so they have a chance of seeing it is, ironically, being loving, to both them and yourself.

If you believe your partner is projecting onto you, the first thing to do is clear any shadow material of your own. It's not OK to tell your partner that they're acting from their shadow merely to avoid your own. Then let them know, clearly and lovingly, the impact that their behaviour is having on you, how you're choosing to respond as a result and raising the possibility of there being shadow there.

Focussing on how your partner's behaviour impacts you – rather than judging them – invites more vulnerability and openness from them (but still be prepared for an initial "fuck off"). And setting boundaries when needed is another invitation for your partner to see themselves.

Ways your partner's shadow can show up:

- Repetitive behaviours or responses that seem triggered or self-sabotaging
- The sense that your partner isn't really seeing you, they're seeing their projection, or that they're projecting something onto you that is NOT in you.

Dealing with someone else's projections is challenging, and handling them takes being grounded, plus awareness, skill and practice. The more you do your ABC and know your own shadows, the easier it will be to be clear around your partner's.

Ultimately, it's up to your partner to deal with their shadows, just as it is for you to deal with yours. Harassing them about it will only drive their behaviour further into shadow.

The most difficult times are when both you and your partner are projecting at the same time, and neither of you can say, "Stop, I need to look inside myself here." In this situation, you just need to wait until one of you is able to do so or ask a therapist for help.

In rarer cases you might find you're not dealing with shadow but with someone who is a significant substance abuser, or has a true personality disorder such as narcissism, psychopathy, or mental illness. This makes it more difficult (in some cases almost impossible) for them to gain any real insight into their behaviour and it's important to get professional help in working out whether this is your situation and how to deal with it.

The information in this chapter will give you a good understanding of, and ability to start looking at your shadows, but you can still ask for help from a good therapist where you need to. Regardless, choosing to stop blaming and come home to yourself through your ABC to see where your shadow might be hidden will help to defuse much intensity in your relationship.

Managing The Other

10.1 Porn vs Romance

Pornography has become the most commonly watched item on the internet by far, and is implicated in any number of negative traits in the bedroom. It's common to demonise porn, because even in our more 'enlightened' society sex is still somehow seen as wrong. The big dose of shame attached to porn causes most of the problems.

Graeme and I believe that romance has just as much of a negative impact on relationships as porn, yet its impact remains unseen simply because it's more socially acceptable. The danger of both these powerful influences is that they equally take you outside of yourself, putting your focus on getting what you want without any effort. That's wonderful in moments of fantasy, but totally unrealistic anywhere else.

Porn and romance are a little like sucking on a dummy or eating junk food. They're very enjoyable at the time, but not so great to live on. If you see them for what they are, there's nothing wrong with either porn or romance now and again. It's when they become a major part of your diet that their influence on your relationship becomes an issue.

Porn

Porn is largely targeted at, and therefore mostly attracts, men in their sexual vulnerability. It validates the very primal and exciting part of them that's often tinged with shame.

Porn gives a man a place to go when sex isn't available in his relationship. It helps to keep the feeling part of him alive and gives him a place to explore his most hidden fantasies without judgment. It allows a fantasy 'escape' from life, which can be really attractive at times.

Porn offers easy access, visual stimulation, variety, novelty, safety and privacy for the user, who doesn't have to worry about performance anxiety or the challenges involved in real and messy relating. In most porn, we see wet, willing and eager women (or men) ready and waiting for men to take whatever sexual pleasure they want. Pounding away hard and fast with somehow permanent erections, they have minimal interest in their partner's true satisfaction. (At least unless you watch the rarer, couples-based porn that has more mutuality).

This type of porn teaches users the stereotypical idea that men are permanently hard and horny, and that women are effortlessly aroused, neither of which are true. It's important to remember that porn creates a fantasy experience for the watcher that ultimately leaves them 'high and dry', because that's all it can ever do: create an illusion of satisfaction. Porn often leaves women feeling shamed and rejected too, although more women are becoming open to it.

Romance

If you're a woman who feels your hackles rise when you think of a man taking the easy way out of intimate relating through porn, take a moment to see his perspective through something closer to home. The romance industry – which is widely available through movies, books, advertising and chats with your girlfriends – exerts an equally manipulative effect on women.

Think of the rich, attractive man who says and does all the right things, intuitively pushing all right buttons for the heroine, and making her swoon with love, lust or both. She's effortlessly desired, pursued and satisfied, even if she teases him to her heart's content first. Of course, he's totally satisfied with whatever she has to offer, and needs nothing more. Even if he dominates her, she remains in the power position, giving her a fantasy relief from challenges in real life.

This story of instant attraction to a perfect man who offers everything a woman's heart desires with little real effort or vulnerability on her part is the female flipside of porn. The perfect images it projects can have a similar impact on women, creating false expectations for men to aspire to and generally leaving them totally uninspired. Ask a man what he thinks about acting like Christian Grey from 50 Shades, and he'll probably tell you that it's too much like hard work – just the same way most women think about acting like a porn star.

Becoming Healthy with Porn

The most effective method for dealing with the negatives of porn is to create your own healthy alternative through the many suggestions in this book. When this happens, the desire for porn is greatly reduced, and may even disappear. There's just no substitute for the real thing; and when real, embodied sexuality is part of your life, porn is relegated to the occasional place where it belongs.

If you're a woman and the man in your life watches porn, start by validating his desire to feel without shutting down his sexuality. Recognise that much of what's triggering you is cultural shame about sex, and don't dump this on your partner. Instead, use your ABC to explore this shame in yourself. Believing in his desire for you and treating it as pure gold will bring him back into desiring your realness. Trust that he *does* desire you – after all, you're real, you have curves, and you're potentially a hell of a lot more fun than a computer screen.

As a couple, your vulnerable challenge is to talk about what lies behind the desire to use porn and make it more human. Snuggle up to enjoy porn together occasionally, and validate yourselves as sexual beings with sex as a normal part of your lives. Learn something from your own and your partner's different sexual desires and accept the genuineness behind both.

Becoming Healthy with Romance

Again, the most effective method for dealing with the negatives of romance is to create your own healthy alternative and learn to recognise *authentic* romance through the many suggestions in this book. When you do this, the desire for 'artificial' romance is greatly reduced. It may even disappear, because – again – there's no substitute for the real thing; and when real, embodied love is part of your life, romance too is relegated to the occasional place where it belongs.

If you're a man who loves a woman who consistently demands romance, start by validating her desire to feel without shutting down her heart. Recognise that much of what's triggering you is gender stereotyping, and don't dump this on your partner. Instead, use your ABC to explore this in yourself. Believing in her desire for you and treating it as pure gold will help her to see and desire your realness. Trust that she ultimately desires you – after all, you're real, you have an open heart, and you're potentially a hell of a lot more fun than any plastic ideal.

Your vulnerable challenge is to talk about what lies behind your partner's desire for romance, and to understand where she's coming from so you can 'get' her more clearly.

You can also occasionally do something romantic for your partner (perhaps from her list of things she'd love to receive) purely for her joy of receiving your genuine offering and the magic it brings. It doesn't need to be flowers or chocolates – just something clearly from your heart. If your choice is something less obvious, make sure you let her know where your gift is coming from in you, so she can really feel it. And if as a woman you desire romance yourself, do something romantic for your partner occasionally too, so they 'get' how good it feels.

A 'Sometimes Food'

If you believe you're addicted to either porn or romance, you need to look at the underlying need, rather than focusing on the behaviour. Focusing on the addiction often overlooks what's really happening. Following the suggestions in this book will certainly have a positive, long-term influence in creating healthy connection and intimacy.

Once you gain a more authentic relationship, artificial games become less attractive.

You'll become more interested in creating something real for yourselves. The idea is to remain embodied and connected with yourselves around these two powerful energies, to ensure you're driving them, rather than have them driving you.

10.2 How to Turn Jealousy Into a Gift

(Without pouring acid onto your partner's car, throwing their belongings into the street or boiling their rabbit!)

> *"Welcome to the wonderful world of jealousy, he thought. For the price of admission, you get a splitting headache, a nearly irresistible urge to commit murder, and an inferiority complex. Yippee."*
>
> Dark Lover, J R Ward

Jealousy. A *little* bit can be a good thing. A twinge of uneasiness at seeing your partner chatting enthusiastically to an attractive member of the opposite sex across the room can create an instant spurt of desire for them within you. But jealousy over the long term is a gut-churning, painful misery, where trust and happiness seem like a distant memory. Though it's not an excuse for lousy behaviour the truth is that jealousy says much more about YOU than about your partner.

It's said that jealousy only hurts the one creating it, whether there's a basis of truth in the jealousy or not. It seems to thrive on the belief that those you're jealous of are somehow happier, more powerful, or more desirable than you. The intensity of these feelings has you constantly focussing on them, often to the exclusion of everything else. Your view of reality becomes warped, making revenge seem like a reasonable response.

Although the perceptions that accompany your jealousy may be distorted, the pain it gives rise to is real.

The problem with jealousy is that it isn't just one feeling on its own. Instead, it's a combination of several different feelings that range from anger to envy, insecurity, loneliness, abandonment and powerlessness. And underlying all of these is usually shame. These feelings drive your thoughts and vice versa.

> *"Jealousy is a disease, love is a healthy emotion. The immature mind often mistakes one for the other, or assumes, the greater the love, the greater the jealousy – in fact they are almost incompatible, one emotion hardly leaves room for the other."*
>
> Stranger In A Strange Land, Robert A. Heinlein

Jealousy hurts so much that you want to get rid of it in any way you can. You want your partner to stop doing whatever it is that makes you jealous, or turn back the clock so that whatever happened hasn't any more. But both these things are outside of your control and it's more helpful to focus on what you *can* control.

What you can do about jealousy:

- Acknowledge your jealousy without making it wrong.
- Understand that your pain is real, and that you can do something about it.
- Remain connected with yourself and don't give your power away to your 'story' or to others who are only too willing to get in on the drama of the situation with you. Otherwise you're just abandoning yourself the way you feel your partner may have.
- Check whether your suspicions are real or imagined (but don't get lost in this step).
- See your partner's actions as being about *them*, not you. See your response as being about *you*, not them.
- Rather than *thinking* your feelings, practice your ABC. Get grounded. Detach from the images you have in your mind and feel. Use your mind to scan your body and notice where and what it is that you're *actually* feeling.

Allow whatever's there to be there and breathe through it. Yes, it can be painful, but getting a handle on it will help. Breathing helps your body to feel safe and helps you to get more present.

- Take a look at each feeling and see what it's telling you
    - Do you fear losing your partner?
    - Are you angry that your partner is betraying you?

- Are you feeling sadness at the loss of perfection in your relationship?
- Do you feel shame at not being enough for your partner?
- Are you envious that your partner is having a good time?

• Let your hurt in at least a little bit and allow it to open your heart. This is the gift of jealousy if you welcome it. It sounds weird, but it works

You'll find your heart is much, much stronger than you've ever imagined if you trust it to care for you.

Ask yourself:

- Is there anything you're avoiding in yourself and your own life by giving jealousy its head?
- Is your partner giving you a not-so-subtle message that you've become emotionally unavailable to them? Without making yourself responsible for your partner's behaviour, can you own your part in this?
- Are there old, unreleased hurts (even about past relationships) that are being triggered for healing? If so, feel them.
- Are you feeling a need to control or possess your partner? If so, where are you feeling out of control or incomplete in yourself?
- If you envy your partner for meeting their needs are you clearly asking for your own healthy relationship needs to be met?
- If you envy your partner for having fun are you giving yourself permission to have fun and create abundance in your own life?

- If you find yourself envying 'the other person' for their beauty, success, sexiness, etc, find this gold in yourself by identifying your own beauty, success and sexiness.

- Can you go underneath your fear, shame and abandonment and find the part of you that is enough?

Talk to your partner:

- Own and express your concerns with your partner. Then really *listen* to their response.

- Discuss your relationship agreements about acceptable behaviour around others. If you don't have any, create some.

- If your partner *is* treating you poorly, set a healthy boundary for yourself about how you'd like to be treated. Let them know ways they can help you feel safe again in your relationship.

- If your fears are unfounded, own your own jealousy and the strategies you're putting in place to deal with it. To be jealous is human – to own and deal with it is divine.

- To counteract any shame or humiliation in jealousy, find ways to nurture and love yourself, giving yourself some of the attention you deserve.

If your partner is known to repeatedly stray outside your relationship without owning it and is unwilling to work with you to heal it, that's different. If you've done your own work, face the fact that they're unlikely to change and do yourself a favour by moving on. This can be the biggest lesson of all. Otherwise what is this saying about you?

Don't make jealousy wrong

The vital thing with jealousy is to feel it and the vulnerability it brings without making it wrong. Breathe into it and welcome it in. If you let it, jealousy will open your heart more deeply to parts of yourself you hadn't known before, because it's a powerful heart opener and teacher.

10.3 When Your Partner's Had an Affair

Infidelity is one of the last remaining taboos in a relationship. The shadow of unfaithfulness still packs a big wallop: it's a really painful blow to your romantic heart to discover your partner has been involved with another person in the very personal and intimate parts of what you'd thought was yours alone.

You might find questions like these rolling around in your head:

- How could they have done this to me? To us?
- Don't they love me anymore?
- What have I done wrong?
- Am I just not good enough?

And for the person who's had the affair, the thoughts can be just as painful:

- How could I have hurt the person I love most in the world?
- How could I have been such a shit?
- How come I *don't* feel guilty?

Infidelity is a real blow to the ideal of 'happy ever after', cutting right to the heart of a relationship.

Infidelity cuts into the heart of your ego self. If you've chosen a relationship for purely romantic reasons, who are you after you've been rejected, when you're no longer 'the one'?

And the other question both people almost invariably ask is, "Can I/we get over this?" You now face the decision of whether to work on your relationship or head out the door. It often seems easier to bolt, but it isn't

10: Managing The Other

necessarily the best option. Understanding the dynamics of affairs in general – and in your relationship in particular – will help you to make a healthier decision.

The first thing to understand about affairs is that they trigger a huge amount of shame and feeling wrong for both the doer and one who's been done to. When this happens, it's important to remember that shame IS just a feeling, and when you recognise and see it for what it is, this reduces its intensity enough to see what's going on more clearly.

Affairs are not new: they've been around as long as relationships. People in otherwise 'happy' relationships have affairs. Even people in so-called 'open' relationships have them. Perhaps the very ideal of a relationship and coupledom invites the situation – people having affairs report striking out for something that's just 'theirs'.

> *"Adultery has existed since marriage was invented, and so too the prohibition against it – in fact, it has a tenacity that marriage can only envy."*
>
> The State of Affairs: Rethinking Infidelity, Esther Perel

That's the second important thing to know. Even though hurt is the end result, the person having the affair probably didn't do it to hurt you. People having affairs don't so much *turn away* from their partners as look for something that's missing in themselves. Affairs are less about the actual sex than about the desire to want and feel wanted – to feel special and important, to feel the mystery of having something forbidden or to feel *fully alive* again.

People who have affairs may:

- Feel disconnected from their partner – as though they're in a relationship, but not really relating

- Feel bored in their relationship OR in their lives
- Not feel sexually desired or desirable
- Not be able to discuss any of this with their partner to find a way forward in the relationship
- Feel undervalued by their partner, unneeded, or overwhelmed by their partner's needs.

Or, occasionally there might be a more serious inability to sustain a relationship at all that results in repeated affairs. This requires more serious attention.

Affairs seem to be an attractive solution to the all of above issues. They especially offer that feeling of edgy aliveness that can become addictive and hard to give up, even when the affair itself is no longer so 'hot'. It seems impossible to find that edginess in an existing relationship that's settled into a routine. It's definitely harder, but not impossible.

And of course, comparing the idea (or the reality) of an affair with your current relationship and partner is not really fair. What you should be comparing are the aliveness and the desirability of an affair with how you and your current partner were at *the beginning* of your relationship, back when the glow was still on it. How did you behave then, how did that contribute to the outcome, and can you find that again now?

So What Should You Do if One of You Has Had an Affair?

The outcome of an affair is up to both of you.

1. If you're not the one who had the affair, you have to let go of the need to punish your partner and play the victim role (as tempting as it might appear to expose them as a traitor all over Facebook). Punishing them will destroy any chance of re-establishing a healthy dynamic.

2. Know that you are the *only* one who can heal your hurt, because it's inside YOU. It's your choice whether to hold onto it or not. Your partner can't do this for you.

    Part of this healing is taking a look at any ways you might have contributed, not to the affair, but to the place in your relationship that made the affair a possibility. Betrayal comes in many forms – indifference, unavailability, avoidance, criticism, manipulation, etc. Owning your part is essential, but it's not an easy thing to do when you feel so wronged.

    Once there's more understanding, forgiveness can start to happen.

3. Your partner can help by showing genuine remorse for the hurt you've felt. Sometimes they may not feel remorse for the affair itself, particularly if it's given them new aliveness and clarity, and brought things out into the open that were killing your relationship. It can be hard to admit, but this is where the most potential lies for healing.

4. Your partner can also help by being willing to restore and maintain your boundaries in the relationship in order to rebuild your trust. But remember: setting boundaries is only part of the healing. If it's all that happens, it's not a solution: it's a time bomb waiting to go off.

5. You also need to resolve the underlying issues that led to the affair. Discover what led to the choice being made, and what can you each do to fill that need within your relationship. Also find the things that you each value about your relationship with each other. Learn how you can bring the aliveness, freedom, connection and mystery into your own relationship.

Sometimes an affair is simply the outward sign of a relationship that needs to end. More often, it can be the beginning of something stronger than ever before. It won't be as easy as walking out the door, but the rewards can be many.

So, can you get over an affair? Possibly. Should you try? Most definitely. Dealing with the affair and at least trying to move forward is far braver and potentially more rewarding than immediately giving up and leaving which is good for your ego but not much else.

10.4 Monogamy, Screwing Around, Open Relationships and Polyamory

As part of their relationship agreements, modern couples often ponder the idea of defining their own relationship boundaries rather than rely on the traditional ones set out for them. Graeme and I chose to include this topic in the book, as it's one we get many questions about. Sometimes the questions are from people who are merely interested, and other times they're from those who are confused and hurting as they try to deal with the impact of challenging their relationship structures. So in this section, we'll outline how dealing with the possibility of others in our relationships is a reality for all of us and what we can do about it.

Now that we have a higher standard of living, live longer and hold higher expectations of our intimate relationships, the idea of one 'forever' person is more challenging than ever before. Fewer of us have only one partner for life, more of us are serial monogamists - having one partner *at a time* over the course of our lives.

People are also more mobile and exposed, out and about in the workforce, with access to online dating sites and a variety of places to interact with others – from the friendly woman at the local coffee shop to the guy on the overseas conference or the woman who pops up in the corner screen of your laptop.

> *"Very often we don't go elsewhere because we are looking for another person. We go elsewhere because we are looking for another self. It isn't so much we want to leave the person we are with as we want to leave the person we have become"*
>
> The State of Affairs: Rethinking Infidelity, Esther Perel

On top of this, sexuality is promoted in almost every ad, video clip or movie you see and every billboard you pass, and morality generally is a little... looser... than it used to be. All of this means that sex seems to simply be more available than it used to be and that perhaps you should be having more of it. Managing this availability is a reality of our modern way of living. Do you shut the spark of sexual attraction down and avoid it in shame, fear and denial? Or can you enjoy it in a way that's safe, energising and a source of strength in your relationship?

Confronting the shame, fear and control that comes up around intimate sexual boundaries in your relationship and talking about it is vital to validate this healthy part of being human.

Given the amazing power of sexual energy, the challenges that arise from sexual desire exist whether it's spoken about or not. As we've said elsewhere, if you don't control your sexual energy, it will control you. Many relationships fail simply because one or both partners fall into shame about their sexual desire, and give up, shut down or covertly have affairs because open discussion seems too difficult. Even though this subject is becoming less taboo fear of judgment from partners and people around them keeps many couples quiet about this subject (unless it's late at night under the influence of alcohol...)

Being in a monogamous relationship in a still largely unhealthy sex culture is hugely demanding. Men still struggle to understand their sexual desire: the primal urges that leak out somehow when they're shut down in feelings of sexual frustration, watching porn, having affairs, domestic anger, closed hearts and depression to name a few. Women also still carry intense shame around their own sexuality, body image, disempowerment and from simply being women. When these shame pieces collide, many relationships collapse under their weight – basically from a lack of healthy support.

Despite the many different theories that abound on this subject, Graeme and I don't have any particular philosophical slant about the morality or supposed naturalness of any particular lifestyle choices, or whether they're right for anyone, let alone everyone. We do believe that it's important to make a conscious choice about where you're at for yourselves. And to be very honest and clear in what you're doing if you choose to explore any, or none, of these options.

Otherwise you'll simply create a big headache for yourselves due to the very high level of conditioning and shadow that lie in this area. We all have this kind of conditioning and shadow to some degree, even for those who were raised by open-minded parents. For most people, the conditioning is familial, cultural, religious, political, generational and gender based.

But when a couple consciously chooses to explore these boundaries – even just through a conversation, or a series of conversations – with honesty, intimacy and vulnerability inside their relationship, they create wonders by bringing the beast out into the open. And a conversation is often all that's required. We believe, based on our own experiences and what we've seen in working with others, that the ultimate experience in a relationship starts with one person first: yourself. When you're grounded in your individual self, having open communication on this topic can be a very powerful experience that transforms your relationship from a place of fear and limitation into one of unlimited love.

The way to start a conversation about your relationship boundaries is definitely NOT "I met this woman/man at a conference in Sydney last weekend and we ended up sleeping together. Now I'd like to talk to you about being in an open relationship so I can continue seeing them. What do you think?" This is a blatant attempt at manipulation and a recipe for disaster. So is agreeing to open relating in the hope of holding onto your partner, or to fix an already unsatisfactory relationship.

Instead, the way to start is to talk about how being around others whilst in a committed relationship is for you and your partner. Share how it is for you that you have, or haven't, thought about sleeping with someone else, as well as hear how this is for your partner.

Be curious and non-judgemental. Come from love and own any fear. This conversation can happen over several months or even years. Be aware that at least one of you is likely to feel fear, or even revulsion at the very idea of this conversation. This doesn't mean the conversation is wrong, or that having it will open the floodgates and leave your relationship fraught with danger. You may even become intrigued or excited.

Either way, it doesn't mean you have to DO anything about it. It simply means that you're taking charge in a very powerful part of your relationship by bringing it out into the open and seeing it more clearly.

It takes a lot of courage and skill to really show up at this depth: to trust in your relationship container and talk about these potentially big unmentionables. It directly challenges your deep sexual and social conditionings, as well as any unresolved inner child wounds, particularly around rejection, jealousy, betrayal, abandonment, shame, unmet needs and your sense of self. In this place, the level of intimacy and vulnerability between you is intensely magnified; and if it's experienced, it will create a genuine expansion of trust, depth and open-hearted connection.

Regardless of the outcome, simply having courage to have these conversations will make a difference, even if it gets rocky initially. Communicating from a place of loving trust and vulnerability, and sharing your secret desires and fantasies can be incredibly freeing (and perhaps fun!). In this place, the love, connection and intimacy can deepen beyond words, helping to bulletproof your relationship from the carnage of unconscious sexual acting out.

So, take a few breaths, use your ABC and explore a little.

Defining Your Relationship Boundaries

1. Begin the discussion about dealing with desire for others by discussing the ideas outlined above. Come back to it every now and again until it becomes a source of comfort and connection between you, rather than an unspoken threat.

2. You might also like to discuss your own beliefs, judgements, desires and fears around the ideas of monogamy, screwing around, open relationships and polyamory. What do these terms mean to you, if anything:

   Some generally agreed definitions are:

   - **Monogamy:** is where two people choose relationship with each other (married or not) and seek all of their romantic and sexual intimacy needs to be met within this relationship.

   - **Screwing around:** is where one or both partners are playing around or actually having sex with others purely for self-gratification (even if they try to call it 'polyamory'). No resulting emotional issues are looked at, and existing ones in the relationship are likely avoided. If this describes you, do yourself and your partner a favour, and be honest enough to own it.

   - **Open Relationship (also known as Negotiated Non-monogamy)** is where one central couple has an agreement to allow each other to have sexual experiences with others outside the relationship. What this agreement looks like is totally unique for each couple, depending on what each person believes they can emotionally handle. Because even though we're talking about sex here, the impact is often bigger than just the physical sexual experience.

   - At a practical level, it can range from allowing each other some online flirting, to a once-only exploration, a free pass on business trips, an occasional one-night stand, or giving permission for regular hook-ups. Some couples have a don't ask/don't tell policy, whilst others use the details of outside experiences as part of the titillation in their foreplay.

- Over time, these sexual relationships can develop into long-term friendships but love is not their basis.

- **Polyamory:** (rather than open relating which is often *called* polyamory) is a belief that humans have unlimited love at their core, and allows this unlimited love to dictate the form of their relationships. It includes loving sexually and/or intimately more than one person at a time. The relationship is seen as a pathway to develop a deeper relationship with themselves and with love itself rather than an exploration of 'romantic love'. Dealing with the emotional impacts of these multiple loves is seen as the path, rather than being separate from it. In fact, Polyamory's nickname is 'Polyagony.'

"In all honesty, after 25 years as a relationship coach in the polyamory community, I'm not at all sure that polyamory can fulfil its potential for sustainable intimacy"

Polyamory In The 21st Century, Deborah Taj Anapol

Graeme and I believe that if you can't get it right with one person, you have little hope with more.

- These different concepts are no longer static and couples can move in and out of different ones at different times in their lives. The point is in making them an active choice.

3. Rather than getting lost in any of these large philosophical ideals, we suggest you begin with something more concrete – looking at your relationship with yourself and your current real-life sexuality.

Exploring Your Sexual Energy Out in the World

Explore what you do with your sexuality when you're out and about in the world. Do you act it out, shut it down, avoid it in fear or shame, or subtly use it to manipulate others to get what you want? Or can you experience it in a healthy way, which is just giving yourself permission to feel and enjoy it for what it is – a pleasurable tingle and aliveness in your body that connects you with yourself and opens your heart if you take charge of it?

- If you feel a spark of attraction around another person, enjoy the moment from *inside* you, without making it about the other person and getting hooked into the need to act it out.
- Simply ground yourself and take a breath into this delicious feeling, exhaling out through your mouth and feeling it spreading through your body, and smile. Own it as your own secret source of power, love, creativity and vitality (or whatever works for you here).
- Spreading your sexual pleasure through your body can help to decrease both its urgency and the need to DO something with it. Moving it up to your heart (where the mind goes, the energy follows) allows you to feel nurtured and fulfilled from within.
- Go home to your loved one alive, ready for more, and yet still fulfilled if it's not available.
- If you're with your partner and you see an attractive man or woman, breathe, relax, enjoy the feeling and give your partner the smile.

This is being in control of your own sexuality in your relationship, without shutting it down, or acting it out in shadow.

The idea of freedom whilst in relationship, sexual or otherwise, is a tempting idea. Getting real about it starts with connecting with yourself and who you really are as a sexual being, rather than fearing or focussing on the glamour of the above labels. This allows whatever you choose to be authentic and valuable to you and your partner. Doing your ABC and working through the suggestions in this book is a great start.

What About Love?

11.1 The Universal and Personal Heart

Ultimately, we know love through our experience of it.

We move now from talking about sex and sexual love to the aspects of love that more directly belong to our hearts.

Love: like intimacy, it's a word that's extremely hard to define; and because it has so many meanings, it can be an elusive concept. The different understandings and experiences of love – especially between men and women – then often contribute to the troubling differences they experience in their loving relationships. Having a *felt sense* of our hearts is a more concrete experience of love that may help to clear some of these differences up allowing you to meet in the middle of love.

To get this *felt sense*, Graeme and I recommend imagining that your heart has two parts: an upper (Universal) and lower (Personal), and then seeing if the following ideas resonate with you.

Universal Heart

The Universal part of your heart radiates Universal Love, which is an expansive feeling that spreads out from the upper part of your heart, opening it *outwards*. This Universal Love creates a desire within you to love, unconditionally accept, connect with and nurture everyone and everything around you. It's about surrendering yourself in the service of others, and it often occurs – although by no means exclusively so – in women.

Universal Love is the more common and socially accepted version of what love is: it's more 'known'. We can see it easily in the selfless devotion of a new mother who gets up in the middle of the night to see to her newborn child no matter how tired she may be. We can also see it in the man who tirelessly devotes himself to caring for a wife with debilitating cancer or dementia. And Graeme and I see it around Byron Bay as love of nature – the birds, bees, trees, oceans, whales, etc.

But this powerful aspect of love has an equally powerful shadow.

Because we're all so conditioned to think Universal Love is what *all* love is, it easily becomes more of a mental concept than an experience. It turns into something we act out because we think we 'should', rather than being a genuine expression of what we're actually feeling. And we can feel equally guilty about situations where we don't feel this love and think we 'should'.

Continually giving out Universal Love can result in our becoming unbalanced and ungrounded, and losing our sense of self because its focus is outside of ourselves. We might see this loss in a mother who becomes desperate at the thought of her children leaving home and feels as though her whole identity will leave with them. It can also happen to anyone who's totally devoted themselves to another person, career, interest or cause at their own expense. A little is healthy, but too much is not (unless perhaps it is chosen as a spiritual path).

A further shadow in Universal Love is that we can be trapped by our egos into expecting the love we give out to be returned in order to 'fill ourselves up' again. This leaves us vulnerable to the pain of missing out when it's not available, leading into our many varied and ugly ways of manipulating in order to receive it.

Graeme and I see this commonly in romantic relationships where each member gives love easily, but only if they're loved back.

And finally, the impersonal aspect of Universal Love that loves everything and everyone equally means it can become overly detached, dispassionate and inhuman. This is not always useful in the very personal world of relationships.

Personal Heart

The Personal or lower part of your heart, by contrast, opens *inwards* and *downwards*, opening your heart to yourself, penetrating you with Personal Love. This Personal Love is experienced through connecting with and nurturing yourself before everyone around you. It keeps your energy inside of you for yourself, energy that you may choose to share with others but not at the expense of yourself.

Personal Love feels grounded, insular and stable. It's less common in either sex, but is still more common in men. It's most frequently seen in things we all 'do' to love ourselves, eg readily standing up for ourselves; asserting clear boundaries; freely enjoying sexual pleasure, and having a strong sense of self. But it's not what we do that creates this self love, self love is the place where we do these things from.

This type of love is less socially acceptable (because we're less compliant in it) and harder to come by than Universal Love. To access it, we need to totally let go and surrender our egos to the unknown inside us – where our Personal Hearts live. In this surrender, we connect deeply to the essence of ourselves in a healthy way. It includes enjoying our sexuality which is a very personal part of ourselves. This love is about the self, yet it is not selfish: Personal Love readily helps us to find compassion and acceptance of others, for we more easily have compassion and acceptance for ourselves.

A shadow of Personal Love is where it's denied and judged as ego when it isn't. Personal Love can be differentiated from ego in the way that it creates outcomes that serve others as well as serving us, rather than being at others' expense. This can be shown as 'tough love', inviting someone to stand up in themselves.

Another shadow is where Personal Love becomes too strong, and we become too self-sufficient – denying ourselves connection and interaction with others.

Not better or worse

It's important to understand that these differences are not about one kind of love being better than the other. Both are equally important and support each other. It does, however, explain why men and women see love very differently sometimes. For example, a mother's love for her child might be seen in her wanting to nurture them and keep them safe, where a father's love might challenge them to take risks, to trust and learn about themselves.

In our relationships, the more we're grounded and open to ourselves in our Personal Hearts, the more love we have to give from our Universal Hearts – and the more freely we can enjoy sexual pleasure.

Universal and Personal Hearts

Try this simple process to experience the difference between these two hearts:

- Close your eyes and take a few deep breaths.
- Imagine a very young baby in front of you, gazing back at you with an expression of innocence.
- Notice feeling your Universal Heart opening and unconditional love pouring out to this tiny, precious being, to the point where all you want is to love, cherish and protect them. You may even have a sense that 'you' become less important than your care of the child. This is the devotional aspect of Universal Love.
- Perhaps you find your Universal Heart is blocked and unavailable to you and you feel nothing here? If this happens, see it as a good beginning: you're seeing what's missing within you. Ask your Universal Heart what it needs or what can you do to support it to open more fully and listen for the intuitive answer.
- Now let go of this image, and imagine literally turning the feeling of love in your heart around, then breathe it in as if you could breathe it down into yourself. Imagine your Personal Heart opening inwards and filling you with Personal Love, whatever this feels or looks like to you.
- What does this love feel like? Can you notice the difference? Do you feel more centred, grounded and clear in yourself?
- Perhaps you feel a resistance to letting this love in? Or perhaps your Personal Heart feels blocked and unavailable to you? If this happens, once more see it as a good beginning – for again, you're seeing what's missing within you. As before, ask this heart what it needs or what can you do to support it more fully and listen for the intuitive answer.

The Universal and Personal parts of your heart are a pathway towards the Infinite Love that includes them both. Infinite Love is a state of

> being, the place of mystery that lies beyond description, yet which we can see through the many concrete ways in which it works in the world.
>
> Return to review the Universal and Personal parts of your heart regularly, and ask for their wisdom until your blocks in each have gone.

11.2 The Differences between Men and Women in Love

Being human is about both loving and being loved. Ultimately, we're all trying to reconnect with the love that already lies within us, for love is at the core of who we are. In this section, Graeme and I attempt to explain differences we see in love between men and women, in order to help close some of the common gaps between the two that cause needless suffering when they're not understood or acknowledged.

It's important to note that some of the following are generalisations from what we've observed in ourselves and many of our clients, while others are based on ancient Eastern philosophy about energies. Either way, they're not hard and fast rules.

Men and Love

A man IS Love and his focus is *expressing* love *outwards* through *doing* and *action*, and *penetrating out* his love into the world, including through his communication and his sexuality. His genitals are on the outside pointing him in the direction he wants to go.

When a man is doing, communicating and making love, he's expressing what is *already in him,* vulnerably putting out into the world his expression of himself, to be accepted or rejected. The conditioning that says his sex is wrong, and even he is wrong, keeps him in shame and disconnected from the love that lies deeper within him. As does the conditioning that shuts him down from feeling, causing him to depersonalize sex, objectify and seek power over women.

A man generally finds it hard to know he is love because he already IS it, and his focus is looking outwards from it. He gets a sense of this love when he sits on the couch without words for hours, yet still 'knows' he's connected with his partner who is there with him.

He fears or feels burdened by a woman's need to 'feel' his love, because he's already there, whether he knows it or not. He desires his partner to find this love, completeness and freedom in herself, as he does.

Without fully embracing his feeling aspect, what a man most commonly feels is loneliness.

A man's challenge is to fully connect with the love that lies within him through fully feeling and experiencing it so he can not only *act* and *give* love, so he can know it within himself. When he feels fully he can access his heart and the gifts it brings: along with the freedom to live from his essence and his inner power, to love from vulnerability and to make love (whether it's lusty and primal or exquisitely tender) without shame or fear. In this place, he will have greater sensitivity to wherever his woman is at and be able to meet her within it without losing himself.

The many understandings and practices in this book will help challenge man's need for protection that keeps him safely focussed outside of himself, yet also keeps him small. Most important of these is the understanding that annihilating his ego (rather than hers) through connecting to his feelings, opening his heart and connecting to his essence means opening to *more* power in himself, not less.

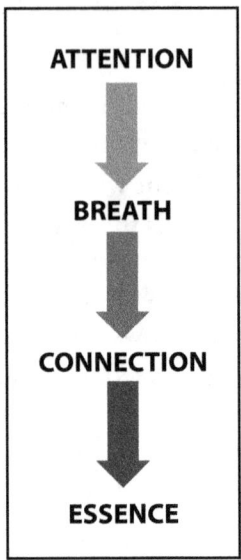

A woman who's willing to support this process by *not* playing small, by wanting more than her man's protected heart, and by not keeping her own heart and sexuality closed to him will be well rewarded an authentic, loving relationship.

Women and Love

A woman IS also Love, but her focus is on *connecting inwards*, through *feeling* and *experiencing* love through connection, communication and receiving. Her internal and hollow genitals reflect this.

When a woman is connecting, communicating and making love, she's searching for what she believes lies outside of herself, vulnerably opening herself up to receive and be filled, leaving herself open to being accepted or rejected. A woman believes she's wrong because she thinks she doesn't have what her man already seems to. This keeps her in shame and disconnected from the love that lies deeper within her. As does the conditioning that invalidates her need to feel and closes her heart.

11: What About Love?

A woman looks to fill the deep yearning that lies within her, yet she needs to connect to herself first.

A woman finds it hard to know that she is love because she's always looking for it outside of herself in order to fill the space that lies within her. She gets a taste of this love when she sits with her man on the couch and he fills her up with his attention. If he doesn't, however, she feels abandoned and separate from love.

Yet as soon as she disconnects from feeling the intensity of her own feelings and looks to a man for his love and approval, a woman is lost to herself. Until she understands that annihilating her own ego (rather than his) and surrendering here is surrendering to the love within her, rather than to him. This means she's opening to more power, not less – again, opening to the awesome power of her open heart. The many understandings and practices in this book are here to challenge her need for protection that keep her safely focussed outside of herself, yet also keep her small.

A woman's challenge is to look inside herself for her love, rather than depending on her man to give it to her. The more she connects to the love within her own heart, the freer she is to be her loving, feisty, playful, changing and intelligent self.

She no longer needs her man to fill her, and she can instead share with him from her own wholeness. She can reach out and share of herself – including her sexuality – without feeling used.

A man who is willing to support this process by not playing the game of providing her with her sense of self through him, and is also willing to stand in his own vulnerability, will be well rewarded an authentic, loving relationship.

All of the Above is Like God's (or the Universe's) Cosmic Joke

We have a system that has us forget who we are (Love) and sends us searching for it in another person. Yet it's only through finding completeness in ourselves that we can fully love and enjoy each other.

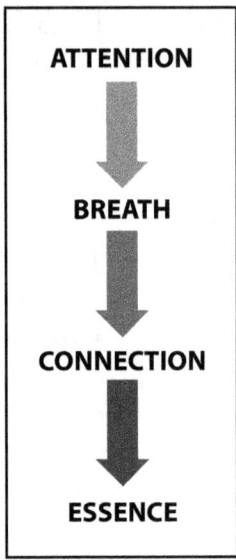

And *that* is the point – no matter how complete we are in ourselves, we'll always seek relationships because that is our human nature: to share in the love, joy and suffering of the human experience.

> **Reflecting on Love**
>
> - Do these ideas resonate with you?
> - Have any lightbulbs gone on?
>
> Discuss your thoughts with your partner and see if they create any changes in the way you see each other.

11.3 The Hidden Person Inside of Us Worthy of Our Love

There are people in every relationship that influence its outcome more than we realise. These are each person's unseen inner children: who they were as a baby, toddler, young child, tween and teenager.

These are the parts of you that were once fully open to life before you learned that this was an unsafe – maybe even scary - way to be. Before you grew up and learned 'the rules': that it's not OK to feel however it is you feel. Before your capacity for wonder, your absolute confidence, and the openness of your heart folded up and closed down.

As your heart became a little less open you started to disconnect from your authentic self. What you felt and what you showed the world started to become different. You started to protect your hurts deep inside of you where they couldn't be seen. This disconnection was a necessary survival skill unless you were lucky enough to have someone to teach you how to care for yourself emotionally.

And in disconnecting from yourself you abandoned, stifled or even killed these parts of your inner child and missed out on lifelong access to this innocent, wondrous, creative, playful and often wise part of you.

The gift of intimate relating is that you get triggered back into feeling these same hidden feelings as an adult, your vulnerability potentially reconnecting you with this long-abandoned part of yourself.

> "The most sophisticated people I know, inside – they are all children."
>
> Jim Henson: The Biography, Jim Henson, creator of The Muppets

It's not unusual for a 60-year-old man to feel the anxiety he felt as a four-year-old when his wife sexually rejects him. Nor is it unusual for a 30-year-old woman to feel the inadequacy she experienced at seven from her teacher asking her a question she couldn't answer in front of the class when her husband challenges her on her budgeting strategies. As strange as it may seem, it's even possible for your partner going out for the night without hugging you goodbye to trigger you into the abandonment you felt in your cot at a few weeks old when your parent went out for the night without doing the same thing.

Our child self underlies the places we most often get triggered into in the depths of intimacy. These triggers are merely incomplete feelings that we didn't have the skill to integrate at the time, and the way to deal with them now is simply to acknowledge them whilst soothing our past selves along with our current selves. This effectively heals the past in the present.

It's normal to poo-poo this idea as ridiculous new age bunkum from the lofty position of your rational adult brain.

Graeme and I have seen the value of recognising this child self thousands of times, both in ourselves and in our clients. There's a part of all of us that feels whole when we acknowledge this part of who we are. We don't even need to go into the story of *why* we feel the way we do: we just make the connection between our adult and child selves, and the rest follows.

> ### Loving Your Inner Child
>
> - When you feel a painful and very familiar triggered feeling, rather than denying it, take a few moments to imagine yourself as a child (if you haven't already been triggered there) and feel the familiar feeling.
> - When the image feels real, imagine yourself putting your adult arms around that child and comforting them, just as you would if there were an actual child standing in front of you who felt sad, scared, ashamed, etc.

- Hug them to your chest and identify with their feelings. As you feel their hurt diminish in the love between you, your own hurt will too. Offer them some words of comfort (rather than the harsh words of judgment you might otherwise say to yourself).
- If the hurt doesn't shift at whatever age you've chosen, go further back to a younger self until it does so. This will be the age at which you abandoned yourself for the 'shoulds' of your external conditioning.
- Then ask them if they have any words of wisdom for you, to help you understand yourself or your situation better. Kids love to be listened to!
- Place an early photo of yourself on your bathroom mirror and look at it daily until you can look at yourself with love.

This is the deepest level of your personality integrating itself. It's reclaiming the part of you that has a child-like capacity for innocence, wonder, awe, joy, sensitivity and playfulness; and making these wonderful qualities available to current-day you, as well the person you're in relationship with. Releasing these old feelings from your childhood can also bring you the extra energy to be found in your child self, for kids have energy to burn.

As you integrate your triggers, you'll no longer need to do this process consciously. Instead, the gifts of your child self will become more available to you without you even having to look for them.

11.4 Letting Love In

It's common in our culture to think that you need to be physically attractive, wealthy, exciting, charismatic, sexy and successful to have a relationship. Then love comes along and blows this theory out of the water when you find someone who loves you just because of the way you laugh, how you snuggle up to them in bed or how your sassiness challenges them. This is the magic of love.

Whilst these magical factors will begin a relationship, sustaining it is much more about what lies *inside* of you. These are qualities you can cultivate by connecting to your essence through the ABC process, which is where these qualities for profoundly satisfying intimate relationships and lovemaking naturally arise from.

 Qualities to Embrace for a Dynamite Relationship

Discuss what each of the following mean to each of you, using an example from your relationship to highlight it. Discuss how you can bring more of these qualities in. Graeme and I believe that they arise most easily though the ABC practice, but you can include your own ideas.

- **Commitment:** When you fully commit to something, heaven and earth moves with you in support.
- **Courage:** Taking action in the face of the fear.
- **Willingness:** The preparedness to act.
- **Presence:** Being aware of and fully experiencing everything both around and within you.
- **Vulnerability:** Openness and availability for connection.
- **Surrender:** A state of ceasing resistance and letting your egoic mind sink into your body and heart without trying to get anything or make anything happen. This means not trying to be someone else, or somewhere else, or with anyone else, other than where you are in the present moment.
- **Humility:** The quality of having a low or modest opinion of your importance.
- **Responsibility:** Owning the thoughts, feelings and actions you choose.
- **Playfulness:** Being light-hearted and full of childlike fun.
- **Trust:** Believing in yourself and your partner.
- **Gratitude:** Being thankful, showing appreciation, respect, giving recognition and acknowledgment.

- **Generosity:** A readiness to give or offer more than is necessary or expected.
- **Empathy:** Understanding and sharing the feelings of your partner (without losing yourself).
- **Compassion:** Concern for your partner's suffering that leads to action to help alleviate it.
- **Kindness:** Being considerate, respectful and generous to your partner.
- **Grace:** Being kind and generous to your partner when they least feel they deserve it.
- **Integrity:** Being honest and adhering to your moral principles.
- **Authenticity:** Being real, genuine and the author of your own life.
- **Inspiration:** Creative ideas that influence you to act.
- **Curiosity:** A strong desire to learn or know.
- **Creativity:** Using your imagination to create something inventive.
- **Bliss:** Complete happiness, utter joy and contentment.
- **Love:** A mystery.

Cultivating these qualities in your relationship encourages you to go beneath the superficiality in life and find what really matters. Rather than seeing your external achievements, status, entitlements and privilege – which all satisfy your ego self – as the be-all-and-end-all in your life, choose to feed your soul (or whatever you believe gives life meaning).

We find that doing this simply as a life choice, rather than in any pious way, helps us to stay more connected with our hearts and with each other. We see and love ourselves as we are, rather than who we might need each other to be. And that is a very restful approach.

Inviting Love In

To help further cultivate these qualities in your relationship, Graeme and I offer the following practices. Use these any time you want to let the rest of the world recede for a time so you can just love and value the preciousness of each other and what you share together.

If, before you begin you don't feel like doing these practices, or you don't feel particularly open in yourself and your relationship, they're still worth doing. Most often, the love you once felt is still inside you somewhere and will show up if you give it the opportunity to.

You can do these practices one at a time or together as a powerful way to connect quickly and deeply. You can also do them as formally or informally as you like.

 Soul Gazing

This practice gives you the gift of truly seeing and being seen, revealing the truth of the love that lies within both of you.

Your resistance to doing this activity may be huge, this resistance is just a sign that the activity *is* so powerful! Don't let your resistance get in the way. Instead, just have a go (playing gentle background music may help.)

- Sit or lie directly facing each other. As we mentioned back in Chapter 5, this aligns your energy centres, heightening your energetic and emotional connection. We also encourage you to try sitting in Yab Yum position (see Chapter 8).
- Using your ABC, centre into yourselves. Then look each other in one eye softly for two minutes. If you feel discomfort arising, simply breathe deeply and stay with it until it passes. It's simply your ego resisting dropping into your heart. Over time, extend your gaze up to 15 minutes for a beautiful connection.
- If you're doing this practice on its own, finish with a melting hug for two or three deep breaths.

11: What About Love?

"The root of joy is gratefulness... It is not joy that makes us grateful; it is gratitude that makes us joyful."

Gratefulness, the Heart of Prayer: An Approach to Life in Fullness, David Steindl-Rast

 **Honouring**

We all love to be respected, acknowledged and appreciated, especially by someone who loves us. This is especially true because we're likely to hear criticism and judgment in our daily lives, most often from ourselves. At times, we can also feel a little uncertain of being loved, simply because we've been too busy to connect, or things have gone wrong at work or with the kids, or we haven't made love for a while.

Done with presence, honouring and appreciation become more than just a mental exercise. They remind us how to feel, how to be in our bodies and how to deeply connect with each other, because they come straight from our hearts. They can even awaken our desire to make love.

- Stay opposite each other as above. Then, if you're the person sharing first, close your eyes, centre into yourself and focus on your heart.
- When you're ready, allow the words arise from inside you. Be OK if this takes a minute or two. The trick is to not to try and work this out beforehand or *think* about it too much. The more you speak from your heart, the more real your words will be.
- Share **five things** that you honour or appreciate your partner for. They can be little or large – it doesn't matter. The main idea is that they're genuine rather than trying to be romantic. Take your time. This is a precious gift you're giving your partner.
- Make sure your words don't carry any hints of negativity or covert sarcasm. This needs to be a totally safe space that you and your partner can trust if you're going to build love in it.
- The person receiving your appreciation should say *nothing*, other than, "Thank you!"

- Finally, share a happy memory from your relationship – one that reignites the feelings all over again, which helps to overwrite any negative re-writing you have going on.
- When you're done, swap over, then finish with a melting hug.

 Merging with Breath

Allowing yourselves to merge even more deeply together will help you to experience a profound sense of connection that's beyond words. It's subtle, you may not feel it at first, take your time here.

- In the same position as above, both centre into yourselves again. Then, with your eyes closed, begin breathing slowly and deeply into your bellies.
- Exhale out through your mouths. Allow yourselves to make "ah" sounds of letting go as you exhale.
- After a couple of minutes, you'll find that your breaths come into union and the boundaries of your bodies soften, allowing you to energetically merge with one another.
- Enjoy the moment.
- To take it deeper, place your foreheads together to connect your third eyes. Each contract your pelvic floor as you inhale and imagine energy rising from your pelvis up your spine to your third eye. And as you exhale, imagine it entering your partner's third eye and descending down their spine into their pelvic bowl. Continue until you feel complete.
- Sit in stillness together for a few minutes, enjoying the effect you've created together, then finish with a melting hug.

 Sleep Together Naked

Sleeping together naked is a simple and beautiful way to let love in. The other benefits from the lushness of skin-to-skin contact that's experienced in sleeping naked are not to be sneezed at either.

For example, over 40 years of research has shown that this type of contact enhances general wellbeing and promotes relaxation and bonding by releasing oxytocin, which is known as the 'cuddle chemical'. The practice reduces your stress hormone cortisol levels too, as well as lowering the risk of depression. Naked snuggling also lowers your blood pressure and enhances your immune system. In short, it's a beautiful gift to give each other.

NB. If being fully naked is too much for you, try as little clothing as possible.

- **Lie physically naked** in bed and hold each other, either spooning, or face to face. You may not stay this way all night, but you can start here.

- **Give yourself permission to really feel the skin on skin** and enjoy it. Breathe through any resistance or arousal that comes up, and relax into yourselves.

- **Make it a 'non-doing' activity.** Resist the urge to stroke or actively arouse yourself or your partner in any way. Give yourselves permission to just be. If you try it, you'll find it's a delicious treat for both of you.

 **Daily Devotion**

You may have seen the Indian Tantra Temples at Khajuraho, which are covered with thousands of highly erotic sculptures that were long considered vulgar or pornographic by the West. And if so, you might have wondered at the meaning behind them.

A student of this temple must meditate on each erotic image until they've come to peace with the lustful desires it inspires before they're allowed to enter the temple itself. A lustful mind will imagine an orgy of sex going on inside, when actually what's inside is the vastness of nothing, where love and peace lives.

This is also the meaning behind the practice of Daily Devotion. It's the practice of joining in sexual union with *no foreplay* and *no orgasm*. It takes you to a place that's *beyond doing* in sex, to a place of being, as in meditation. Non-doing is an important key in your sexual practice, for if you can't let go of doing and striving in sex, you'll never experience the magic of sexuality in union with love and with spirit (whatever this means to you).

To commence the practice:

- Get into a position that's comfortable – scissors is good (See Chapter 8). Or you can also lie on your sides with rear entry.
- Come into sexual union without foreplay, using lubricant to encourage 'soft entry', the woman threading man's Lingam between her thumb and forefingers into her Yoni.
- If you need to use a condom, try a female condom which allows for soft entry. Alternatively, try manual stimulation before applying a regular condom, using just enough movement to keep it in place whilst holding it firm at the base. If you do this, keep the practice time at the shorter end, and avoid going to sleep. A third alternative is to cut open a disposable glove and lay it between your genitals, simply resting them on the outside.
- Move just enough to sustain the physical connection. Even if, as the man, you lose your erection, just having your genitals laying close together will have an energetic effect. If you do this practice last thing at night, you can even fall asleep this way.
- Simply breathe, be present, and occasionally open your eyes. In the beginning, it will feel weird, but eventually you'll discover that there's 'no orgasm like no orgasm'. You may also experience a range of other phenomena such as energy movements, moments of exquisite peace, bliss, connection etc.
- This Daily Devotion can be done anytime. At the beginning or end of the day is nice, or when you just want to connect for anywhere between 10 minutes and an hour. It's also a nice way to start if you haven't made love for a while.

It's important to note that this is a *separate* practice to lovemaking, and *not* a manipulation into it. If you want to move into lovemaking, break your contact and agree to start again. Or you might mutually decide at

11: What About Love?

> the start to use it as a gentle entry into lovemaking, particularly if you have dryness, pain or erection challenges.
>
> This practice allows men to let go of performance anxiety and women to relax with no expectation of having to give. The practice will also re-energise your sexual desire by building an energetic connection between your genitals. Both of you will move beyond mere orgasm focus, which is where you need to go if you want to take your sexuality to its highest level. Doing this allows you to no longer be controlled by sex, and instead to enjoy it without need and become comfortable with letting love join in.

Love needs space to enter into. Moving from external status to internal rest, allowing your souls to join through your eyes, opening your hearts though sharing gratitude, merging with breath, joining in non-doing sexual union, and even just non-doing will allow love in.

Putting these practices into your relationship, whether together or separately, will introduce a sense of something larger than just the two of you melding you together and smoothing the pathway. How you define this tangible intangible is then up to you.

Shine and Sustain

12.1 Creating a Solid Relationship Framework

Whether you and your partner are new to your relationship or you've been together for years, creating a relationship agreement offers you a solid relationship framework. This framework eases times of challenge, as well as building in the juice to keep things interesting.

Most people only focus on their relationship with the dreaded 'Honey, we need to talk' conversations. In this chapter however, you'll actively find ways to make your relationship better, giving yourselves the chance to discuss it when things are going well, and allowing you space to discover more about yourselves and each other.

You'll create a strong yet dynamic relationship container that recognises the illusion of security, whilst at the same time creating something for you to believe in for the long run. It will help you and your partner to feel like you're on the same team, rather than being opponents. Finally, actively creating space in your relationship for what you DO want will stop it from trying to get your attention by creating crises in ways you don't.

How do You Create the Relationship You Want?

Once, we wouldn't have even asked this question ...

Instead, we'd just do what everyone else, including our parents, did – we'd fall in love with a person of the opposite sex, get married to them for the rest of our lives, have some kids along the way, and cross our fingers that it would all somehow turn out OK.

But relationships have changed

Traditional beliefs about relationships are fading faster than a politician's election promises. Now we have not only monogamous male/female couples who are married with or without children, but also couples living together with or without children, step parents, single parents, blended families, couples choosing not to have children, same sex relationships, serial monogamists, open relationships, together-but-living-separately relationships, friends with benefits, etc.

For all of its faults, the strength of marriage as an institution is the external force it exerts on a couple to stay together no matter what. Now that this external pressure has been reduced due to easier divorce it's easy to fall into the trap of living with one foot half out the door. Yet if we simply rely on the external pressure that marriage provides to do all the work for us, it's all too easy to take our relationships and our partners for granted, creating the dreaded boredom and loss of passion found in many long-term relationships.

Have you ever asked yourself why you're in the type of relationship you're in, and whether it's working for you? This isn't about *who* you're with, but the form of your relationship itself. We're in a place in society's evolution where there's no one standard relationship map, so we're free to create a context for our own.

The choice is yours

Instead of leaving it to society to determine how your relationship might look, you now have the power to make your own choices and create a relationship that will really work for you. This may of course include the tradition of marriage, but even marriage can now look as individual as you want it to.

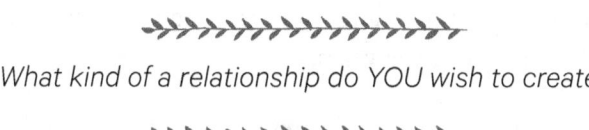

What kind of a relationship do YOU wish to create?

Make an overt commitment to your relationship, be active in the process, and put the chips on yourself. If you make a habit of taking action rather than reacting, and trust in the best in each other, what you want is more likely to show up. This is what living in your heart will invite. Along with a relationship blueprint – a plan for your success – your dreams are far more likely to come true. It's not about figuring it all out in advance. Instead, it's about actively navigating the journey and trusting in the pieces that arise along the way. It's about believing in that plan, committing to it and putting your desires into action.

If you *don't* have a plan when you're dealing with something as powerful and magical as a relationship, it's easy to get lost in the details – the problems and the suffering – and miss the joys along the way. Having a bigger-picture plan helps you to avoid sweating the small stuff in the daily ups and downs of life. It gives each of you a little breathing space to be yourselves through the safety of the plan you have together.

NB. A relationship agreement is useful even within the formality of marriage, as it bonds a couple at a more personal level.

We create plans for our workplace

We all think it's normal to plan and set goals that help us to achieve our desired outcomes in our personal and business lives. So why not do the same in our relationships? The clearer the plan, the more likely we are to get to the outcomes we want.

Of course in your relationship, even more than in business, you need to expect the unexpected and change along with circumstances. This means your plan will evolve over the years.

Plus, simply talking about your desires, needs, values and dreams as you put a plan or agreement together can teach you all sorts of things that you never knew about your spouse or partner, and vice versa. So the most important thing about a plan for the relationship you desire is to actually have one.

A healthy relationship is a conscious creation where the people in it actively choose the kind of relationship they want. Both individuals get to decide what their ideal looks like, remembering, as we said in the Introduction, that the only 'normal' in any relationship is the setting on the washing machine. Each individual can decide to include as few or as many aspects of what they want in a relationship to make up their own unique design.

Simple or complex...

At its simplest, a relationship agreement may simply be an agreed intention to live together always and to be there for each other as the highest priority. At its broadest, a relationship agreement can include all aspects of your two selves – personal, physical, psychological, emotional, sexual and spiritual. Each can create a deeply committed, conscious, loving, open-hearted, bonded connection with a balanced healthy sexual partnership.

The differences between these two very different approaches (and everything in between) don't actually matter. The fact that you're talking about and agreeing on what's right for you is what's important.

Making active choices and setting outcomes forms a very powerful container for your relationship. It creates your relationship from a triangle rather than a twosome: the triangle of you, your partner and the relationship itself. This takes the focus off you as two individuals competing with each other for your individual needs, and instead places it on the relationship – for when the relationship's needs are met, so too will be the needs of the individuals within it.

The power of commitment

> *"The moment one definitely commits oneself, then providence moves too. All sorts of things occur to help one that would never otherwise have occurred."*
>
> Ascent of Everest, Sir Edmund Hilary

Creating an active commitment to your relationship brings unseen powers to support it. This is particularly so in your sexual relationship – active commitment helps fears to lift and creativity to rise.

So if you were to develop a relationship plan of your own, what would it look like? What are your beliefs and values about relationships? What would you like more of? What's most important for you? What would the ultimate relationship for you look like? And if you discussed this with your partner/spouse, what would their thoughts be? Where would you align? Where would you be different?

The Only Way to Know for Sure is to Ask...

When Graeme and I got together, we'd both been in traditional marriages before, and had decided that we didn't want to recreate the past. So we wondered what we were now going to create for ourselves. Even asking this question was powerful. It meant taking charge, rather than just doing what was expected.

My biggest fear at that time was the lack of security in being out of wedlock, even though I knew from experience that being married didn't necessarily provide security. Graeme's challenge was how to make an authentic commitment that represented who he now was.

So rather than a once-only ceremony, we developed a practice of having an ongoing relationship agreement where we make an active and regular commitment to being together (married or not) which we review annually. We each decide what we want the relationship to look like, and then meld our desires together. We each take responsibility for the aspects we want to include. This active process creates our relationship strength *from the inside,* rather than from the external idea of a marriage. This active commitment is helping us to find the safety, freedom and aliveness we desire, as well as the longevity.

Intentions are Even More Powerful than Goals

A goal is a predetermined destination that comes from your ego's idea of what you already know exists. Graeme and I encourage you to replace your idea of goals with that of intentions. Because your focused intentions also set the infinite organising power of the universe (which is unseen) in motion along with what you already know that can be put into action.

Intentions also allow you to let go of the need for total control, and instead see opportunities that you can take to fulfil your desires as they arise. These opportunities often create better outcomes than the goals your ordinary, everyday mind comes up with. This can then manifest more of your (currently hidden) potential – both in your relationship

12: Shine and Sustain

and within yourself. An example of an intention, formed in the positive is 'We lovingly support each other in achieving our individual dreams and goals.'

> *"We must be willing to let go of the life we have planned to have the life that is waiting for us."*
>
> Reflections On The Art of Living, Joseph Campbell

 Create Your Own Relationship Agreement

Begin with the places where you agree. The places where you differ are the gold in your relationship, and you can add these in as you get clearer on them over time.

First, each person separately considers what's important to them in a relationship.

This is not necessarily based on your current relationship, but on your own ideas about 'relationship' itself. Ask yourselves:

- What do you value in a relationship?
- What are your expectations of it?
- What do you love about it?
- What are your needs in it?
- What inspires or motivates you in it?
- Who do you want to be in it?
- What would you love to create?
- Reflect on some of the unconscious habits you have in your relationship: things you find yourself doing without even realising it because they're so familiar. Examples might be only making love on Sundays or eating dinner in front of the TV. Are these habits supporting you, or is it time to bring in some new ones,

such as adding in a spontaneous time for loving, or having dinner by candlelight once per week?

Each person then makes a list of all the things they desire in a relationship.

These can be things that already exist in your relationship as well as things you'd like to add in, *whether you believe they're possible or not*. This process is about taking risks, allowing yourself to be seen, and opening to the magic of possibility. You'll never know if you don't put it out there!

The first time I did this with Graeme, I felt very scared of being rejected – but I said I wanted to start living with him full time. I was delighted to find this was his as-yet-unspoken desire too. NB. Write your lists as if they're already happening, eg 'We love and live together', as this tells your unconscious mind that it's already true, and allows your mind to help you manifest your reality.

Finally, share your lists with each other (re-read the section on Communication in Chapter 5 first if desired).

- If you're being real in this, there will be areas that both delight and challenge each of you.
- Begin with making ALL suggestions OK, even if you don't agree with them – and honour each other for taking a risk, as this creates a safe space to explore in.
- Ignoring any areas of disagreement combine the remaining items to form your current relationship agreement.
- Write out your agreement and put it somewhere you can both see it.

NB. With the remaining areas of contention, work together over time to see how each need or desire, *however opposing they may initially appear,* could be met. And as we showed in Chapters 4 and 9, you can meet these challenges in a way that's good for your relationship as a whole.

12: Shine and Sustain

If you believe the higher purpose of your relationship is to polish your rough diamond selves into shining gemstones, it's easier to see what there is to gain or learn from each other.

For example, when Graeme and I first got together, we each had had limited sexual experiences, but didn't want to give up our growing relationship with each other in order to go out and have more. So we agreed that we'd support each other in exploring any lingering desires in this area together (rather than doing it covertly), and viewed dealing with any issues this brought up as part of our relationship agreement at the time. This agreement may not be to your particular taste – nor does it need to be – but for us, it certainly provided plenty of juice for both personal and relationship growth.

Having a relationship agreement means that there are fewer unspoken rules and frustrated desires operating in your relationship. It doesn't mean you need to override your personal values, but it may mean you need to challenge what they mean to you. Having a relationship agreement offers space to brainstorm and get creative about your outcomes. The only thing that ultimately works in areas of challenge are win/win solutions. The previous chapters in this book should certainly have sparked your appetite for discussion and for positive change.

Review your agreement regularly to keep your relationship focussed and alive. Try a minimum of once per year, plus whenever challenges to the agreement come up.

The most important thing is to begin the discussion!

12.2 Trust the Process

Change in the cycle of life never ends. Look at photos of your children – it's easy to see them growing and changing. Then look at the photos you've taken over your own life: even as an adult, you continue to change with time, along with the world you live in.

Your relationship is the same. It's never stationary: like nature it's always changing, either growing or dying. Still, your ego self wants what it wants, which is to avoid suffering and be happy NOW! For change to become sustainable, and for your relationship to deepen into something you truly trust and believe in, it takes more than an instant or two. Most of the time you know this, no matter how many bright and shiny 'quick fixes' your ego might be attracted to along the way. But it can be tough to remember in the tight places that happen in long-term, intimate relationships. Taking time to connect with your whole self helps you to remember what your ego self continually forgets.

*Sometimes immediate change does happen,
but then seems to disappear...*

When creating change it can seem that the new connection you felt, the new way your partner was treating you, or your own new habit of looking for the best in your relationship too easily falls by the wayside. This doesn't happen because the change wasn't real, or because you or your partner weren't trying.

Instead, it's because you have an internal thermostat, just like the one in your fridge, that regulates your psyche. When you open the door and put a whole bunch of fresh food in, the motor works overtime to return the fridge to its set temperature. Your psyche also wants to try and return you to your internal set point because it's familiar. It's important not to think you've failed, but instead to understand that it takes practice to raise the overall set point in your psyche so that the change becomes your new normal. So instead of focussing on where you've failed, look for where you might have grown, no matter how small it might be.

12: Shine and Sustain

The Dynamics of Relationship Change

There's a special dynamic of change that happens in relationships. We're not talking about small changes here, like finding a new restaurant to try, or spending more time together on Saturdays. This is about deeper, more lasting and life-altering change. Most times, this kind of change doesn't happen in *both* people at the *same* time. More often, one person will make a shift and the other person will be left to shift (or not) in response. This is particularly challenging when the one left behind doesn't understand, agree with or support the change that has occurred.

 Real Behaviour Changes Invite a Change in Your Partner

Yvonne decides to get healthy, and starts regularly going to the gym, eating more healthily, and passing up the extra glasses of wine she used to enjoy with Mark during dinner. Even though this is a healthy change, it takes away an intimate ritual they used to enjoy. It also shines an uncomfortable light onto Mark's less healthy lifestyle choices, which he now has to face.

Steve starts to actually share more about what's happening for him emotionally with Sue. This challenges Sue to change the way she relates to him as well, getting more vulnerable than she ever imagined being.

This is a 'pivotal point' where your differences challenge your partner to grow. Over time, couples get used to this dance of change and welcome it, understanding that it's a process. Rather than seeing it as an ending, they know it's an opportunity to grow in their relationship. They also experience 'sweet spots' when everything seems magical, knowing the only thing to do here is enjoy it.

Change doesn't have to be about ultimatums

Graeme and I often see one person in a relationship who draws a line in the sand for themselves and says, "I can't do this anymore. I need things to change," or, "I feel suffocated in my relationship, and this makes me resist intimacy with you."

These are healthy boundaries rather than ultimatums, which are a 'You must... or I will...' statement. Ultimatums are an attempt to manipulate your partner into to giving you what you want and are a form of emotional abuse. Instead, expressing a healthy boundary is a recognition of where you're at – one that helps both you and your partner to see and feel your situation more clearly. Such a boundary leaves it up to each person as to how to respond.

 Each Partner from Above Can Now Choose Their Response

Mark now has a choice to join Yvonne in her lifestyle changes or re-affirm his own choices for himself without disrespecting Yvonne's by trying to cajole her into an extra glass of wine.

Sue sees that she now has to drop her familiar complaints about Steve's emotional unavailability and really listen to him and respond from her own vulnerability if she wants to nurture Steve's new habit.

Don't be afraid of things falling apart

When you start to create change, or when it's forced upon you by circumstances or your partner's choices, it can seem like everything you know is falling apart and even falling into chaos. It's important to understand that this is part of the process of shaking things up. It's about letting go of past unhealthy structures and creating space for something new – usually something truer and more authentic – to arise.

12: Shine and Sustain

This breakdown gives you a chance to realign your lives and rise from the ashes as your more powerful, resourceful and loving selves. You can be guided in this process by your ABC practice keeping you grounded and aware, and following where the most energy is, as this will bring you the best outcomes.

You can't 'do relationship' from outside of it

Being in a relationship is about getting your hands dirty, and you can't do it by sitting safely on the fence and leaving it all up to your partner. You need to recognise your part and make your relationship a focus in your life, putting the necessary time and energy into it. Otherwise it will just drain away, leaving you scratching your head and wondering what happened.

Remember you can't do your partner's part for them

If you find yourself continually focussing on where your partner is at and what they're doing or not doing, our question for you is, "Where are you?" No matter how much you might want to focus on them and think it will help, too much gets in the way.

All you can do is YOUR part, and there will be enough in *that* to keep you busy for a lifetime. Also, if you try to rescue your partner, you'll limit their opportunities for their own growth. This doesn't mean you can't protect or support them, but being continually in their space doing it for them will be the death of your relationship.

There's never one 'broken' partner who needs to be fixed

*We commonly see couples who believe that one partner has all the 'issues', and if **they** get fixed, the relationship will be fine.*

Each of us is a result of our own life experiences and choices. If either partner places undue emphasis on the other's faults, or constantly pressures them to fix themselves, it shames that person for being who they are. Equally, it can force one partner into an unhealthy therapist role. Even worse they might put their partners down because they believe they themselves are so much more evolved. This is an egoic spiritual narcissism, not love.

The 'unbroken' partner needs to remember that their partner is a mirror and look more closely at what they themselves are putting into the relationship. They need to examine where *they* might be enabling their partner's behaviour or manipulating them to avoid their own vulnerabilities. Choosing to stand up within themselves instead will invite healthy change from the other person, and put the relationship back on an even keel where it has a chance to become whole.

Working together can be about doing your own thing

Even in a relationship where both people recognise that things aren't working and agree to work towards change together, the process isn't usually actualised by both people in the same way or at the same time. Most often, one person will gain some insight and make a shift, leaving their partner feeling out of their comfort zone, and perhaps digging their heels in, trying to force the other person to go back to the way things were. This resistance may be quite unconscious, so it's important not to blame them for their position.

> ### Understanding the Process of Resistance
> *James makes a shift to being more present in his lovemaking, is able to last longer and access more pleasure in himself. His wife Abbey then drops into a place of not feeling good enough as her own blocks to deeper sexual pleasure show up. As a result, she pulls away from sex.*

> *Abbey requires a period of adjustment to James' change, and it's important that he doesn't shut down in the face of her resistance. After coming to terms with her own discomfort and seeing that James isn't leaving her behind but is instead inviting her deeper from a place of love, she can make a step forward of her own.*

Real change isn't always about instant happiness

As you can see, if the changes are real, the process will probably involve as much discomfort as happiness. For every action, there is a reaction; and even a negative reaction is a sign that significant change is happening. Things can seem worse rather than better for a time if the reactive partner shifts into greater resistance. This is where the person making the change needs support to hold their position (with compassion but not collapsing) whilst their partner catches up in their own way.

> ### The Value of Standing Firm in our Change
>
> *Margaret, a mother who'd always been there for everyone else and now finds herself drained of energy and momentum, decides to put herself first and say 'no' more often to others and 'yes' more often to herself.*
>
> *She needs to stand firm in herself whilst her family gets used to not having their needs attended to in the old, automatic ways. They need to learn new ways of coping. It can take time for her family to see that the changes are good for Margaret, and that she's happier as a result. When they 'get' this, they'll be spurred on to support her.*

Healthy Intimacy is Where Differences Bring Value

In the vulnerability of a relationship, you can want your partner to make the shifts YOU want them to make – the ones that suit your needs. But ultimately, if the shift is authentic, it's healthier for each person to find their own solutions. This is better because it allows an opening to new things in their fullest expression, rather than contracting or distorting them in any way. It also brings surprising new energy for *both* people in the relationship.

This doesn't mean you can't share your opinion and express your needs, but you leave the end decision to your partner and trust that who they shift into will teach you something.

Being Willing to Be in the Unknown

Your challenge in change is to be willing to be in the unknown, without any guarantee of an expected or obvious outcome, and to hold the fort while this change occurs and is integrated into the relationship.

> ### Allowing Room for Inspiration to Arise
>
> *Neil is stressed and depressed in his career. Cathy would like him to take Sundays off to play golf, when what Neil would really love to do is take some time out to just sit on the couch and discover what's meaningful in life for him outside of the rat race.*
>
> *This idea is frightening and challenging – financially and emotionally – for both for Neil and Cathy. Yet if they can agree on how to manage it and for what time period, the rewards of such introspection can be profound – a return to life and career with renewed vigour and vitality in all areas for Neil, and a happier relationship for Cathy.*

What Happens when You Change and Your Partner Doesn't?

What if you've done the hard work, given it your best shot, and your partner is still resistant? You probably feel indignant about their apparent unwillingness to change, justified in your fear of them being unable to do so, or just hopeless at the seeming impossibility of it.

It's important to ask yourself some hard questions here:

- How fully have you *really* changed? Are you truly going there, or just tinkering around the edges? Real change has a clarity and a solidness that's hard to argue with. Can you feel that clarity within you?
- Are you asking your head or your heart? Are the changes you've made bringing you to a greater wholeness, or are they simply about gratifying your ego?
- Are you wanting your partner to make a change that suits you rather than something that's authentic for them, so they're rightly resisting it?
- Are you pushing too hard? Sometimes change needs space to happen in, and this means letting go of trying and letting the change move through.

Real change in one half of a relationship *forces* a reaction in the other, even if it's a negative one, such as holding more firmly to their position. So even if only one person makes the choice to change in the relationship, if the change is real, their partner will be forced to shift somehow as a result. A negative response is still positive, because it means real momentum is happening.

If you're the one who's embracing change, trust that your partner will, in time, see the negative consequences of their own resistance and where they could choose to step up. Or you might need to see where *your change* is leading you astray, so you can shift in a different way.

> ### Sometimes it's Just Fear of Change Itself that Gets in the Way
>
> *Ian discovers a passion for travel and Debbie discovers a desire to help those in need. This separation initially feels like a betrayal of the connection in their relationship. Over time however, they learn to combine these interests by travelling to both Indonesia and South America and doing some aid work whist they're there, making their connection stronger and more fulfilling in ways they never previously imagined.*

This is where it can be helpful to have a third person outside of your relationship – a compassionate friend or counsellor who supports each of you in the process of understanding both sides of what is happening.

Think of Growth as a Seed You Plant in the Ground

When you plant a seed, you choose a good spot with plenty of light, access to water and richly fertile soil. You make a hole, place the seed in it, cover it over with soil and water it. Then you have to wait. This period of waiting is one of being in the unknown. You *believe* the seed will sprout and grow, but at this point you can only *trust* that your efforts will result in a healthy, abundant plant with flowers, fruit or vegetables.

You trust enough to go about your life, even forgetting about the seed for a few days, weeks or even months (depending on the type of seed). Then eventually, voila! There you have a shiny green sprout, popping its head up through the soil, and bursting with new life.

But when you begin to make changes in your relationship, you somehow forget about this growth process and expect results straight away. If you don't get them, you start interfering in the process. You CAN experience many immediate and exciting changes – but for deeper changes to arise and stick, it takes *trust* that they'll happen, *action* to see them through, *support* to help them manifest in an optimal way, and *time* for them to eventuate.

In reality, creating change happens just a few steps at a time, or even with one step forward and two steps back. So, the Number 1 lesson in change is to be active but gentle with yourself.

How Growth Occurs In a Relationship

Our idea of how it should occur:

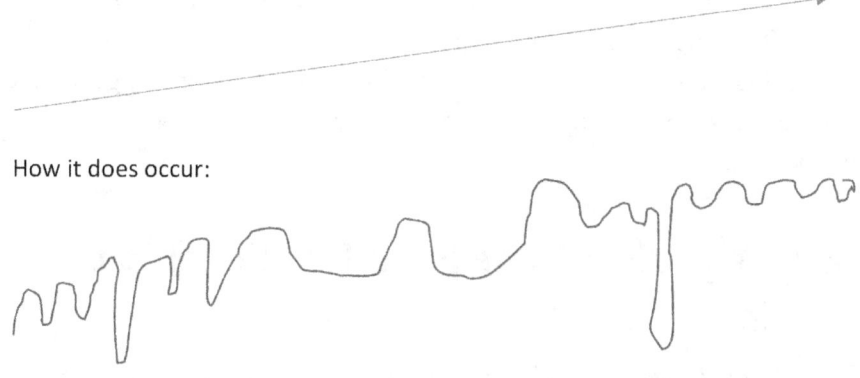

How it does occur:

Diagram 12.1 How Growth Occurs In a Relationship

In our very efficient modern world, we believe that all problems have solutions if we try hard enough. With the self development ethos of 'fixing ourselves', it can be challenging to see that we're never actually going to get to a place where we're perfect and everything around us is permanently heaven on earth.

We can have many, many moments of heaven, for sure. But then time moves on and the next moment might bring something totally different – happiness, pleasure, gratitude and achievement; or equally fear, resentment, jealousy or failure. Accepting that we and our relationships are always in this process of change and choosing to be in the driver's seat as much as possible is the way to create more moments of value.

Finding resilience in being OK no matter what, is true achievement (just don't bullshit yourself)!

Fully accepting where we are – rather than wanting to be somewhere else – actually invites positive change, because it teaches us that we can trust in life. Trusting in life helps us to get up off the floor and have another go, finding ways to be with suffering so that it becomes meaningful rather than endless, and having the patience to wait for the sun to come out again.

12.3 When is it Time For a Relationship to End?

In this book, Graeme and I have talked much about how your relationship is really about yourself rather than the other person. We've said that relationship challenges are your own stuff, to be looked at in yourself. Does this mean there's never a time when your relationship with your partner needs to end? The answer is no. Sometimes it does.

Relationships take hard work: often much harder work than we ever imagined. Pain, suffering, loss of faith, hatred and even loss of love can all be part of a long-term, committed relationship at times. There's a common belief that if a relationship takes work, it's wrong for us, but our relationships are the only place this belief surfaces. In other areas of achievement such as work or sport, we assume that lasting success absolutely involves hard work and commitment. It's the emotional intensity that makes relationships so challenging and just because we come up against some tough places doesn't mean it's time to throw in the towel.

12: Shine and Sustain

At the same time however, new paradigms and new ways of being require the destruction of the old. Sometimes, just admitting, "I don't know how to try anymore. I have to give up." can be the best thing you can do.

Sometimes moving forward requires quitting.

I admit that I've given up trying before in my relationship with Graeme – a scary thing for someone with attachment issues to do, but I did it. In fact, we've both given up at times. Mostly, though, that 'giving up' was about totally giving up our old ways of being and admitting what was real: that our hearts were closed, or that in our fear we'd been faking it, rather than actually moving out. Each time we did so, a whole new layer opened up in our relationship as a result.

Being willing to leave your relationship is a good thing. It stops you and your partner from taking it for granted. It allows you to trust that you'll be OK no matter what, so you can let go of holding on too tight. You can look at that person across from you and know that every day you are both choosing to be there.

Just remember that being willing to leave doesn't mean it's OK to use that willingness as a threat to manipulate your partner into meeting your demands.

Couples *can* decide to take time out from their relationship, literally separating for a while. The vital thing to know about this kind of separation is that you need to keep doing your inner work on yourselves and your relationship while you're separated.

If you merely take time out from your relationship to 'fix it' without doing the work and only focus on all the shiny, new things around you (and after moving away from the struggle, many things will look bright and shiny!) your relationship has an almost 85% chance of ending.

Some clients of ours have taken conscious time out, enjoying the bachelor pad they've never had or using the space to see themselves more clearly. And even those who were almost at the point of divorce have come back with very creative solutions for their relationships – including a six-month cruise around the Pacific on a catamaran. Others have remarried each other even after divorcing. If you do the work, anything is possible.

However, it's time to question your relationship's future if:

1. There are repeated episodes of emotional or physical abuse that aren't addressed by the abuser in any real way. Anyone can make a mistake once or twice and heal it, but anything ongoing is intolerable.

2. You find yourself constantly on the defensive and having to justify yourself. You find yourself continually being gaslighted – told that nothing is wrong when you firmly believe there is. Or you might notice you're the one continually going out of your way to make your partner wrong. And in each of these situations, the person involved isn't willing to look at these behaviour patterns.

3. You don't have support from someone who will be there with you in the tough spots: either a friend or a counsellor/therapist.

4. You're seeing a therapist and it isn't helping. Not all therapists are great ones. See another one – one who specialises in relationships, as this offers a very different dynamic to working with a single individual, before assuming your relationship needs to end.

5. You've looked within and made significant changes in yourself (see *Trust The Process* earlier in this chapter), knowing that if you don't make these changes now, you'll only have to do them in the next relationship – but your partner is unwilling or unable to join you.

6. You look within yourself – or even better, you look into your heart – to ask whether you can do this anymore, and the answer is a serious 'no'. Rituals have become chores, communication goes nowhere, your partner treats you with contempt (a sign of a closed heart), or you find yourself treating your partner that way. You've given it time,

but the flat spot hasn't passed, and you've ceased planning any kind of future together. In this case, the ultimate decision is yours and you're the only one who can make it.

Knowing that you've worked to your limits to make the relationship survive can make leaving an easier decision. It can also allow the separation to occur with a lower level of animosity and a higher potential for understanding, learning and compassion.

Sometimes ending a relationship can allow partners to be better friends with each other than they ever could be before, which is especially wonderful where children are involved. Other times, of course, this isn't possible. But Graeme and I see couples more and more often now who do the surprising and get into a new kind of relationship with each other after ending their old, painful ways of relating. When this happens, they find a totally different place of connection.

Whatever happens, doing your inner work makes it easier in the long run.

12.4 Signs You're Creating a Sacred, Intimate Relationship

How do you keep your belief in your intimate and sexual relationship alive over the years? Well, by now you will hopefully have learned many new tools and gained many new insights for making this possibility happen. You understand yourself, your partner and the reality you're creating much better. There is still one other choice you can make that brings a magic of its own.

This is believing that an intimate relationship itself is a sacred act and acting according to that belief. Sacredness here means connected with God (whatever that means to you) or a higher purpose and deserving of respect.

The person you choose to be in intimate relationship with – a relationship outside of birth, culture, work or obligation – forms a major part of your life. So it makes sense that you honour yourself, your partner and your choice consciously and respectfully. It's easy to get blasé about your relationship, but if you've seen anything throughout this book, it's that there are major benefits to getting well and truly involved in something that's real, loving and achievable. Sacredness is more than a mental concept, it's a (surprise, surprise) felt sense more than anything, one that feels like an unarguable truth. This felt sense is supported by what you're able to see happening in your relationship.

Signs that You're Creating a Sacred Intimate Relationship

1. You embrace your relationship's wholistic ecosystem at the levels that work for you: mind, body, feeling, sexuality, meaning and magic.

2. You're 100% committed to making your relationship happen because you know this is what it takes. You prioritise time together, whether this is to talk, share common interests, have fun, enjoy each of the layers of intimacy, deal with your challenges, make love or just hang out together.

3. You understand that you can only be in a relationship with your partner to the extent that you're in relationship with yourself. You nurture your self-connection with regular ABC practice.

4. You're willing to take 100% responsibility for your part in the relationship you're creating. You own your thoughts, beliefs, values, feelings, assumptions and projections as being what you're *choosing* to project onto the screen of your life.

5. You realise that you're going to fuck things up at times and you understand that it's not avoiding mistakes but the willingness to clean them up and learn from them that creates a great relationship.

6. You have a relationship agreement in place that you both review regularly, and that helps you to follow a fulfilling path through the uncertainty of life together. This agreement supports expression of your individuality whilst nourishing your togetherness.

7. You not only know yourself, but you also know your partner intimately too. You know their personality, their fears, their joys, their needs and their desires nearly as well as your own, because you care about them and who they are.

8. Your heart open lovemaking nurtures your connection, fosters intimacy and desire, building a bond between you that's beyond words.

9. You know what you have in common and you can tolerate the uncertainty of your partner being different to you and having different interests, desires and needs. Your differences add flavour rather than fracture.

10. You can support your partner being wonderful at something – be it work, sport, play or even lovemaking – because you know you'll receive benefit from it too, and will rise to meet them in your own wonderful ways.

11. You practise connecting, communicating and lovemaking when things are good between you, so that these strengths can hold you together when things get tough.

12. You have a greater sense of your own authenticity, knowing that authenticity equals moments of freedom, fulfilment and access to greater life force energy. You both live comfortably inside your own skins and know the importance of maintaining healthy boundaries.

13. You regularly assess how you're being in your relationship, where you're coming from in your words and actions, and how they're being received – all as an act of love.

14. You feel gratitude for every time you notice that you or your partner are able to respond, rather than react; to choose, rather than resist; and love, rather than fear.

15. You willingly embrace all your feelings as a positive part of yourself, your sexuality, your heart and soul, and your relationship.

16. You use the learnings of your body, feelings and intuitive wisdom as well as the power of intellectual reflection to navigate through your relationship challenges.

17. You have a concrete connection with your heart and live from it as often as possible, trusting it to guide and nurture you.

18. You know that love is a felt state of being that you can choose to access in yourself and share in with your partner, rather than something you have to 'get' from them.

19. You know the value of healing the past as it arises so its shadows don't negatively impact on what you're creating in the present.

20. You choose to cultivate love as a practice, rather than carry it as an expectation. You're willing to allow yourself to be seen in your truth, vulnerability and imperfections, valuing your relationship more than protecting your ego.

21. You respect your sexuality as a powerful pathway to creating love, connection, nurturing, pleasure and bliss. You take responsibility for co-creating your own pleasure in lovemaking and cultivate the sensuality of your body outside the bedroom, keeping the fires of your passion stoked. You manage your sexual energy in a way that brings to the relationship, rather than drains from it.

22. You fall in love with your breath knowing the gifts it can bring, apart from just keeping you alive. It helps relieve stress, it brings you into the present moment, it helps you feel and shift your emotions and connect you to your heart. It also activates, increases and spreads your feelings of connection and sexual pleasure.

23. You see your relationship as a place to grow – in fact, you know this is why you've chosen each other. You cultivate courage and take risks in trusting yourself, your partner, the relationship and love itself.

24. Over time, you find fewer issues that challenge you, bringing a greater ease between you and your partner. You have greater emotional resilience and find yourself seeking your partner from a desire for connection, joy and pleasure.

25. You take time out to celebrate your relationship by choosing to do rewarding things together on a regular basis.

26. You find you're a better person for having been in this relationship than you could have ever been alone. The abundance that you find in your relationship serves as a source of energy and support that you share with your family, friends and the world around you.

27. As you no longer focus on fixing your partner, you also stop trying to fix your kids. Instead, you focus on stepping into your authentic self (with boundaries intact), knowing that as you do so, you're providing the best role model possible for them. We've seen this approach positively impact the children of many clients, and even their parents and friends.

28. You see so many layers of possibility in your relationship, intimacy and lovemaking that you desire to choose it for a lifetime, trusting in the magic you're creating.

The practices in this book are designed to get you into the present moment of your relationship – out of living in your head and into relating with your partner in real time. They're there to help you penetrate into the deepest recesses of each other's being and begin to explore, despite the title of this book, a mystery that can never be fully solved.

Your relationship is actually a mystery to be lived, not a problem to be solved.

The joy, the mystery, the beauty, the tragedy and the transforming: they're all there waiting for you in your intimate relationship. Given a chance, love can be a constant adventure, a never-ending journey into yourself and into your partner. Remember that your past is not your potential – your now is unlimited and your conditioning is not who you are.

You now have an abundance of choices to help you create the intimate relationship and love life you desire, whether it's planning your relationship agreement, becoming emotionally aware, getting more real in your communication, trying something new in the bedroom, finding greater connection with yourself, taking time out to celebrate what you have, topping up your intimacy bank account or seeing your partner as someone new all over again by letting go of the past and loving them in this moment now.

A study of 5,716 middle-aged people showed that those with the highest self-regulation abilities were over 50 times more likely to be alive without chronic disease than those with the lowest scores. The choice is yours: what is it that you're going to choose for yourself, your relationship and your love life in this moment, right here, right now?

Your relationship doesn't need to be perfect to be perfect for you.

The Japanese have an art form called Kintsugi, where broken pottery is collected and lovingly repaired with gold-dusted adhesive, to make it into a new and more valuable piece. In the West, we repair things to be 'as good as new', but for the Japanese, the repair is part of the journey and transformation. They celebrate the breakage as part of the object's history, rather than as the end of the story.

People fight, fuck up and generally cause damage to each other in a relationship – that's a given. But if you both then lovingly repair (we would say 'grow') yourselves and each other from that damage, you create something new, worthwhile and uniquely yours. And your willingness to grow shows love, understanding and a deep commitment to taking care of each other – with each gold dusted repair line becoming your story of love.

12: Shine and Sustain

"If nothing saves us from death, may love save us from life."
Selected Poems, Pablo Neruda

Annette, Graeme and Oztantra

Annette Baulch and Graeme Sudholz are specialist couples counsellors. Since 2006, they've facilitated Oztantra couples sessions, weekend workshops, Ultimate Couples Getaways and Ecstasy & Intimacy retreats for couples seeking more intimate and heart-connected relationships in Australia and overseas. They're known for changing lives through changing relationships and are quietly achieving an enviable success rate in helping couples to stay happily together. The remainder have invariably left it too late before seeking assistance, so it's recommended you ask for support sooner rather than later as it makes a difference.

A couple themselves since 2002, they've created a depth of connection, intimacy, trust, honesty, pleasure, passion and purpose beyond their wildest dreams that thrives in the challenges of daily reality.

Annette and Graeme teach about relationship and sex in a personal, open-hearted and knowledgeable way that allows their clients to feel both heard and met. They're happy to meet couples wherever they're at – from simply wanting to spice up their sex life to illuminating love in their darkest corners.

They both have Diplomas in Counselling, and they're grateful to have trained with some of the world's best practitioners of emotional intelligence, Tantra and relationships: Dr Jo Horwood, Nicholas De Castella, Charles & Caroline Muir, Oceana & Icarus, Bodhi Avinasha Deborah Anapol, PhD, and have been influenced by hundreds of others through the works that line their bookshelves. They've been invited to happy clients' weddings and anniversary celebrations that would not have happened without their support.

You can visit Annette and Graeme at www.oztantra.com and www.comingtogetherbook.com.au.

Suggested Reading

Passionate Marriage by David Schnarch

Emotional Intimacy by Robert Augustus Masters

Tantra: The Art of Conscious Loving by Charles & Caroline Muir

Hold Me Tight by Dr Sue Johnson

Facing Codependence by Pia Melody

Attached: The New Science of Adult Attachment and How It Can Help You Find—And Keep—Love by A Levine. & R Heller

Being In Love by Osho

Tantra: Osho The Supreme Understanding by Osho

The Heart of Tantric Sex by Diana Richardson

Transcendent Sex: When Lovemaking Opens the Veil by Jenny Wade

The Gifts of Imperfection by Brene Brown (anything by Brene is worth reading)

Spiritual Bypassing by Robert Augustus Masters

The Dance of Fear by Harriet Lerner

Tantric Orgasm For Women by Diana Richardson

Women's Anatomy of Arousal by Sheri Winston

Activate Your Female Power by Sharon Moloney, PhD

Women, Food & God by Geneen Roth

Urban Tantra by Barbara Carellas & Annie Sprinkle

Vagina by Naomi Wolf

Wild Feminine by Tami Lynn Kent

The New Male Sexuality by Bernie Zilbergeld

Manhood by Steve Biddulph

Crossing The Souls River by William O. Roberts

He'll Be Ok- Growing Gorgeous Boys Into Good Men by Celia Lashlie

Sex Secrets of Escorts by Veronica Monet

www.ingramcontent.com/pod-product-compliance
Lightning Source LLC
Chambersburg PA
CBHW071851290426
44110CB00013B/1105